THE EUROPEAN UNION UNDER TRANSNATIONAL LAW

For almost a decade the European Union has been stuck in a permanent crisis. Starting with domestic constitutional crises, followed by an imported financial crisis, it has evolved into a fully formed political crisis. This book argues that none of the crises are exclusively internal to the EU and the responses to date, which have taken inward looking approaches, are simply inadequate. Resolution can only come when the EU engages more fully with transnational law.

This highly topical book offers an innovative dual focus on both transnational and EU law together. It sets out the relationship between the two frameworks by exploring practical concrete problems that transnational law has posed to the EU. These problems are explored from the perspective of four key tenets of both systems, namely the rule of law, democracy, the protection of human rights, and justice. It does this by advancing the theoretical framework of principled legal pluralism. In so doing it offers clear normative guidance as to how the relationship between EU and transnational law should be developed and fostered.

Volume 84 in the Series Modern Studies in European Law

The European Union under Transnational Law

A Pluralist Appraisal

Matej Avbelj

·HART·

OXFORD · LONDON · NEW YORK · NEW DELHI · SYDNEY

HART PUBLISHING

Bloomsbury Publishing Plc

Kemp House, Chawley Park, Cumnor Hill, Oxford, OX2 9PH, UK

HART PUBLISHING, the Hart/Stag logo, BLOOMSBURY and the Diana logo are
trademarks of Bloomsbury Publishing Plc

First published in Great Britain 2018

First published in hardback, 2018
Paperback edition, 2020

A catalogue record for this book is available from the British Library.

Library of Congress Cataloging-in-Publication Data

Names: Avbelj, Matej, author.

Title: The European Union under transnational law : a pluralist appraisal / Matej Avbelj.

Description: Oxford [UK] ; Portland, Oregon : Hart Publishing, 2018. | Series: Modern studies in
European law ; volume 84 | Includes bibliographical references and index.

Identifiers: LCCN 2017039015 (print) | LCCN 2017040732 (ebook) |
ISBN 9781509911547 (Epub) | ISBN 9781509911523 (hardback)

Subjects: LCSH: European Union. | International and municipal law—European Union
countries. | International law—European Union countries. | Rule of law—European Union
countries. | Human rights—European Union countries. |
Legal polycentricity—European Union countries.

Classification: LCC KJE5075 (ebook) | LCC KJE5075 .A97 2018 (print) | DDC 341.242/2—dc23

LC record available at https://lccn.loc.gov/2017039015

ISBN: HB: 978-1-50991-152-3
PB: 978-1-50993-825-4
ePDF: 978-1-50991-151-6
ePub: 978-1-50991-154-7

Typeset by Compuscript Ltd, Shannon

To find out more about our authors and books visit www.hartpublishing.co.uk. Here you will find
extracts, author information, details of forthcoming events and the option to sign up for our newsletters.

Acknowledgements

This book has had a long period of gestation. The actual work on it began in late 2013, when I was awarded a generous research grant by the Slovenian Research Agency for a project dedicated to the 'The Post-modern Challenges of Transnational Law for the European Union'. This grant permitted me, while still teaching as an associate professor of European law and working as an academic dean at the Graduate School of Government and European Studies at the Nova Univerza in Slovenia to devote much more time to the research in this extremely interesting, highly topical, but theoretically still relatively uncharted terrain.

However, the roots of the ideas and arguments contained herein can be traced back a whole decade earlier, to my studies and research at NYU School of Law and, in particular, the European University Institute. It was there that my interest in EU law and legal pluralism was born and has later culminated in a study of the relationship between the EU and transnational law from a pluralist perspective, which is what this book is essentially about. Over this relatively long period of time, the ideas contained in this book have been tested, rejected and reformulated in a number of different academic fora, lectures and conferences, including at the University of Amsterdam, the University of Michigan Law School, the Mississippi College School of Law, Harvard Law School's Institute for Global Law & Policy, University College Dublin, the Centre for Law and Public Affairs in Prague, the WZB in Berlin, the National University of Singapore Law School, the University of Vienna, the University of Cambridge, the University of Edinburgh and at my two home institutions: the Graduate School of Government and European Studies and the European Faculty of Law. It was there where a number of talks, workshops and a special conference were organised to discuss the challenges of transnational law to the EU.

In these academic venues and events, I have benefited, in particular, from my exchanges with Neil Walker, Mattias Kumm, Gianluigi Palmobella, Daniel Augenstein, Alun Gibbs, Maria Varaki, Cormac Mac Amhlaigh, Verica Trstenjak, Zoran Oklopčič, Michal Bobek, Filippo Fontanelli, Maria Cahill, Jan Zobec, Daniel Halberstam, Jan Komarek, Andrew Glencross, Christoph Möllers, John Haskell, Dimitry Kochenov and Vojko Strahovnik. Futhermore, Giuseppe Martinico and David Roth-Isigkeit deserve to be especially commended. They have read the entire manuscript and provided extremely valuable feedback. I would also like to thank the extremely supportive and efficient team of Hart Publishing, in particular Sinead Moloney, Emily Braggins, Jon Lloyd and Tom Adams, who have helped me to improve this manuscript, where possible, and to finish it in good time. The research assistance of Alesia Koletič deserves to be mentioned too. Finally, I need to acknowledge a generous grant by the Humboldt Foundation. In the final phase of the project, it permitted me to work as a Humboldt Senior Research Fellow at the WZB in Berlin, bringing the book to its successful completion.

As befits academic thinking, which has been developing over a longer period of time, parts of the arguments contained in this book have already been published before. Chapter 1 thus draws on 'Transnational Law between Modernity and Postmodernity' (2016) 7 *Transnational Legal Theory*. Chapter 3 builds on 'Theory of European Union' (2011) 36 *European Law Review*. Chapter 4 borrows a few pages from 'The UN, the EU, and the *Kadi* Case: A New Appeal for Genuine Institutional Cooperation' (2016) 17 *German Law Journal*; while Chapter 5 was already published as 'Integral Pre-emption of EU Democracy in Economic Crisis under Transnational Law' (2015) 4 *Cambridge Journal of International and Comparative Law*.

Last, but certainly not least, this preface cannot be completed without acknowledging the tremendous and unwavering support of my wife Martina. She has stood beside me in the course of writing of this book in particular, as well as in my too often excessively time-consuming academic endeavours more generally. While the ideas for this book have been evolving, we were also blessed with three sons: David, Luka and Jakob. Their unbounded energy, joy and untainted interest in the world around them have been an immense source of inspiration (as well as a cause for exhaustion) for me. It is thus, for obvious reasons, that this book is dedicated to my family.

Contents

Introduction

THE LAST DECADE has been one of the most turbulent times in the process of European integration. In this period, the EU has literally risen to the stars and fell back from the heavens. The beginning of the new millennium was marked by enviable achievements. The EU carried out a successful enlargement to the East. It adopted a single currency and the economic growth was booming. The objective, laid down in the Lisbon strategy, was to make the EU 'the most competitive and dynamic knowledge-based economy in the world, capable of sustainable economic growth with more and better jobs and greater social cohesion'. This goal ought to have been met by 2020. However, the developments that took place since 2000 have made the attainment of this objective anything but possible. Rather than becoming the leading economy in the world, since 2009 the EU has been in a permanent state of economic crisis and, while this has been tamed, it is far from resolved. Its consequences for the most affected Member States in the South and in the East have been grave. They have shaken up the foundations of the well-ordered societies that these Member States have at least tried or pretended to be.

The outcome has been a deep political crisis. This has unleashed an unprecedented wave of populism, resulting in a backlash against the national and supranational elites. In several Member States, democracy and the rule of law have come under strain. The achievements of constitutional democracy have been rolled back and the very value foundations on which the EU has been built have been seriously undermined. The unfavourable geostrategic environment, both to the EU's East and South, has exacerbated the crisis. The influx of refugees and migrants from the Middle East added a humanitarian dimension to this. The unprecedented terrorist attacks in several Member States complemented the crisis with a security component. All this has, directly and indirectly, influenced British voters to decide in favour of leaving the EU. The Brexit decision has thrown the EU into a bigger political turmoil, straining integration to the point at which its very existence seems to have come into question.

Not unexpectedly, in this unhappy decade the main preoccupation of academic and political actors alike has been to identify the remedies for the crises just described and to return the EU to the path of stability, growth and prosperity. The question most typically asked, both in theory and in practice, has therefore been what can or should be possibly done within the EU, its institutions and on behalf of its Member States to develop an effective response to the crises. The crisis-resolution focus has thus been an internal one. It has centred almost exclusively on the improvements in the organisational structure of the EU and its overall functioning. This book takes the opposite approach. Its point of departure is that the internal focus, while justified, is simply inadequate. Neither the origins of the several crises referred to above nor the solutions to them are exclusively internal to the EU. On the contrary, there are jurisgenerative actors beyond the EU of varying legal status: public, private and hybrid, which importantly affect the EU's internal functioning as a whole and challenge its capacity to function as a well-ordered polity. These actors operate transnationally and the norms created by them have been called transnational law.

It is against this highly topical backdrop that this book proceeds by focusing on the relationship between the EU and transnational law. EU law and transnational law have already received quite an extensive treatment in legal scholarship. However, they have rarely (if at all) been addressed together. Thus, not only is this book topical, it is also novel and its focus is original, at least in a double sense.

First of all, it is original since transnational law is a relatively recent phenomenon and its challenges to the EU are therefore qualitatively new and under-researched. While the literature on the law beyond the state and on other types of non-statist law has been flourishing at least since the late 1990s, it has been predominantly focused on the question of meaning of new types of law(s) and governance through law for the state (law). The same question, however, has not been posed with regard to the EU, which is itself a non-statist, post-national and therefore transnational entity. Thus, the question of the relationship between EU law and transnational law has not been asked before. It is hence an original question in need of a compelling answer, which would fill the void that is both theoretical and practical.

However, the focus of the book is original in yet another way. Traditionally the challenges to the functioning of the EU have come from the Member States. These internal challenges and the answers to them have been gathered in a huge and still-growing body of literature devoted to EU constitutional law *sensu lato*. Transnational law, on the other hand, poses challenges to the EU, which are external; they are operating in an outside-in rather than an inside-out direction, which is where the traditional focus has been centred thus far. Yet, this is not to argue that the internal constitutional challenges of the EU have been resolved. On the contrary, it is to claim, as this book does, that while the internal challenges have not been sufficiently addressed yet, the newly emergent external challenges are making this task even more difficult. To have a holistic understanding of the process of European integration, it is therefore necessary to complement the internal constitutional dimension with the external transnational dimension.

This book therefore addresses the question of the relationship between EU law and transnational law. The interest in this relationship does not merely grow out of an abstract, theoretical curiosity as to how to structure, relate and conceive of these two phenomena together. It is instead derived from concrete practical problems that transnational law has recently posed to the EU with respect to the rule of law, democracy, human rights protection and justice. These four values stand for qualitative standards that any polity has to meet in order to qualify as a well-ordered political community. The EU is no exception. It has proclaimed these standards as its foundational legal values, enshrined in Article 2 of the Treaty on European Union (TEU). As the rule of law, democracy, human rights protection and justice are thus at the heart of the functioning of the EU, they must be chosen as a natural point of departure for case studies, in which the impact of transnational law on the EU will be examined and theoretical conclusions will be drawn.

This conclusion is reaffirmed by the fact that the EU, largely due to its specific legal and political nature, has not been particularly good at implementing its foundational values. The literature blaming the EU constitutional structure for all kinds of deficits in the rule of law, democracy, human rights protection and justice is burgeoning. However, the present, apparently insufficient capacity of the EU to address and remove its constitutional deficits is bound to deteriorate further because of transnational law's external influence. One of the main normative concerns of the book is therefore how to prevent and/or reverse a negative spiral, in which the internal and the external dimensions of the EU's functioning keep feeding the vicious circle of its rising constitutional deficits.

However, to meet this objective, this book first needs to climb the theoretical conceptual hurdle concerning transnational law. While the interest in transnational law has been growing progressively, it still remains an opaque and ill-defined concept. This can be attributed to different factors. The most important of these is the fact that transnational law escapes the theoretical confines of the conventional understanding of law. Transnational law often goes by undetected because it simply does not count as law in conventional modernist terms.[1] Simultaneously, transnational actors and their practices strongly challenge the formal and substantive contours of the conventional concept of law too. The latter has thus grown increasingly inadequate even to describe the legal landscape beyond the state. In order to put transnational law on the legal map, the conventional concept of law needs to be adapted. This calls for a fresh theoretical perspective, which this book offers by way of advancing the theory of principled legal pluralism.

The theory of principled legal pluralism is the backbone of the book and drives it towards four main research objectives. First, the book provides a revised pluralist understanding of the conventional concept of law. Second, on that basis it develops a compelling, rigorous conceptual account of transnational law and of the EU. Third, the book argues that the relationship between EU law and transnational law is, as a matter of description and explanation, best conceived of in terms of principled legal pluralism. Finally, it is demonstrated on the basis of concrete, practical interactions between the EU and transnational law in the domains of the rule of law, democracy, human rights protection and justice that these internal constitutional values of the EU are best secured if and when the relationship between EU law and transnational law is conducted following the normative prescriptions of principled legal pluralism.

---

[1] M Avbelj, 'Transnational Law between Modernity and Postmodernity' (2016) 7 *Transnational Legal Theory* 406.

The book is divided into eight chapters. Chapter 1 is a descriptive and conceptual chapter focusing on the phenomenon of transnational law, its evolution and its simultaneously contested and under-theorised nature. It puts forth its own conceptualisation of transnational law *sensu lato* and *stricto sensu* by neatly distinguishing between public, administrative and private bodies of transnational law depending on the degree of the public authorities' involvement in the creation of transnational norms. The proposed conceptualisation of transnational law raises questions about the transnational law's *real* legal character and it reveals a considerable misfit between transnational law and the conventional concept of law in both of the latter's dimensions: the formal and the substantive dimensions. This discussion paves the way to the main theoretical contribution of the book.

Chapter 2 thus advances the theory of principled legal pluralism. It explains why there is a need for a fresh theoretical approach, how it differs from the existing leading theoretical approaches in the field, both constitutional and pluralist, and what its core elements are. The chapter argues that the theory of principled legal pluralism provides a compelling conceptualisation and an accurate description of transnational and EU law. Furthermore, it claims that principled legal pluralism is also a very persuasive explanatory and normatively attractive account both of transnational law and EU law, as well as of the relationship between the two. The rest of the book is dedicated to the substantiation of these claims, both on the theoretical/conceptual level as well as on the basis of concrete practical case studies.

Chapter 3 hence develops a legally pluralist conception of the EU as a union. This is a special pluralist constitutional form, consisting of three layers: the national, the supranational and the common whole that, at the time of writing, draw together 29 autonomous legal orders and an equal number of polities. In contrast with other (proto-)federal regimes, which are held together by a degree of social homogeneity and/or hierarchical legal structure, the union is a heterarchical structure, which in the absence of homogeneity is viable due to the normative spirit of pluralism that it is permeated by. The theory of principled legal pluralism proves itself as a theory, which can accurately describe and persuasively explain the project of European integration and also, in normative terms, contributes towards its viability. Additionally, it provides a theoretical anchor for the concept of the union, which is a unique constitutional form that this book is launching in the contemporary EU legal scholarship.

Having developed the conception of transnational and EU law, the book then examines through the theoretical lens of principled legal pluralism the relationship between the two in the domains of the rule of law, democracy, human rights protection and justice. The book first analyses to what an extent this relationship, as it stands, complies with the requirements of principled legal pluralism. To the extent that such a descriptive and explanatory fit is found to be lacking, the book provides normative prescriptions as to how the relationship could be structured in a pluralist way to better meet the objectives of the rule of law, democracy, human rights and justice. With regard to each of the four standards, a different type of transnational law is focused on in order to also test whether the modalities of the relationship between EU law and transnational law depend on the category of transnational law involved.

Chapter 4 is thus concerned with the rule of law under the influence of international law, which is an example of public transnational law. The latter's impact on the rule of law in the EU is examined on the basis of the notorious *Kadi* case. As is well known, because of the peculiar interplay between the EU internal constitutional structure and international law, Mr Kadi was caught in a legal limbo, falling short of formal, substantive and sociological requirements of the rule of law. It is argued that had the relationship between EU law and international law been conducted pursuant to the prescriptions of principled legal pluralism, the rule of law conditions in the EU as well as Mr Kadi's rights would have been much better secured.

Chapter 5 focuses on the impact of transnational private corporate law and transnational private administrative law on democracy in the EU. It shows that during the economic crisis, the interaction between these two forms of transnational law and the internal constitutional structure of the EU has led to a pre-emption of democracy across the institutional, substantive and economic domains at the national and supranational levels of the EU. Credit rating agencies have acted as the gatekeepers of the global financial markets, which have relied more on their ratings than on the political assurances of states and the EU in need of fresh capital. The resulting outcome has been a standoff between the EU and transnational law. This has had a corroding effect on democracy in the EU, which, in the absence of funds, cannot perform its basic function of being a system of government based on veritable self-determination. The chapter explains how, by following the normative prescriptions of principled legal pluralism, the relationship between the EU and transnational law should be reshaped in a way that will better serve and protect the objectives of democracy in the EU.

In Chapter 6, the book focuses on transnational law's effects on human rights protection in the EU. In the centre of analysis is the right to privacy at the intersection of EU law and two disparate hybrid and private transnational legal regimes of *lex sportiva* and *lex informatica*. Peering through the lens of theory of principled legal pluralism, the relationship is analysed on the basis of the leading cases of the Court of Justice of the European Union (CJEU) in the fields of *lex sportiva* and *lex informatica* (including the most recent Google and Facebook rulings). It is revealed that the relationship's actual pluralist character depends on several factors, such as the maturity and robustness of a transnational legal order, as well as its primary purpose (economic or other). The chapter also drafts pluralist guidelines to optimise the objectives of the disparate legal orders involved and, in particular, the protection of human rights of the affected individuals.

Chapter 7 addresses, by way of the last case study, the implications of transnational law for justice in the EU. The question of justice is a perennial one, but it has surprisingly received almost no attention in the relationship between EU and transnational law, despite the fact that in recent years, the dilemmas of justice in the EU have also been exacerbated due to transnational law and its actors. As a groundbreaking contribution, this chapter thus discusses three different ways in which transnational law has been contributing to injustice in the EU. The first example is injustice as a lack of justification, which results directly from transnational law as a whole. The second example is economic injustice caused indirectly by sector-specific economic transnational law. Finally, the last example is injustice as an affront to human dignity also stemming, albeit even more indirectly, from specific segments of mostly private transnational law. The discussion once again demonstrates that if the admittedly dynamic and complex relationship between EU law and transnational law is conducted pursuant to the normative guidance of principled legal pluralism, this results in less injustice being created in, by and outside of the EU.

Chapter 8 wraps up the discussion by outlining the main theoretical and practical outcomes of the book. In so doing, it, finally, also pauses with the actual viability of principled legal pluralism in the contemporary world order. The latter has increasingly been witnessing a come-back of the old and the emergence of the new monisms. They pose a considerable threat to a pluralist normative scenario defended in the following pages and, in that way, also to the values of the rule of law, democracy, human rights protection and justice in the EU and beyond.

1

The Emergence and Growth of Transnational Law

I. REACHING BEYOND THE EXCLUSIVE STATIST FOCUS IN EU LAW

SINCE THE END of the Second World War, the legal landscape has undergone profound empirical changes. Most importantly, the state has lost its monopoly over law-making. It has ceased to be an exclusive source of the law. The statist jurisgenerative function has been transformed, supplemented and sometimes even replaced by other sites of law-making beyond the state.[1] The initially circumscribed and exclusively state-dependent international law has grown in its scope, has deepened the *ratione materiae* and has fragmented across a plethora of public functional regimes.[2] The role of the state in international law, while still central, has thus subsided. Alongside a range of international organisations and international adjudicative bodies, the state has become one of the many actors in international law.[3] Some international regimes have even won functional independence from their founding member states. Among these self-contained regimes, the supranational legal order of the EU, which has resulted mostly out of a decades-long judicial construction by the EU's top court, the European Court of Justice, is the best-known and most developed example.

The EU has been advanced and championed as a model for the post-national, global governance of tomorrow, destined to complement and rescue rather than supplant its Member States.[4] It ought to provide a constitutional framework for a mutual engagement of states, facilitating the pursuit of common objectives, which would be more than a sum of insular national interests and half-baked

---

[1] The literature explaining the process of transformation of the state under the impact of globalisation is burgeoning and there is no aim to do it justice here. For an overview, see P Glenn, *The Cosmopolitan State* (Oxford, Oxford University Press, 2013) 181–86.

[2] See, for example, Report of the Study Group of the International Law Commission, 'Fragmentation of International Law: Difficulties Arising from the Diversification and Expansion of International Law', April 2006, legal.un.org/ilc/documentation/english/a_cn4_l682.pdf.

[3] R Domingo, *The New Global Law* (Cambridge, Cambridge University Press, 2010) 61: 'The death throes of the state certainly are changing the distribution of world power, yielding to new political actors all clamoring for a bigger role on the world stage.'

[4] J Monnet, *Memoires* (New York, Doubleday & Company, 1978); C Bickerton, *European Integration: From Nation-States to Member States* (Oxford, Oxford University Press, 2012).

interstate compromises. The latter has been the method of international law, which has been, as a result, marred by inefficiency, lack of trust and hence too often deprived of its very legality. However, while the EU's uniqueness has made it attractive to other sites of regional cooperation, it came at a price. In the world of states, this neither statist nor international *sui generis* polity has had to deal with an increasing number of crises: the constitutional, the financial, the economic, the political, the rule of law, the security and the humanitarian crises. However, the approach to these crises, with regard to the identification of their causes as well as with regard to their possible solutions, has remained deeply embedded in the statist paradigm.

The EU institutions, the Member States and observers alike have acted as if the causes and the solutions of the crises remain in their hands or at least in the hands of a joint co-operation with the other states making up the international community. As the case studies later on in this book will demonstrate, the ongoing economic crisis has at least disproved this myth. The most vital axis of the EU functioning might still be the one between the Member States and the supranational institutions, but to focus on it exclusively overlooks the complete picture. If the states have been weakened by transnational actors, their capacity to dominate the functioning of the EU must have been affected too. This calls for a double reorientation of our focus. First, we should be concentrating on the EU as a whole, which is more than the sum of its national and supranational parts. Second, as the causes of the crises are not exclusively internal to the EU, but a complex mix of endogenous and exogenous factors, these must be factored in too.

This is because since the 1990s, we have been witnessing an unprecedented increase in the law-making powers of non-statist actors at a transnational level.[5] Beyond the states, other transnational actors (private, public and hybrid) have emerged, which act more or less autonomously, free of the states' influence, while simultaneously heavily influencing their own functioning. Scholars have become increasingly cognisant of this phenomenon, but their focus has remained on the impact of transnational law on the states. The same impact with regard to the EU has been studied much less or even not at all.

In other words, the declining role of the states has also resulted in their circumscribed capacity for bringing about the solutions to the crises of the EU. There are important external transnational non-statist actors, which influence not just the functioning of the states—where the focus has traditionally rested—but also the EU. This is why this book shifts the focus from the relationship between EU law and (Member) States to EU law and transnational law. In so doing, it does not want to diminish or even to deny the importance of the internal functioning of the EU and the contribution of the (Member) States to it, but it does insist that a more

---

[5] This has prompted one academic observer to proclaim that 'we live in an age of transnationalism'. See G Shaffer, 'Transnational Legal Ordering and State Change' in G Shaffer (ed), *Transnational Legal Ordering and State Change* (Cambridge, Cambridge University Press, 2013).

accurate picture can only emerge through a more holistic approach, which brings in the external dimension and the influence of non-statist transnational actors. The book's objective, therefore, is to fill the gap in the EU scholarship by exploring the relationship between the EU and transnational law. This exploration begins by first laying down the concept of transnational law.

II. THE CONCEPT OF TRANSNATIONAL LAW

The concept of transnational law,[6] as a law in-between,[7] is elusive.[8] It was first used in the 1930s by Max Gutzwiller, but then only as a label.[9] Conceptually it was endowed with more substance in 1956 by Philip Jessup, who defined transnational law:

> [T]o include all law which regulates actions or events that transcend national frontiers. Both public and private international law are included, as well as other rules which do not wholly fit into such standard categories.[10]

This is obviously a very broad, perhaps even over-inclusive definition. Not only is any law beyond the state considered as transnational law, but the latter includes also 'other rules', which apparently do not need to be necessarily legal. This poses a problem of the utility of a concept that is so broad as to lose any distinctiveness.[11] It also raises a more acute objection as to what makes transnational law legal in the first place. These two critiques, especially if taken together, are fatal. They deprive us of the capacity to define transnational law *in abstracto*, which in turn makes it impossible to map out actual phenomena as transnational law in practice.

The legal character of transnational law depends on the kind of concept of law one subscribes to.[12] This book joins those who agree that transnational law

---

[6] This section draws heavily on M Avbelj, 'Transnational Law between Modernity and Postmodernity' (2016) 7 *Transnational Legal Theory* 406.

[7] K Tuori, 'Transnational Law: On Legal Hybrids and Perspectivism' in M Maduro, K Tuori and S Sankari (eds), *Transnational Law: Rethinking European Law and Legal Thinking* (Cambridge, Cambridge University Press, 2014) 11; P Zumbansen, 'Transnational Legal Pluralism' (2010) 1 *Transnational Legal Theory* 141; N Walker, 'Beyond Boundary Disputes and Basic Grids: Mapping the Global Disorder of Normative Orders' (2008) 6 *International Journal of Constitutional Law* 373; H Hongju Koh, 'Why Transnational Law Matters' (2005–06) 24 *Penn State International Law Review* 745.

[8] Scott has identified three conceptions of transnational law: see C Scott, 'Transnational Law as Proto-concept: Three Conceptions' (2009) 10 *German Law Journal* 859.

[9] C Tietje and K Nowrot, 'Laying Conceptual Ghosts of the Past to Rest: The Rise of Philip C. Jessup's Transnational Law' in C Tietje, A Brouder and K Nowrot (eds), *The Regulatory Governance of the International Economic System* (2006) 50 *Halle-Wittenberg: Beitrage zum Transnationalen Wirtschaftsrecht* 27.

[10] Philip C Jessup, *Transnational Law* (New Haven, Yale University Press, 1956) 1, 3.

[11] For a critique, see R Dibadj, 'Panglossian Transnationalism' (2008) 44 *Stanford Journal of International Law* 253.

[12] For a discussion of the concept of law in the transnational environment, see, R Cotterrell, 'Transnational Communities and the Concept of Law' (2008) 21 *Ratio Juris* 1; B Kingsbury, 'The Concept of "Law" in Global Administrative Law' (2009) 20 *European Journal of International Law* 23; A Somek, 'The Concept of "Law" in Global Administrative Law: A Reply to Benedict Kingsbury' (2009) 20 *European Journal of International Law* 985.

is its own, autonomous and separate field of law.[13] Therefore, and contrary to what is typically attempted, transnational law cannot be subsumed either under international law or under comparative law without changing the two beyond recognition.[14] Perhaps the best way of conceptualising transnational law is by introducing a distinction between its broader and a narrower understanding.[15] The former, the transnational law *sensu lato*, encompasses any law whose effects extend beyond the state, whereas the latter, the transnational law *stricto sensu*, relates only to the body of transnational law that does not originate, either directly or indirectly, from the organs of the state. The transnational law *stricto sensu* is thus transnational law without a state.[16] By following this distinction, whereby the guiding criterion is the authorship or at least influence of the state in the making of transnational legal rules, a map of transnational law *sensu lato* could be drawn as follows.

Transnational law		
Public	**Administrative**	**Private**
International law	Public	New *lex mercatoria*
Supranational law	Hybrid	Transnational corporate law
Private international law	Private	
Transnational human rights regimes		

The map is composed of three parts. Transnational law *sensu lato* can be: public; administrative and private. Public transnational law consists of international law, supranational law, private international law and transnational human rights litigation regimes. International law includes legal norms that govern the relationships between states as well as between states and international organisations. International law belongs to public transnational law because it exists in the legal realm beyond the state and is exclusively created by public entities, either directly or indirectly by the states in their engagement in international law-making through international organisations.

---

[13] TC Halliday and G Shaffer, 'Transnational Legal Orders' in TC Halliday and G Shaffer (eds), *Transnational Legal Orders* (Cambridge, Cambridge University Press, 2015) 20.

[14] L Cata Backer, 'Principles of Transnational Law: The Foundations of an Emerging Field', lcbackerblog.blogspot.com/2007/03/principles-of-transnational-law.html.

[15] For a similar distinction, see G-P Calliess, 'Reflexive Transnational Law: The Privatisation of Civil Law and Civilisation of the Private Law' (2002) 23 *Zeitschrift fur Rechtssoziologie* 185. Calliess defines transnational law as a third-level autonomous legal system beyond municipal and public international law, created and developed by the law-making forces of a global civil society, founded on the general principles of law as well as societal usages, administered by private dispute resolution service providers and codified (if at all) by private norm-formulating agencies. See also G Shaffer, 'Transnational Legal Process and State Change' (2012) 37 *Law and Social Inquiry* 229, as well as G Shaffer (ed), *Transnational Legal Ordering and State Change* (Cambridge, Cambridge University Press, 2013).

[16] To paraphrase Teubner's global law without a state, see G Teubner, 'Foreword', as well as 'Global Bukowina': Legal Pluralism in the World Society' in G Teubner (ed), *Global Law without a State* (Dartmouth, Ashgate, 1997).

Supranational law is an example of an autonomous legal order, separate both from national legal orders as well as from international law. Its most developed, but probably not exclusive example is the law of the EU. Originally created as a regional international organisation, it has, through the institutional practices that have been (explicitly or tacitly) sanctioned by the Member States, created its own legal order, with its own constitutive rules, principles and practices that in many ways depart significantly from the general international law. The supranational law of the EU is part of public transnational law as it is situated in the legal space beyond the Member States. As masters of the founding treaties, they remain in control of the constitutional set-up of the EU and continue to keep hold of its law-making powers, even though they have long lost the monopoly over them due to the erosion of the consensus requirement, the special independent role of the Commission and the growing powers of the European Parliament.

The next example of public transnational law is private international law. The latter is state-made law, which regulates the choice of law and determines the competent jurisdictions over cases involving cross-border elements. Private international law belongs to transnational law because of the remit of its application. It is state law, eg, part of statist legal hierarchy, which applies to transnational situations. In that way, it differs from international and supranational law, which originate from states, without being part of the national legal hierarchy; rather, they are situated in the transnational legal space from where they regulate and affect transnational as well as national situations.[17]

Finally, public transnational law also includes those national regimes which provide for universal jurisdiction. The best-known example of this kind is the US Alien Tort Claims Act. Following the *Filártiga* ruling,[18] this has enabled foreign claimants to bring courts actions in the US for torts committed in violation of international law in a third country.[19] The *Filártiga* decision has opened the gates[20] widely for the so-called transnational litigation of the violations of human rights committed mostly by transnational actors in the environments where the appropriate forum for seeking judicial redress was either de jure or de facto missing. The regime for transnational human rights litigation belongs to public transnational law because its legal basis derives from the state and because it is effectuated in the courts of the state. They decide on the cases of pure transnational origin, which come under their jurisdiction solely by virtue of the plaintiff's tort action against an individual over whom the judging state has obtained a personal jurisdiction.[21]

---

[17] This distinction between transnational law which 'only' applies to transnational situations and transnational law which is a transnational construction and flow of legal norms relies on G Shaffer, 'Transnational Legal Process and State Change' (2012) 37 *Law and Social Inquiry* 229, 233–234.

[18] *Filártiga v Peña-Irala* 630 F 2d 876 (2d Cir. 1980).

[19] For an early discussion of this case, see A-M Burley, 'The Alien Tort Statute and the Judiciary Act of 1789: A Badge of Honor' (1989) 83 *American Journal of International Law* 461.

[20] They have been recently basically closed by the Supreme Court ruling in *Kiobel v Royal Dutch Petroleum Co* 133 S Ct 1659 (2013).

[21] See Burley (n 19) 461.

It is thus characteristic of public transnational law that states continue to exercise relatively direct control over the transnational law-making process. However, this control is incrementally weakening as we move to the field of administrative transnational law.[22] This corresponds to global administrative law as defined by Kingsbury, Krisch and Stewart,[23] and later developed further by Sabino Cassese and others.[24] However, while only some rules of global administrative law have global effects or scope of application,[25] they all have transnational effects, which thus favours the use of the term transnational law rather than global administrative law. Administrative transnational law thus exists in transnational administrative space governed by transnational administrative bodies which might be of a public, hybrid (public-private) and private character.[26] Accordingly, administrative transnational law is broken down into three groups: public, hybrid and private administrative transnational law.

Before looking more closely at each of these groups, let us examine what exactly the adjective 'administrative' adds to transnational law. Classifying transnational rules as administrative designates their mezzo-level legal character and specific (eg, administrative) function. Administrative transnational rules are adopted within the permissible legal scope defined by the law of the state, international law, supranational law or private contractual regimes for their respective actors. Administrative transnational rules are thus always derived from pre-existing legal bases from which they must trace their origin and validity. The function of transnational administrative rules is to administer, execute or to make possible the execution of policies contained in more abstract and general rules through the setting of regulatory standards.[27]

As stated above, transnational administrative law can be public, hybrid or private. Public administrative transnational law is created by the organs of the state, international organisations or supranational organisations. State organs can create transnational administrative law on two levels: first, on the domestic level by adopting regulatory decisions with transboundary effects—Kingsbury, Krisch and Stewart have dubbed this mode of transnational administrative

---

[22] For a prominent account that argues that the EU is, in fact, an example of (supranational) administrative law, see PL Lindseth, *Power and Legitimacy: Reconciling Europe and the Nation-State* (Oxford, Oxford University Press, 2010).

[23] B Kingsbury, N Krisch and RB Stewart, 'The Emergence of Global Administrative Law' (2005) 68 *Law and Contemporary Problems* 15.

[24] S Cassese (ed), *Research Handbook on Global Administrative Law* (Cheltenham, Edward Elgar, 2016).

[25] ibid 18–19; see also Shaffer, 'Transnational Legal Process and State Change' (n 15) 232: 'The concept of transnational law has been developed, in parallel, to address legal norms that do not clearly fall within traditional conceptions of national and international law, but are not necessarily global in nature.'

[26] See Kingsbury, Krisch and Stewart (n 23).

[27] ibid 17: '[transnational] administrative action is rulemaking, adjudications, and other decisions that are neither treaty-making nor simple dispute settlements between parties'.

law-making 'distributed administration';[28] second, states also create transnational administrative rules in the transnational administrative space beyond the state by taking part in formal, semi-formal and informal transnational regulatory networks in which they co-operate with other states and/or international and supranational organisations. Therefore, this second mode of primarily state-driven transnational administration through transnational regulatory networks[29] can, depending on the actors involved, be statist, international, supranational or combined.[30]

Public administrative transnational law also emanates from the international administration[31] in international organisations addressing the regulatory questions in the fields of the economy,[32] finance, the environment[33] and security.[34] With reference to international administration, Kingsbury, Krisch and Stewart distinguish between international administration with direct[35] and indirect regulatory effects.[36] It is also created by the supranational administration which takes place in the supranational organisations, such as the EU. Within the latter, one should emphasise the system of comitology as an example of a well-developed supranational regulatory network composed of committees consisting of the representatives of the state, supranational and expert interests.[37] However, the latter very frequently come from the private sector, which brings the system of comitology very close to hybrid transnational administrative law.

Hybrid transnational administrative law is created in the transnational administrative space beyond the state jointly by public (statist, international, supranational) and private actors. Private actors can be representatives of various transnational civil societies;[38] they can be drafted from different expert groups, scientific communities and associations, they can be representatives of businesses etc. Transnational civil society has been composed mainly of transnational

---

[28] ibid 19.

[29] ibid 20.

[30] ibid 20–23.

[31] ibid 21.

[32] ibid.

[33] ibid 19. According to the authors, environmental regulation is partly the work of non-environmental administrative bodies such as the World Bank, the Organisation for Economic Co-operation and Development (OECD) and the World Trade Organization (WTO), but increasingly far-reaching regulatory structures are being established in specialised regimes such as the prospective emissions trading scheme and the Clean Development Mechanism in the Kyoto Protocol.

[34] ibid. Administrative action is now an important component of many international security regimes, including the work of the UN Security Council and its committees, and in related fields such as nuclear energy regulation (the IAEA) or the supervision mechanism of the Chemical Weapons Convention.

[35] ibid 21.

[36] ibid.

[37] GJ Brandsma, *Controlling Comitology* (Basingstoke, Palgrave Macmillan, 2013).

[38] RD Lipschutz, 'Reconstructing World Politics: the Emergence of Global Civil Society' (1992) 21 *Millennium, Journal of International Studies* 390 has defined a transnational civil society as 'the self-conscious constructions of networks of knowledge and action, by decentred, local actors, that cross the reified boundaries of space as though they were not there'.

religious actors and transnational sector-based NGOs. Historically religious communities predated the modern Westphalian state, whose emergence then led to an intricate relationship between the laws of the state and of the church.[39] With the progress of the process of secularisation, especially in the West, the religious communities were in a temporary retreat. However, the late twentieth century has witnessed a revival of religious actors and communities, which have seized the technological advancement to enhance and strengthen their cross-border networks, mostly through application and development of religious 'soft power'.[40] In so doing, transnational religious actors have exerted increasing influence over sovereign states, international politics, order and dis-order, the latter in particular in the Islamic part of the world.[41]

At the same time, we have also witnessed an immense growth of the transnational sector-based non-governmental organisations (NGOs), both in terms of numbers as well as in terms of their geographical reach. Transnational NGOs have been defined as 'a group of persons or of societies, freely created by private initiative, that pursue an interest in matters that cross or transcend national borders'.[42] NGOs should be distinguished (although the line is sometimes blurred) from intergovernmental organisations (IOs), which come into being through intergovernmental co-operation, as well as from the transnational corporate actors (discussed below) because they are not profit seekers.[43] NGOs exercise four core functions in the transnational realm: they contribute to the development, interpretation, judicial application and enforcement of transnational law.[44] They also work together with representatives of states, international and supranational organisations in a variety of standard-setting bodies or run the so-called certification programmes.[45] Depending on the degree of involvement and influence of the public actor on the decision-making process, these hybrid standard-setting or certifying bodies can be more or less public.

In case of standard-setting and certifying bodies in which states or other public entities are absent from the decision-making process, we can speak about

---

[39] This has been fittingly described as the '*locus classicus* of thinking about the multiplicity of normative orders'. see M Galanter, 'Justice in Many Rooms: Courts, Private Ordering, and Indigenous Law' (1981) 19 *Journal of Legal Pluralism* 28.

[40] J Haynes, 'Transnational Religious Actors and International Order' (2009) 17 *Perspectives* 47.

[41] 'How ISIS Works' *New York Times* (16 September 2014) www.nytimes.com/interactive/2014/09/16/world/middleeast/how-isis-works.html; also, on Al-Qaeda as an example of transnational Islamist terrorism, see K Dalacoura, *Islamist Terrorism and Democracy in the Middle East* (Cambridge, Cambridge University Press, 2011) 40–65.

[42] S Charnovitz, 'Non-governmental Organizations and International Law' (2006) 100 *American Journal of International Law* 350.

[43] ibid.

[44] ibid 352. The author, however, limits the scope of NGOs only to international law; see also T Muller, 'Customary Transnational Law: Attacking the Last Resort of State Sovereignty' (2008) 15 *Indiana Journal of Global Legal Studies* 19.

[45] L Cata Backer, 'Private Actors and Public Governance beyond the State: The Multinational Corporation, the Financial Stability Board and the Global Governance Order' (2011) 18 *Indiana Journal of Global Legal Studies* 767.

the emergence of private administrative transnational law.[46] Examples quoted in the literature include: the International Accounting Standards Board (IASB); underwriting laboratories; the Motion Picture Association of America; the Financial Industry Regulatory Authority (FIRA); the International Standardization Organization; the International Electrotechnical Commission (IEC); the Forestry Stewardship Council (FSC); the Fair Labor Association; Fairtrade International; the International Council of Chemical Associations; the International Social and Environmental Accreditation and Labelling Alliance; the Internet Corporation for Assigned Names and Numbers (ICANN); the Codex Alimentarius Commission; *lex sportiva internationalis*; *lex constructionis* etc. Most of the rule-makers in the field of private administrative transnational law are thus founded as private, non-governmental, not-for-profit entities, although they can be recognised or authorised by the legislature or the executive in the country of their incorporation. The rules produced by these private actors are administrative because they bind or regulate through acceptance the collective practices of numerous entities in designated sectors without their prior assent to these rules. Private administrative transnational law is thus not the contract-based law of horizontal application between consenting parties, but carries with it elements of verticality and authority, which are not founded on consent.

This is also how private administrative transnational law differs from the last group of transnational law: private transnational law. Private transnational law is normally contract-based.[47] It emanates from consensual agreements and practices of participating private parties engaged in horizontal, non-authoritative relationships, defined by at least the formal equality of parties. One example of this type of private transnational law is the so-called new *lex mercatoria* (law merchant).[48] Stone Sweet has fittingly defined it as 'the totality of actors, usages, organizational techniques, and guiding principles that animate private, transnational trading relations'.[49] The new *lex mercatoria* consists of two distinct but related bodies of norms: substantive and procedural norms. The first of these encompasses rules, principles and standards of the nascent transnational contract law.[50] The second governs and institutionalises the (largely arbitral) procedural mechanisms for

---

[46] EC Ip, 'Globalization and the Future of the Law of the Sovereign State' (2010) 8 *International Journal of Constitutional Law* 644.

[47] Cata Backer (n 45) 769: 'These regulatory regimes are not effectuated using the well-known tools of state regulations—positive law and judicial and administrative decisions. Rather, contract serves as the means by which the "law" of this system is memoralized and made binding.'

[48] For an overview of the development of the *lex mercatoria* and the new *lex mercatoria*, as well as on the diverging theoretical opinions on it, see K-P Berger, *The Creeping Codification of the New Lex Mercatoria* (The Hague, Kluwer Law International, 2010).

[49] A Stone Sweet, 'The New *Lex Mercatoria* and Transnational Governance' (2006) 13 *Journal of European Public Policy* 629.

[50] ibid 633–35. These can also form a coherent body of legal norms in a designated functional field, such as the laws regulating the carriage of goods by sea (*lex maritima*); see, for example, W Tetley, 'The General Maritime Law—The *Lex Maritima*' (1994) 20 *Syracuse Journal of International Law and Commerce* 133, 133–34.

resolving disputes related to transnational trade.[51] Driven by the functionalist agenda of facilitating transnational trade, both bodies of rules of the new *lex mercatoria* were initially practice-based. They have therefore evolved spontaneously to be incrementally taken up and codified by private transnational specialised associations and chambers of professional interests.[52] To ensure the autonomy of the new *lex mercatoria*, this codification has been deliberately done without involving national governments. However, the states, while still the principal and ultimate enforcers of the new *lex mercatoria*,[53] have for a variety of instrumental reasons,[54] as well for the simple reason of their incapacity to provide functional means to foster transnational trade,[55] recognised this autonomy and created ever more room for it.

Another type of private transnational law derives from the self-regulatory activities of the organs of transnational corporations. This is the so-called transnational corporate law, which consists of the norms regulating the internal governance of a corporation as well as the relationships between corporations.[56] Due to their growing economic power and increased mobility of capital, multinational corporations have increasingly outgrown the regulatory territorial boundaries of particular states and have circumvented their monopoly on power. They are nowadays increasingly able to forum shop for the best national regulations and, especially in relationships with developing countries, can impose their standards and regulatory expectations over the national laws of those countries. In many ways, the transnational corporations have become their own, autonomous rule-makers. Their rules, developed independently of national legal and political influences, usually come into being and are enforced through contracts and very often take the form of soft law with effects functionally paralleling that of hard law.[57] Internally, these rules, created by the governing bodies of the corporations alone[58] or in collaboration with the stakeholders in the corporate supply chain, tend to govern the overall corporate activity of an enterprise.[59] Externally, these rules come into

---

[51]   Stone Sweet (n 49) 635–37.

[52]   The most important among them is UNCITRAL, as well as the International Chamber of Commerce etc.

[53]   Which leads the so-called traditionalists to argue that even the new *lex mercatoria* is still state-dependent law; see Stone Sweet (n 49) 637.

[54]   ibid 639–40. The author mentions three reasons: to attract transnational trade; to relieve the national judiciary of an overload of cases; and to attract financially stimulating transnational arbitral bodies.

[55]   ibid. The author believes that 'state-supplied institutions governing trade probably reached their functional limits no later than in the 1960s'.

[56]   With regard to the distinction between internal and external transnational corporate rules, I am drawing on Cata Backer (n 47).

[57]   ibid 765.

[58]   The most well-known act of this sort are the codes of corporate governance. They are normally drafted by non-state actors, such as NGOs, private industry institutes or corporate actors. See P Zumbansen, 'Neither "Public" nor "Private", "National" nor "International": Transnational Corporate Governance from a Legal Pluralist Perspective' (2011) 38 *Journal of Law and Society* 50.

[59]   Cata Backer (n 45) 762.

being and regulate on a voluntary participative basis the relationships among the community of enterprises.[60] Transnational corporate law thus stands for the private, autonomous, increasingly institutionalised law-making capacities of transnational corporations, conducting their business across national frontiers on the transnational and even global plane in selected, narrow or all-encompassing functional economic domains.[61]

III. THE CHALLENGES OF TRANSNATIONAL LAW

The emergence and growth of transnational law has brought about a number of practical challenges, not just to the functioning of the states, but, inevitably, also to the EU. Several of them will be focused on later on in this book. However, before doing so, it needs to be acknowledged that the challenge has not been merely practical, but also theoretical. Transnational law has impacted on the very way the law as such is being conceived of, practised and normatively guided. To describe this in the words figuratively used by Zumbansen:

> [T]ransnational law works itself like a drill through the few remaining blankets hastily thrown over an impoverished and internally decaying conceptual body [of modern law].[62]

The law as it has been classically conceived of and practised since the Peace of Westphalia—the modern law—has been the law of states, a statist law. Now the state has obviously lost its monopoly over law-making. The breaking-up of the statist legal monopoly through the emergence of transnational jurisgenerative sites described above has created a plurality of legal orders and orderings.[63] The era of legal monism has been replaced by the era of legal polycentricity.[64] This has, in turn, led to an empirical transformation of the foundational concept of modernity[65]—the concept of sovereignty. Traditionally, sovereignty has been

---

[60] ibid.

[61] ibid 756. See also G-P Calliess and P Zumbansen (eds), *Rough Consensus and Running Code: A Theory of Transnational Private Law* (Oxford, Hart Publishing, 2010) ch 4.

[62] P Zumbansen, 'Transnational Law' (2008) 9 *CLPE Research Paper* 739.

[63] The distinction is Shaffer's ((n 5) 7): 'The concept of legal ordering is used to assess the construction, flow, and impact of transnational legal norms. The term transnational legal order is conceptualized as a collection of legal norms and associated institutions within a given domain that order behavior across national jurisdictions.'

[64] Tuori (n 7) 24: '"Polycentricity" connotes a multiplication of sources of law; the fact that new participants have been granted access to legal discourse, where the ever-changing content of the legal order is determined.'

[65] Pursuant to J Bartelson, *A Genealogy of Sovereignty* (Cambridge, Cambridge University Press, 1995) 5–6, sovereignty is a fundamental assumption about authority, the source of knowledge about the political world on the basis of which this world is constructed, ordered and changed; see also M Loughlin, 'Ten Tenets of Sovereignty' in N Walker (ed), *Sovereignty in Transition* (Oxford, Hart Publishing, 2003) 80.

understood and practised as an absolute, indivisible, unitary property of a territorially delimited state, which ultimately autonomously and exhaustively governs its internal affairs and enjoys equal independence externally in relation to other states.[66] With the emergence of new, non-statist, non-territorial, largely functional jurisgenerative entities, sovereignty has evolved from an exclusively territorial to a functional concept, creating not just a possibility for but also the actual practice of a plurality of sovereigns within the same territory.[67]

The shift from territoriality to functionality has gone hand in hand with the blurring of the public-private divide.[68] In contrast to that in the past, the contemporary law with third party (and hence public) effects is increasingly created by private or hybrid actors rather than by public actors alone.[69] In this empirical legal evolution from an exclusively territorial to a functional phenomenon, with a plurality of sources of law (both public and private) within the same territory, another central tenet of statist law could not have escaped unaffected. Legal hierarchy has been significantly undermined, perhaps even abandoned, as putative legal orders and regimes have made and recognised increasingly plausible claims of relating inter se in a heterarchical rather than a hierarchical way.[70]

All these developments have eventually undermined the law's central value of order, both in its formal and substantive dimensions. The legal order's formal requirements of coherence, stability and consequently of predictability and certainty have been threatened by the described plurality of jurisgenerative sites and fragmentation of laws in the absence of a clear-cut hierarchy.[71] In substantive terms, this has undermined the assumption of the uniformity of the law's substantive standards, epitomised by human rights. Legal monism has thus evolved into formal legal plurality marked by a substantive value diversity rather than uniformity.

Last but not least, the emergence and growth of transnational law have even triggered the rethinking of our legal thought—of the very way we reason in and about the law. This has traditionally been embedded in the monistic mindset, whose supreme substantive value is order, relying on the procedural apparatus of

---

[66] J Bodin, *Six livres de la Republique* (1576).

[67] M Avbelj, 'Theorizing Sovereignty and European Integration' (2014) 27 *Ratio Juris* 356.

[68] For a recent analysis, see H-W Micklitz, 'Rethinking the Public/Private Divide' in Maduro, Tuori and Sankari (n 7); I-J Sand, 'Globalization and the Transcendence of the Public/Private Divide—What is Public Law under Conditions of Globalization?' in C M Amhlaigh, C Michelon and N Walker (eds), *After Public Law*, (Oxford, Oxford University Press, 2013).

[69] P Jurcys, PF Kjaer and R Yatsunami (eds), *Regulatory Hybridization in the Transnational Sphere* (Leiden, Brill, 2013).

[70] Teubner appears to be the first to identify and theorise the trend of law's hierarchy self-deconstruction resulting from the process of globalisation; see G Teubner, 'The King's Many Bodies: The Self-Deconstruction of Law's Hierarchy' (1997) 31 *Law and Society Review* 763, 772; G Teubner and A Fischer-Lascano, 'Regime-Collisions: The Vain Search for Legal Unity in the Fragmentation of Global Law', (2004) 25 *Michigan Journal of International Law* 999.

[71] See P Zumbansen, 'Defining the Space of Transnational Law: Legal Theory, Global Governance, and Legal Pluralism' (2012) 21 *Transnational Law and Contemporary Problems* 314.

binary logic. Glenn confirms this by observing that ever since Plato, but reinforced by the modernist legal thought since the Peace of Westphalia, Western lawyers have been adhering to the pattern of 'hierarchical dualism' underlined by the laws of identity, of non-contradiction and of the excluded middle.[72] However, to grasp the richness of the law beyond the state, and transnational law in particular, it is necessary to look at the spaces in-between the existing legal dichotomies. But in order to do so, the present binary logic has to be supplemented[73] by fuzzy or multivalue logic,[74] which allows for a multivalent approach and brings back in the long-excluded middle.[75]

Transnational law has thus essentially challenged and undercut all the tenets of the classical statist law. It is important to understand that this challenge has been real rather than just theoretically imagined. As explained by Teubner, the profound legal changes derive from the world's material structure rather than from the ideational superstructure of a legal theory.[76] They have been caused by the empirical forces of globalisation.[77] Legal theory, for its own part, has been a notable laggard in coming to terms with these empirical developments. Contrary to Dewey's warning, much of contemporary legal theory remains divorced from facts.[78] When faced with an increasingly complex, multilayered, multidimensional, crosscutting, centrifugal, autonomy-fostering, increasingly particularistic but at the same time closely mutually interdependent legal landscape (or even landscapes), there still persists a theoretical tendency to simply wish these developments away and to resist any theoretical adaptation.[79]

It is clear that this strategy cannot work and is bound to fail. Theories cannot be divorced from practice and at the same time viable practices need to be grounded in sound theories.[80] However, the latter are presently notably missing. Since

---

[72] HP Glenn, 'Transnational Legal Thought: Plato, Europea and Beyond' in M Maduro, K Tuori and S Sankari (eds), *Transnational Law: Rethinking European Law and Legal Thinking* (Cambridge, Cambridge University Press, 2014) 62–63.

[73] ibid 68. Glenn makes it clear that fuzzy logic is inclusive of rather than in contradiction to the binary logic: 'Multivalent logic can be used where it is appropriate to do so, without entailing the abandonment of historically useful binary distinctions in domestic law.'

[74] JC Beal and G Restall, *Logical Pluralism* (Oxford, Oxford University Press, 2006).

[75] Glenn (n 72) fn 52.

[76] Teubner (n 70) 770.

[77] ibid. Recently, Teubner has slightly modified his claim: 'The problematic of societal constitutionalism was not caused by globalization, but earlier by the fragmentations of the social whole and the automatization of the fragments during the heyday of the nation state. This has now been considerably aggravated by globalization.' G Teubner, *Constitutional Fragments: Societal Constitutionalism and Globalization* (Oxford, Oxford University Press, 2012) 6.

[78] V Nourse and G Shaffer, 'Varieties of New Legal Realism: Can a New World Order Prompt a New Legal Theory?' (2009) 95 *Cornell Law Review* 61, 84.

[79] Loughlin ((n 65) 93) has probably been one of the most adamant writers opposing the radical transformation thesis, blaming those 'progressive' theoretical approaches either of conceptual fallacies, deriving from the misunderstanding of the main concepts (most notably sovereignty), or of exaggerating the actual scope of factual change.

[80] Nourse and Shaffer (n 78) 84: to argue the opposite means, according to Dewey, falling prey to a false dichotomy between theory and practice.

'reality does not—and never will—wait for theory',[81] Nourse and Shaffer were right in noting that:

> [T]here is no more urgent time than now to reach for a new legal theory, [to develop] new analytic and theoretical tools to understand a world in which we have come to see ourselves as both highly vulnerable to institutional collapse and yet capable of effecting change.[82]

Thus, in order to accurately understand the meaning of transnational law, the full extent of the challenge that it presents to the EU and to develop a meaningful response to it, a theory against which all these practices will be examined and assessed needs to be developed first. It is to this task that the next chapter turns.

---

[81] Domingo (n 3) 54.
[82] Nourse and Shaffer (n 78) 64.

2

The Theory of Principled Legal Pluralism

I. A NEW THEORY FOR A NEW LEGAL POLYCENTRICITY

THE PURPOSE OF this chapter is to develop a new theory to frame the new polycentric legal reality brought about by transnational law. In so doing, it is motivated both by epistemic and normative reasons. In epistemic terms, the chapter should result in a conceptual apparatus that will enable us to comprehend as fully as possible and to describe as accurately as possible the present legal polycentricity. However, in normative terms, this conceptual apparatus should be employed to foster the positive normative outcomes as opposed to the negative ones deriving out of it. Obviously, I am not unaware of the critiques that such an endeavour is either unnecessary or impossible. While the necessity, as argued in the preceding chapter, is plainly there, the judgement on the viability of such a new theory, as an exercise in social construction,[1] cannot be passed in advance. The viability of devising a new theory for the legal landscape of the twenty-first century is uncertain until it is tried.

Several framing attempts to lay the ground for a new theoretical take on the transformed legal landscape have already been in circulation.[2] All of them have, naturally, proceeded from what is presently available, which is a deeply entrenched statist-legal episteme and its correlative repository of state-related legal concepts. The attitude to this statist paradigm has broadly fallen into the two opposing camps of affirmative continuity and negative discontinuity. Among the theoretical debates on whether and to what an extent it is possible and desirable to adapt a historically state-concentrated discourse of constitutionalism and public law to the polycentric legal realm, Neil Walker has broadly

---

[1] PL Berger and T Luckmann, *The Social Construction of Reality: A Treatise in the Sociology of Knowledge* (London, Penguin, 1971); JR Searle, *The Construction of Social Reality* (New York, Simon & Schuster, 1995).

[2] Neil Walker, for example, has distinguished between several candidates for what he has called meta-principles of legal authority: state sovereigntist, global hierarchical, unipolar, regional, integrity, legal-field discursive and pluralist meta-principles. See N Walker, 'Beyond Boundary Disputes and Basic Grids: Mapping the Global Disorder of Normative Orders', (2008) 6 *International Journal of Constitutional Law* 386.

identified four different attitudes: double scepticism,[3] selective scepticism, either to transnational public law[4] or to transnational constitutionalism,[5] and double affirmation.[6]

Sceptics are blamed for nostalgia on the one hand and for defeatism on the other. They are said to undermine each other (selective ones), while simultaneously they necessarily have to and indeed do reckon with the statist categories even beyond the state.[7] On the other hand, the double affirmists are faced with critiques of hegemonic triumphalism and have to respond to a number of empirical and normative objections.[8] This prompts Walker to conclude that 'we can know and should know no final resolution'.[9]

While this open-ended conclusion certainly has its merits in terms of keeping the discussion going rather than closing it down from some allegedly optimal or exclusively right theoretical standpoint, it nevertheless leaves room for yet another and possibly better outcome. It is submitted that scepticism about the translation of the existing modern legal paradigm (constitutionalism and the private/public divide) beyond the state need not relate exclusively to nostalgia about the past or pessimism about the future. On the contrary, the belief about the insufficiency of the existing modern statist legal paradigm, structured around the central concepts of constitutionalism and public law, can be informed by an optimistic, indeed an affirmative view of the present and the future. Rather than pondering on the existing paradigm's capacity to translate beyond the state, which has too often proven to be an unproductive, even frustrating enterprise, why not try to develop something new, something which is not necessarily in conflict with the old?

In so doing, there is no need, as Walker persuasively advises us against, to rethink and remake the world *ab initio* and holistically.[10] It is only necessary to draw together, as inclusively as possible, in a constructive collaborative rather critical dialectical approach the whole array of conflicting as well as overlapping theoretical

---

[3] N Walker, 'The Post-national Horizon of Constitutionalism and Public Law: Paradigm Extension or Paradigm Exhaustion' in C Mac Amhlaigh, C Michelon and N Walker (eds), *After Public Law* (Oxford, Oxford University Press, 2012), 245. Double scepticism denies the capacity of translation beyond the state both to the constitutional and public law, and it does so mainly for two reasons: cultural and epistemic. Walker associates the former with Dieter Grimm's position and the latter with that of Martin Loughlin.

[4] ibid 255. Walker quotes Teubner's work on societal constitutionalism as an example of this position. See G Teubner, *Constitutional Fragments: Societal Constitutionalism and Globalization* (Oxford, Oxford University Press, 2012).

[5] Walker (n 3) 252. This position is associated with the movement of global administrative law.

[6] See ibid 257–261, whereby Walker distinguishes between those, like him, who adhere to the idea of a post-national constituent power and those who defend the idea of cosmopolitan public law—most notably Mattias Kumm.

[7] ibid 248.

[8] ibid 261.

[9] ibid 263.

[10] ibid 262.

views in all those segments in which they are not incompatible.[11] Hence, a constructed new theory, which will be neither exclusive nor comprehensive,[12] would thus, since 'there can never be a legal tabula rasa',[13] draw on the existing modernist legal paradigm, but would upgrade it conceptually, descriptively, analytically and normatively to a new theory. The argument that this chapter will defend is that this new theory for the polycentric legal landscape of the twenty-first century is principled legal pluralism.

II. FROM PLURALISM TO LEGAL PLURALISM

Pluralism is by no means an easy or an unequivocal concept. To begin with, there is no single version of pluralism, but many. In fact, there is a pluralism of pluralisms.[14] As such a multifaceted concept, pluralism has found resonance in various fields, including philosophy, sociology, the political sciences, cultural studies and law. In the absence of a single pluralist tradition,[15] we can thus distinguish between three different branches of pluralist thought: value, political and legal pluralism.[16] The first of these, usually associated with Isaiah Berlin, claims that there is 'a plurality of valuable ideals, pursuits and aspirations for which human beings yearn'.[17] The second concerns the plurality of claims to political authority in a particular (usually territorial) domain.[18] The third relates to the co-existence of the plurality of claims to ultimate legal authority.[19] The latter two are, of course, closely intertwined.[20]

Due to the pluralist character of a pluralist tradition, it is hard to define, both among the proponents as well as critics of pluralism, a quintessential element that all pluralisms would share across the board. Nevertheless, there has been no absence of attempts. Pursuant to Muniz-Fraticelli, pluralism properly so called is

[11] Neil Walker, 'Reconciling MacCormick, Constitutional Pluralism and the Unity of Practical Reason' (2011) 3 *Ratio Juris* 373, referring to MacCormick's lifelong preference for a constructive/collaborative approach to legal study.

[12] Principled legal pluralism does not want to replace all the other theoretical pluralist attempts to cope with legal polycentricity, nor is it claiming to be able to explain the totality of phenomena of which this legal polycentricity is constituted. Its theoretical ambition is therefore relatively modest. It offers a new theoretical account, drawing on and supplementing existing ones to better describe, explain and normatively guide the contemporary legal poly-centricity.

[13] Walker (n 3) 262.

[14] R Michaels, 'Global Legal Pluralism' (2009) 5 *Annual Review of Law and Science* 243.

[15] VM Muniz-Fraticelli, *The Structure of Pluralism: On the Authority of Associations* (Oxford, Oxford University Press, 2014) 13.

[16] J Gray, 'Pluralism and Toleration in Contemporary Political Philosophy' (2000) 48 *Political Studies* 323.

[17] Muniz-Fraticelli (n 15) 15.

[18] ibid 18. This is most notably associated with the tradition of British political pluralists: Maitland, Runciman, Ryan, Figgis, Laski, Follet and Barker.

[19] J Griffiths, 'What is Legal Pluralism?' (1986) 24 *Journal of Legal Pluralism and Unofficial Law* 1.

[20] Muniz-Fraticelli (n 15) 17–28.

composed of three elements: plurality, incommensurability and tragic conflict or tragic loss.[21] Accordingly, pluralism is believed to stand for a plurality of (value, political and legal) sources, which are incommensurable as they cannot be categorically ranked, and consequently always present a potential for conflict that ends up in a genuine loss for everyone involved in the conflict.[22] This conception of pluralism as a loss is not shared by those, such as Sartori, who believe that:

> [P]luralism affirms the belief that diversity and dissent are values that enrich individuals as well as their polities and societies.[23]

According to this positive conception of pluralism as an opportunity, which is philosophically grounded in the idea of transversal reason[24] and which also informs (as we shall see) my own understanding of legal pluralism, pluralism presents a potential for gain in our understanding of the world, due to its more accurate description, more persuasive explanation and more appealing normative guidance. However, to do so, it is necessary—and this is I believe the essential determinant of all pluralisms—to depart from the monistic mindset, eg, from methodologically comprehending the world exclusively in binary terms and stipulating order, usually in the sense of uniformity, as its highest normative ideal. It is precisely this element of pluralism which exhibits its potential to capture more fully the existing legal polycentricity.[25]

To narrow the debate, in what follows, our focus will not rest on pluralism *sensu lato*, but on legal pluralism. However, this is an evasive concept too. Not only (as we shall see below) has it meant different things to different authors in different periods of time, it is, as Melissaris has argued, a unique idea, conjoining the

---

[21] ibid 11.

[22] ibid.

[23] G Sartori, 'Understanding Pluralism' (1997) 8 *Journal of Democracy* 58, 58.

[24] Transversal reason has been defined by Welsch as a fundamental mode of reason conceived as a purely procedural medium, consisting exclusively of logical principles, directed at internal self-reflection and transcending the plurality of rationalities. See W Welsch, 'Reason and Transition: On the Concept of Transversal Reason', https://ecommons.cornell.edu/bitstream/handle/1813/54/Welsch_Reason_and_Transition.htm?sequence=1&isAllowed=y. Accordingly, it is transversal reason that 'makes clear to us the multitude of rationalities so that we can recognize their complex conditions as the real constitution of rationality ... It shows that this situation of ... unavoidable and unsurpassable nature of disorderliness ... It enables us to understand that this constitution is not a loss, but an enhancement of rationality. Contrary to traditional prejudice, it doesn't mean chaos, baselessness or ruin. Transversal reason [like pluralism based on it] involves itself in this disorderliness. It attempts to think with it, instead of wanting simply to head it off or merely to "cope with it". In a confused situation only transversal reason still offers orientation. It shows how one can move steadily on wavering foundations and in the midst of disorderliness'. W Welsch, 'Rationality and Reason Today' in DR Gordon and J Niznik (eds), *Criticism and Defense of Rationality in Contemporary Philosophy* (Amsterdam, GA, Rodopi, 1998) 17–31, also available at: http://www2.uni-jena.de/welsch/papers/W_Welsch_Rationality_and_Reason_Today.html.

[25] For an example of a very early but largely forgotten version of this argument developed by Santi Romano, see F Fontanelli, 'Santi Romano and *L'ordinamento giuridico*: The Relevance of a Forgotten Masterpiece for Contemporary International, Transnational and Global Relations' (2012) 2 *Transnational Legal Theory* 67, 79.

strands of legal theory and jurisprudence on the applied and meta-level.[26] Legal pluralism is not just a legal discourse, it is a discourse about other discourses about the law, as well as a prescription in concrete or abstract terms about how particular cases are to be resolved in light of these discourses.[27] Hereinafter, legal pluralism will be used in all four possible senses. Having said that, legal pluralism as a legal theory can be, in the most general terms, defined as a concept which refers to legal systems, networks or orders co-existing in the same geographical space.[28] The many variants of legal pluralism as a meta-legal theory tend to be divided into two groups: classical legal pluralism and new legal pluralism.[29] The post-colonial or anthropological account of legal pluralism is part of the classical legal pluralism, whereas so-called new legal pluralism encompasses the anti-state legal pluralism, global-transnational legal pluralism, constitutional pluralism and others.[30]

The origins of legal pluralism can be traced back to the empirical studies of post-colonial societies in the 1960s.[31] Legal anthropologists who studied these environments discovered that a substantial part of social and conflict resolution evaded official procedures and were instead conducted pursuant to traditional norms and customs that sometimes clearly conflicted with the 'modern' law of the colonial power.[32] These findings gave rise to a critique of hegemonic ex-colonial forces, in particular of their disregard, even contempt, for the indigenous law and for local traditions,[33] which resulted in the first version of legal pluralism, aptly branded as post-colonial or anthropological legal pluralism.

The message imparted by anthropological legal pluralism was gradually extended to all modern societies, in particular criticising the false ideology of unitary positive law of a state that was claimed to be representative of all legal phenomena.[34] Sociolegal studies refuted this claim by showing that a systematic, homogeneous positive law, bound to a central legislator and jurisdiction, co-exists with habits that are collectively binding by way of the repeated practice of wide-spread recognition and which carry the potential for consolidating, transforming or even altering the positive law.[35] Other social actors (not exclusively the state) have the authority to create collectively binding norms beyond the political process itself and aside from the political legislator.[36] This branch of legal pluralism

---

[26] E Melissaris, *Ubiquitous Law: Legal Theory and the Space for Legal Pluralism* (Farnham, Ashgate, 2009) 25.

[27] ibid.

[28] W Twinning, *Globalization and Legal Theory* (Cambridge, Cambridge University Press, 2000) 83.

[29] S E Merry, 'Legal Pluralism' (1998) 22 *Law and Society Review* 872.

[30] The following draws on Matej Avbelj, 'The EU and the Many Faces of Legal Pluralism' (2006) 2 *Croatian Yearbook of European Law and Policy* 377.

[31] Twinnig (n 28) 83.

[32] ibid 84.

[33] ibid.

[34] ibid.

[35] E Ehrlich, *Grundlegung der Soziologie des Rechts* (Munich, Duncker & Humblot, 1989).

[36] L Pospisil, *Anthropology of Law: A Comparative Theory* (New Haven, HRAF Press, 1971).

therefore already had a broader scope of application and, for its attack on the dogma that the law posited by the state is the only source of law, has become known as anti-state legal pluralism.

Gradually, however, the ambit of legal pluralism has been extended beyond the state. It has been persuasively demonstrated that legal pluralism within the state is only a subspecies of legal pluralism and that individuals nowadays regularly find themselves governed by a variety of regulatory orders which overlap, interact and often conflict.[37] Santos described these different intersecting legal spaces super-imposed, interpenetrated and mixed in our mind and actions as interlegality.[38] Accordingly, this even broader conception of legal pluralism has led to a recognition that local, national, regional, international, supranational, transnational and global orders could all apply to the same situation.[39] It has been convincingly shown that many jurisgenerative activities take place on the sub-state level and increasingly also beyond the state. This latter kind of legal pluralism has been named global[40] or transnational legal pluralism.[41]

Finally, there is also constitutional pluralism.[42] This has mainly been developed in the EU context[43] in order to describe, explain or even justify the legal nature of European integration featuring a plurality of constitutional sites, both national and supranational, that co-exist in a heterarchical rather than in a hierarchical manner, each of them making at least a plausible claim to sovereignty, defined as ultimate legal and political authority.[44] In addition, constitutional pluralism comes in a number of variants with differing objectives.[45] Some of them are concerned with the preservation of constitutionalism in a new pluralist constellation and therefore belong to the constitutional camp. One could refer here to Walker's epistemic pluralism,[46]

---

[37] J Vanderlinden, 'Return to Legal Pluralism: Twenty Years Later' (1989) 28 *Journal of Legal Pluralism* 154.

[38] B de Sousa Santos, *Toward a New Common Sense: Law, Science and Politics in the Paradigmatic Transition* (New York, Routledge 1995) 472–73.

[39] Twinnig (n 28) 85.

[40] R Michaels, 'Global Legal Pluralism' (2009) 5 *Annual Review of Law and Science* 243; PS Berman, *Global Legal Pluralism* (Cambridge, Cambridge University Press, 2012).

[41] P Zumbansen, 'Transnational Legal Pluralism' (2010) 1 *Transnational Legal Theory* 141.

[42] Its founding fathers are Neil MacCormick and Neil Walker; see N MacCormick, 'The Maastricht Urteil: Sovereignty Now' (1995) 1 *European Law Journal* 259; N Walker, 'The Idea of Constitutional Pluralism' (2002) 65 *Modern Law Review* 317.

[43] But see D Halberstam, 'Constitutional Heterarchy: The Centrality of Conflict in the European Union and the United States' in JL Dunoff and JP Trachtman (eds), *Ruling the World* (Cambridge, Cambridge University Press, 2009), who has identified the elements of constitutional pluralism in the US constitutional system too.

[44] N Walker, 'Late Sovereignty in the European Union' in N Walker (ed), *Sovereignty in Transition* (Oxford, Hart Publishing, 2003) 17.

[45] M Avbelj, 'Questioning EU Constitutionalisms' (2009) 9 *German Law Journal* 1; see also D Halberstam, 'Systems Pluralism and Institutional Pluralism in Constitutional Law: National, Supranational, and Global Governance' in M Avbelj and J Komarek (eds), *Constitutional Pluralism in the European Union and Beyond* (Oxford, Hart Publishing, 2012) 85–125.

[46] Walker (n 42).

Maduro's harmonious constitutional pluralism,[47] Kumm's (now) cosmopolitan constitutionalism[48] and Halberstam's systemic pluralism.[49] In contrast, others have laid emphasis on pluralism, playing down or even denying constitutionalism the capacity to retain its relevance in the changed pluralist circumstances.[50] While initially most of these debates centred on the EU, they have gradually migrated beyond it and have started taking root in international law as well as within the so-called discipline of global law.[51] It is here where constitutional pluralism and global-transnational legal pluralism meet, merge and develop into two disparate directions. One travels the constitutional path, the other the pluralist one.[52]

It follows from what has been presented above that legal pluralism has played several roles. Legal pluralism has been a political, descriptive, analytical and normative project. As a political project, legal pluralism has been used as a means, a trigger and a facilitator of social change. Its newly developed conceptual tools, imaginative models have been used by forces inside the state and in colonial contexts to politically attempt to achieve their legal emancipation.[53] As a descriptive project, legal pluralism has acted as a mirror that has reflected the changes in sociolegal practices,[54] whereas in its analytical stage, it has also contributed to the explanatory unmasking of the true scope of the sources of law other than just the state, as insisted upon by the modern legal paradigm.[55] Finally, once the centrality of the state has been removed, legal pluralism has also faced a normative task of reacting to the new polycentric legal realm.

When looking at and critiquing the different forms of legal pluralism, it is first important to distil their true ambitions. For example, a critique that laments legal pluralism as a descriptive project for the lack of its normative orientation simply misses its target and therefore the point. Koskenniemi's critique of legal pluralism might run this risk. He has dismissed legal pluralism for having ceased to pose demands on the world,[56] by flatly accepting the world as it is and celebrating

---

[47] MP Maduro, 'Contrapunctual Law: Europe's Constitutional Pluralism in Action' in N Walker (ed), *Sovereignty in Transition* (Oxford, Hart Publishing, 2003).

[48] M Kumm, 'The Cosmopolitan Turn in Constitutionalism: On the Relationship between Constitutionalism in and beyond the State' in J L Dunoff, J P Trachtman (eds), *Ruling the World* (Cambridge, Cambridge University Press, 2009).

[49] Halberstam (n 43).

[50] N Krisch, *Beyond Constitutionalism* (Oxford, Oxford University Press, 2010); M Avbelj, 'Can European Integration be Constitutional and Pluralist—Both at the Same Time' in Avbelj and Komarek (n 45).

[51] N Walker, *Intimations of Global Law* (CUP 2014); R Domingo, *The New Global Law* (Cambridge, Cambridge University Press, 2010).

[52] M Avbelj, 'Global Constitutionalism as a Grammar of Global Law?' (2016) 3 *Critical Quarterly for Legislation and Law* 217.

[53] Twinning (n 28) 84.

[54] Griffiths' (n 19) purpose was to develop a descriptive conception of legal pluralism.

[55] ibid 1, stressing the need to pierce the ideological veil of 'legal centralism'.

[56] M Koskenniemi, 'The Fate of Public International Law: Between Technique and Politics' (2007) 1 *Modern Law Review* 23.

its own (eg, legally pluralist) descriptive accuracy. This type of critique can only be addressed to those forms of legal pluralism that have conceived of themselves as a normative project and, as such, have satisfied themselves with the celebration of the newly discovered plurality existing as a social fact that calls for no further action. By contrast, such a critique cannot be made of legal pluralism, whose ambition is 'only' descriptive and analytical. Recognising plurality as it is, by arriving at the better, more accurate description of the world, as well as the explanatory thrust of legal pluralism, which reveals that this plurality has a social root[57] resulting out of 'a conscious challenge to the unacceptable features of that general law and the powers of the institutions that apply it',[58] are welcome contributions of legal pluralism as a descriptive and/or analytical project. They more than suffice for making legal pluralism a coherent and persuasive descriptive and/or analytical project in its own right.

Nevertheless, I believe that legal pluralism can achieve even more. It can be taken beyond its descriptive and analytical dimensions, which have been prevalent so far,[59] and can also develop a more pronounced normative side.[60] I am arguing that legal pluralism as an integral project (eg, descriptive, analytical and normative) would also need to demonstrate and provide normative guidelines as to how this polycentric legal landscape is to be made operational. How are these numerous legal sites to interact, engage and enter into a meaningful co-operation, to the extent possible, so as to witness the emergence of a functional rather than a dysfunctional national, international, supranational and transnational legal arena? In other words, the argument is that legal pluralism has to complement its descriptive and explanatory dimensions, where its advantages are clear and appreciable, with a normative stance by turning itself into a roadmap to be of assistance to the actors in the polycentric legal world. For its greater theoretical plausibility, I believe that legal pluralism has to contribute to the viability of the actual social practices that it frames.

The main challenge encountered by legal pluralism as a normative project is therefore how to get from plurality to pluralism.[61] Several pluralists have recognised that this is anything but an easy task and have remained relatively reserved

---

[57] G Teubner and A Fischer-Lascano, 'Regime-Collisions: The Vain Search for Legal Unity in the Fragmentation of Global Law', (2004) 25 *Michigan Journal of International Law* 999 have argued that plurality 'derives from real actions of fragmented and operationally closed functional systems of a global society, which, in their expansionist fervor, create the real problems of the global society, and who at the same time make use of global law in order normatively to secure their own highly refined sphere logics'.

[58] Koskenniemi (n 56) 19.

[59] PS Berman, 'Global Legal Pluralism' (2007) 80 *Southern Californian Law Review* 1166 has argued that 'pluralism is thus principally a descriptive, not a normative, framework'.

[60] For a similar critique, see Sabine Muller-Mall, *Legal Spaces: Towards a Topological Thinking of Law* (Berlin, Springer, 2013) 2.

[61] See, for example, N Walker, 'Constitutionalism and Pluralism in Global Context' in Avbelj and Komarek (n 45) 28, who has queried: 'what makes the basic *plurality* of constitutional orders pluralistic in nature?'

about the capacity of pluralism to deliver in these legal normative terms. Teubner, for example, has warned against an illusory integration of a differentiated global society and has consequently remained of the opinion that in legal pluralism, law can only at best offer a kind of damage limitation.[62] Drawing on his autopoietic systems theory,[63] his legal pluralism almost by necessity remains normatively circumscribed. In his descriptive account of the polycentric legal world, different legal regimes forming a plurality are perceived as deterministically self-closed and as such necessarily contribute to the fragmentation of the legal terrain.[64] In this pluralist model the many contemporary legal regimes forming a plurality can only establish pluralist relationships among themselves in a very limited way through a specific network logic emerging out of conflicts law.[65]

Similarly, Krisch has argued that the relationships within the plurality of legal orders are ultimately much more susceptible to the, pragmatic case-by-case accommodations rather than to legal and principled ordering.[66] For him, in pluralism, there is no common legal point of reference to appeal to in order to resolve disagreements.[67] Along with MacCormick, he therefore believes that taking pluralism seriously, that is, by approving of the so-called radical legal pluralism,[68] requires acquiescing to the fact that in the event of conflicts between different legal sites in a pluralist realm, the law ultimately runs out and makes way for politics.[69] Conflicts are, accordingly, solved through convergence, mutual accommodation or not at all.[70] As will become apparent below, Krisch's account of legal pluralism deeply informs my own take on legal pluralism, but, unlike me, he is willing to concede much less space to legal rather than political normativity in structuring the pluralist relationship between different jurisgenerative sites.[71] In other words,

---

[62] Teubner and Lascano (n 57) 1045.

[63] G Teubner, 'Autopoiesis in Law and Society: A Rejoinder to Blankenburg' (1984) 2 *Law and Society Review* 83.

[64] Teubner and Lascano (n 57) 1014 have claimed that transnational actors 'are so closely coupled, both in terms of organization and self-perception, with their own specialized regimes in the legal periphery that they necessarily contribute to a global legal fragmentation'.

[65] ibid 1004.

[66] Krisch (n 50) 298.

[67] ibid 69.

[68] N MacCormick, *Questioning Sovereignty: Law, State and Nation in the European Commonwealth* (Oxford, Oxford University Press, 1999).

[69] Krisch (n 50) 298 emphasises the reshape of relationship between law and politics (in favour of politics), speaking against legalisation. Compare, for example, the following: 'Postnational pluralism recognizes the blurred separation of layers of law but does not seek to reorganize them in an over-arching legal framework, as does constitutionalism. It envisages a heterarchical structure in which the interaction of different layers is not ultimately determined by one legal rule but influenced by a variety of (potentially conflicting) norms emanating from each of the layers. Between the different layers, there is no common point of reference in law; their relationship is fundamentally open and depends, in large part, on political factors.'

[70] ibid 69.

[71] ibid 17, advocating a break 'to eschew constitutionalism's emphasis on law and hierarchy and propose more pluralist models, which would leave greater space for politics in the hierarchical interplay of orders'. See also N Krisch, 'Global Administrative Law and the Constitutional Ambition' in M Loughlin and P Dobner (eds), *The Twilight of Constitutionalism* (Oxford, Oxford University Press, 2010), 245.

Krisch's post-national pluralism is much more political and pragmatic than legal and principled.[72]

Others have tried to square this normative circle between plurality and pluralism with the help of constitutional devices. However, in so doing, they have found it hard to avoid the monistic strain.[73] Neil Walker has remained the most circumspect about these dangers. He has subscribed to the so-called epistemic pluralism,[74] recognising the very epistemic irreconcilability of a plurality of claims to legal authority that can nevertheless be managed within the meta-constitutional framework[75] of shared understandings whose thickness depends on the type of polity, and can be further institutionally connected through a number of existing and still to be envisaged bridging mechanisms between different legal sites.[76] Maduro draws on this, but goes further, requiring more procedural engagement and pluralist dialogue between the different sites of plurality, insisting on the universalisability of their arguments to the point that the irreconcilability of a plurality of claims is overcome.[77] Already implicit in his account is a relatively thick idea of shared values.[78]

Halberstam in his systems pluralism makes it explicit: 'some minimally shared purpose or basic compatibility is necessary'[79] for the long-term viability of this plurality. He locates this in the liberal enlightenment idea of limited self-governance through law;[80] in short, in constitutionalism. While Halberstam pluralises constitutionalism to the greatest extent possible,[81] he is eventually still unwilling to abandon the very constitutional register in favour of pluralism. In his eyes, pluralism without constitutionalism would be reduced to a mere plurality.[82] Kumm is even more circumspect in pluralising constitutionalism. He makes the constitutional requirement of commonality even thicker and more explicit. He is

---

[72] This also makes it a more all-encompassing theory, which is not limited exclusively to legal questions in a narrower sense, but ventures further into the domains of political science by addressing the challenges of democracy and legitimacy in a post-national constellation. Principled legal pluralism is in this respect a more circumspect legal theory.

[73] Walker (n 61) 27.

[74] Walker (n 42).

[75] N Walker, 'Flexibility within a Meta-constitutional Frame: Reflections on the Future of Legal Authority in Europe' (2009) 12 *Jean Monnet Working Paper*.

[76] Walker (n 61) 22.

[77] Maduro (n 47) 525.

[78] ibid. The claims have to be universalisable to all the participants, and must be conducive and should ultimately lead to an agreement on the specific outcomes.

[79] Halberstam (n 45) 107.

[80] ibid 109.

[81] For his concept of 'plural constitutionalism', see D Halberstam, 'Local, Global and Plural Constitutionalism: Europe Meets the World' in G de Burca and JHH Weiler (eds), *The Worlds of European Constitutionalism* (Cambridge, Cambridge University Press, 2012).

[82] 'Using constitutional language, by contrast, can help us understand how multiple autonomous legal orders, each with their own tie-breaker, can nonetheless stand in a relationship of mutual legal commitments to one another.' See the exchange between Halberstam and Weiler in de Burca and Weiler (n 81) 290.

still devoted to the recognition of plurality, but makes it part of a denser constitutional framework.[83] His normative ambition thus requires a shared commitment to the universal[84] constitutional principles of legality, subsidiarity, due process, democracy and human rights protection.[85] These provide a foundation for public law practices as well as a common framework to mediate conflicts between the plurality of claims to legal authority.[86] Like that of Halberstam, Kumm's approach also privileges constitutionalism over plurality and would be better described not as constitutional pluralism, but as pluralist constitutionalism.[87]

Having briefly reviewed the normative accounts of legal pluralism, both pluralist and constitutional, it becomes clear why so many legal pluralists satisfy themselves only with the descriptive and analytical legal projects. It also explains why legal pluralism when couched in normative terms has either remained mainly political and pragmatic and therefore legally very thin, or it has drifted towards constitutionalism and its overly thick normative, monist and therefore no longer really pluralist nature. Legal pluralism as a normative project is a difficult one because of an inherent instability of its pluralist solutions, which are constantly torn between two monisms: that of an insular plurality and that of a new singular monolith.[88] Legal pluralism can fail as a normative project so that we end up with a disconnected plurality, or it can be too successful, resulting in a new aggregate monism. As Walker has argued, the claim to move beyond plurality to pluralism remains a precarious one.[89] Admittedly, this is the case, but this does not absolve us from giving it yet another try.

In what follows, I will make a case for legal pluralism that should be legal, principled and normative. It will start from an idea that legal pluralism is much more than plurality;[90] it is a connected plurality.[91] It is, first of all, about the recognition of plurality—a multitude of entities of a particular legal kind—and, second, a perspective that integrates this legal plurality into a common pluralist whole without, however, consuming its constitutive parts. This type of legal pluralism should be neither normatively undernourished nor overfed. It should find a finely tuned path in the middle. I am arguing that this could be achieved by a theory of principled legal pluralism.

---

[83] M Kumm, 'Rethinking Constitutional Authority: On the Structure and Limits of Constitutional Pluralism' in Avbelj and Komarek (n 45) 64.

[84] Kumm (n 48) 322.

[85] ibid 310, 315.

[86] ibid.

[87] Others have used this term before; see, for example, WA Galston, 'Pluralist Constitutionalism' (2011) 28 *Social Philosophy and Policy* 228 JHH Weiler, 'Prologue: Global and Pluralist Constitutionalism—Some Doubts' in de Burca and Weiler (n 81) 14.

[88] Walker (n 61) 18–19.

[89] ibid 29.

[90] On the need to distinguish between pluralism and plurality, see N Walker in M Avbelj and J Komárek (eds), 'Four Visions of Constitutional Pluralism' (2008) 2 *European Journal of Legal Studies* 325, 336.

[91] M Delmas-Marty, *Le Pluralisme Ordonné* (Paris, Seuil, 2005) 13–26.

III. THE THEORY OF PRINCIPLED LEGAL PLURALISM

The theory of principled legal pluralism's point of departure is a refined concept of law. For something to count as law, it must pass a threshold of plausibility, eg, it must be first intelligible as law to be recognised as law by relevant social actors and epistemic communities. The idea of intelligibility, as endorsed by Muniz-Fraticelli, thus becomes a primary criterion of legality.[92] It serves as 'a coherentist criterion of recognition'.[93] Accordingly, 'a normative system is a legal system if it is intelligible to other legal systems as a legal system'.[94] In that way, not every normative order can be considered as law, but at the same time the state is not its only source either. As we have seen in Chapter 1, other entities have made (and have been recognised as making) plausible claims to autonomous law-making.

In a second step, legal pluralism focuses on the relationship inside the just-described plurality of legal orderings. For the identified legal regimes do not merely co-exist, and even if they did, legal pluralism would insist on establishing connections between them. Legal pluralism following the dictates of transversal reason requires and is all about self-reflexivity. Different sites of law have to be open to the claims of other sites and be willing and capable of reconsidering their own foundations as a response to their environment.[95] Different legal orders have to transcend their self-perceived exclusivity, resulting from and simultaneously engendering 'hypertrophic self-confidence'.[96] In the absence of reflexivity, legal pluralism would be reduced to a mere plurality. Simultaneously, the requirement of reflexivity is not unlimited. Its limits are defined by each legal order for itself. For legal pluralism to exist, every legal order has the right to shield its irreducible epistemic core against the claims of another legal order.[97]

The prerequisite of the advocated conception of legal pluralism is thus a normative spirit of pluralism, which stands for a double commitment: to the plurality and to the common whole, both at the same time. If legal pluralism is taken seriously all the way down, this commitment cannot be unlimited and the conflicts between the entities forming up a plurality are therefore not excluded.

---

[92]   Muniz-Fraticelli (n 15) 50.

[93]   ibid 153.

[94]   ibid 150.

[95]   Compare with Melissaris (n 26) 79, who has insisted that 'it is possible to at least *try* to transcend one's context and raise claims to universality, as long as one is always aware of the corrigibility of these claims'. See also JL Cohen, *Globalization and Sovereignty: Rethinking Legality, Legitimacy and Constitutionalism* (Cambridge, Cambridge University Press, 2012), who has named this attitude reflexive monism; and Z Oklopčić, 'Provincializing Constitutional Pluralism' (2014) 5 *Transnational Legal Theory* 331, 358, who has suggested that this reflexivity should be conceived in the spirit of self-irony: 'The monist perspective here would be self-ironic, as it would understand its own legitimacy as critically informed by the judgment of the external audience.'

[96]   Welsch (n 24).

[97]   Walker (n 44) 28; M Avbelj, 'Supremacy or Primacy of EU Law: (Why) Does it Matter?' (2012) 6 *European Law Journal* 744, 752.

If they do take place, however, legal pluralism requires them to be performed in light of normative spirit of pluralism, eg, by defending particular claims on their own epistemic legal basis, but with a commitment to a larger picture of the legal common whole.

As the conflicting claims will sometimes be irreconcilable, which is an inescapable consequence of epistemic plurality, principled legal pluralism imposes no demand of making compromises by all means. Principled legal pluralism thus shares with Walker's epistemic pluralism the pluralism-defining condition of epistemic plurality. However, it departs from it by demanding both less and more of pluralism. On the one hand, as will be explained in more detail below, principled legal pluralism demands more from pluralism by grounding it into a monistic substantive foundation of human dignity. On the other hand, principled legal pluralism requires less from pluralism by refusing to make it part of a constitutional register due to the latter's mostly conceptual difficulties, but also ideological and utopian features, exhibited in its ambition to serve as the theory for the post-statist legal polycentricity.[98]

Principled legal pluralism also distinguishes itself from Maduro's approach to constitutional pluralism. This is not just due to Maduro's (like Walker's) continuing faith in the viability of the constitutional discourse beyond the state, but primarily to his insistence on the requirement of universalisability. The latter, as advocated by Maduro, simply asks too much of pluralism, essentially depriving it of its very pluralist character.[99] Principled legal pluralism thus does not anticipate that the theories of deliberation and justification, on which the courts of different legal orders base their decisions, must be universalisable to all the other participants in Maduro's meaning of the term.[100] Principled legal pluralism equally does not require that each theory must be constructed so as to adjust and adapt to competing theories,[101] and finally, as stated above, principled legal pluralism does not expect that different epistemic and substantive theories employed by different jurisgenerative sites must be conducive to an agreement on specific outcomes.[102] Taking plurality seriously might make the requirement of an agreement on specific outcomes theoretically impossible, but it certainly makes it practically unfeasible. Buying into an idea of transversal reason and abstracting away the assumption of

---

[98] For a compelling explanation why constitutionalism is not a suitable theory for a post-national legal constellation, see N Krisch, 'The Case for Pluralism in Postnational Law' in de Burca and Weiler (n 81) 205–19; and, more broadly, Krisch (n 50). For a similar critique applied to a particular EU context, see M Avbelj, 'Can European Integration be Constitutional and Pluralist Both at the Same Time?' in Avbelj and Komarek (n 45).

[99] Compare Maduro (n 47) 525: (1) the theories of deliberation and justification on which the national and European courts base their decisions must be universalisable to all the participants; (2) each theory must be constructed so as to adjust and adapt to competing theories; and (3) they must be conducive to an agreement on specific outcomes.

[100] ibid.

[101] ibid.

[102] ibid.

universal-unitary basis of reason that is allegedly prone to universally valid unitary solutions,[103] principled legal pluralism's expectations are procedural, requiring mutual openness, self-reflexivity and commitment to the common pluralist whole composed of a totality of very particularistic jurisgenerative sites.[104]

For this reason, in contrast to some other pluralist accounts, most notably that defended by Kumm, principled legal pluralism does not nurture hopes that there are some universal substantive principles that, if really and correctly used,[105] can help resolve almost any conflict. However, the duty of legal regimes in conflict is to justify their ultimate positions, taking into account the interests and claims of the opposing legal order. To paraphrase Welsch, this should be done transversally through reciprocal interpretation.[106] A legal order should reconstruct a claim of another legal order within its own framework in order to discover the inevitable situatedness and framework dependedness of each claim. On this basis, it would gain a detached view of its own position, opening itself up to the consideration of alternatives and (perhaps) identifying flaws or lacunae in its own argument. It would reach a final, but always situational and temporally-specific decision, after having 'frankly and extensively considered all potential objections to one's own description of the situation and determination of the position'.[107]

The approach required by legal pluralism, even at the moment of conflict, is therefore a principled one; a mere pragmatic accommodation will not satisfy the conditions of normative spirit of pluralism.[108] By being simultaneously normative, principled and legal, this account of legal pluralism is importantly different from the other conceptions of legal pluralism discussed above. However, in so doing, principled legal pluralism drifts closer to the constitutional approaches. Indeed, there are several similarities between my idea of legal pluralism and the so-called pluralist constitutionalism, but there are also important differences.

To start with, principled legal pluralism and pluralist constitutionalism share the same foundation—respect for equal human dignity—but they seem to be drawing different conclusions from it. Constitutionalist approaches rely on equal human dignity as a foundation for the universality of human rights and uniformity of other substantive standards that the rule of law has to be infused with.[109]

---

[103] Welsch (n 24).

[104] This is almost analogous with universalisability as understood in the context of de Burca's notion of 'mutual perspective-taking: the obligation always to take account of the position of the other in reaching decisions which have implications for that other, and to articulate one's own position as far as possible in terms which are cognizable to the other'. However, note that de Burca has dubbed her account as soft constitutionalism, delimiting it from pluralism by understanding the latter as a mere plurality rather than pluralism properly so-called. See the exchange between de Burca and Weiler in de Burca and Weiler (n 81).

[105] Contra Kumm (n 48).

[106] Drawing on Welsch (n 24) 6.

[107] ibid 15.

[108] Contra Krisch (n 50).

[109] For a critique, see J Tully, *Strange Multiplicity: Constitutionalism in an Age of Diversity* (Cambridge, Cambridge University Press, 1995).

In so doing, constitutionalism eventually ends up being substantively monist.[110] On the contrary, legal pluralism takes the same foundation of equal human dignity as a licence for diversity. While we all have equal human dignity, this consists of the right of every individual to self-fulfilment in his or her chosen and therefore different way.[111] Human dignity is therefore a prerequisite for plurality and simultaneously a limit on it. It demarcates the scope for a legitimate plurality, consisting of all those differences that are respectful of equal human dignity. At the same time, human dignity is not just a precondition of plurality, but also of pluralism. It is constitutive of normative spirit of pluralism, which turns plurality into pluralism. In the absence of respect for equal human dignity, the normative spirit of pluralism can never evolve.

In short, legal pluralism, as conceived of here, is not without foundation[112] and therefore should not be equated with relativism or nihilism. It comes with a single, thin foundation of equal human dignity, which is the source of all other possible, socially constructed diverse foundations.[113] This contrasts it with persistently modernist constitutionalism, which, on my reading, even when entirely severed from its statist pedigree (whose plausibility is debatable in the first place), comes with a much thicker foundation grounded in the universal rather than cosmopolitan ethos and therefore—to a certain extent at least—assumes and protects the substantive uniformity of rights, values and social forms of organisation.[114]

Pluralist constitutionalism and principled legal pluralism join in their quest for containing politics.[115] Politics, as a synonym for power, has to be exercised in a non-arbitrary and therefore principled way in accordance with the law. The principled approach, insisted upon both by constitutionalism and the account of legal pluralism defended here, should thus be contrasted with two other forms of decision-making. It must be distinguished from an exercise of naked power, which as a brute force is not just unprincipled but evidently unlawful, and also from arbitrary ad hoc compromise-making, which can be lawful, although it is certainly unprincipled.[116] The lack of principles in arbitrary ad hoc compromise-making is

---

[110] For a review within the EU context of various forms of constitutionalism with a pluralist ambition that end up essentially monist, see Avbelj (n 45).

[111] Domingo (n 51) 134: 'Thus, law and dignity go hand in hand, like person and dignity. Without the person, there is no dignity, and without dignity, there is no law.' See Constitutional Court of Republic of Slovenia, Tito Street Case U-I-109/10: 'Human dignity is the fundamental value which permeates the entire legal order and therefore it also has an objective significance in the functioning of authority not only in individual proceedings but also when adopting regulations.'

[112] Compare with T Isiksel, 'Global Legal Pluralism as Fact and Norm' (2013) 2(3) *Global Constitutionalism* 160, who critiques pluralism for being contingent on other values and not a value in itself. However, while this is true, there are hardly any values that are entirely self-dependent.

[113] For a comprehensive treatment of human dignity, see C McCrudden, *Understanding Human Dignity* (Oxford, Oxford University Press, 2014).

[114] Tully (n 109) 58 has therefore critiqued constitutionalism for being an empire of uniformity.

[115] MP Maduro, 'Three Claims of Constitutional Pluralism' in Avbelj and Komarek (n 45) 330.

[116] This resembles what Dworkin has called checkboard laws; see R Dworkin, *Law's Empire* (Cambridge, MA, Harvard University Press, 986) 179.

an encroachment on integrity. Integrity is, following Dworkin, an intrinsic political value in a community of principle where 'collective decisions are matters of [moral] obligation, not mere power'.[117]

Thus, both pluralist constitutionalism and principled legal pluralism assume that they derive from and regulate communities of principle underpinned by the value of integrity. The latter is a reflection of human dignity, its constitutive, inherent part. He or she who loses integrity has been deprived of his or her human dignity too.[118] However, there is a difference between the two theoretical accounts both in relation to the nature of a single community as well as (and even to a greater extent) to the relationship inside the plurality of different communities of principles. Drawing on its statist legacy, pluralist constitutionalism assumes that its communities of principle rely on a single coherent scheme of principles.[119] This scheme of principles is thick, substantively homogeneous and indeed uniform to a large extent. In contrast, principled legal pluralism anticipates from a community of principle, which can also be constitutional in character, to have a thinner, more heterogeneous and, indeed, internally pluralist scheme of principles. However, the main difference between constitutionalism and pluralism can be seen in their treatment of the relationship between the many communities of principle, eg, in the extent and scope of the transcontextual principles bridging the plurality of legal entities. Constitutionalism endorses many principles, which are thick and considered to be substantively universal.[120] Depending on the variant of constitutionalism, this leads them into solutions which are formally monist,[121] substantively monist[122] or both.[123]

However, principled legal pluralism requires only two transcontextual principles: a substantive and a procedural principle. The substantive principle consists of the respect of equal human dignity. This is a prerequisite for the recognition of legitimate diversity, which any entity making up the pluralist common whole has to meet. Failing to recognise equal human dignity *ex ante* disqualifies an entity from partaking in the pluralist common whole. Such an entity is unable to genuinely develop the normative spirit of pluralism: a dialectically open self to oneself and to the other. On the other hand, the procedural principle draws on the substantive principle and requires the above-described mutual openness, commitment

---

[117] ibid 214, as opposed to a rulebook community which, following Dworkin, compromises convictions along the lines of power.

[118] Compare, L McFall, 'Integrity' (1987) 1 *Ethics* 1, 20.

[119] Dworkin (n 116) 214.

[120] Kumm (n 48).

[121] Weiler's socio-teleological constitutionalism could be quoted as an example. See JHH Weiler, 'In Defence of the Status Quo: Europe's Constitutional Sonderweg' in JHH Weiler and M Wind (eds), *European Constitutionalism beyond the State* (Cambridge, Cambridge University Press, 2003).

[122] Kumm's (now) cosmopolitan constitutionalism is of such a kind; see, for example, M Kumm, 'The Jurisprudence of Constitutional Conflict: Constitutional Supremacy in Europe before and after the Constitutional Treaty' (2005) 11 *European Law Journal* 262.

[123] See, for example, I Pernice, 'Multilevel Constitutionalism in the European Union' (2002) 27 *European Law Review* 511.

to plurality and to the common whole as well as dialogical reflexivity. This procedural principle is encapsulated in a thin version of a principle of integrity. Dworkin was right in arguing that the many political communities as sovereign entities each speak with their own voice and not in harmony with other sovereigns,[124] but this does not (necessarily) mean that integrity as proposed here does not hold among political communities, but only within them.[125] Indeed, there is no need to pursue harmony between territorial or functional sovereigns, but they must stick to integrity both in their internal and external affairs if they are to build a viable legally pluralist world structure.[126] To argue the opposite risks violating human dignity of which integrity is a necessary condition and a consequence.

IV. THE ADVANTAGES OF A THEORY OF PRINCIPLED LEGAL PLURALISM

Principled legal pluralism defended in this chapter comes with a number of advantages. The first among them is epistemic. The conceptual and normative framework of legal pluralism gives us access to better knowledge about the contemporary world.[127] It enables us to eschew false consciousness[128] that has misled some into an ideological and others into a utopian representation of the world, or that has instigated conceptual acrobatics, resulting in a hasty reinterpretation and transformation of the generally well-established concepts beyond the plausible threshold of their conventional meaning, sometimes making them almost unrecognisable.[129]

Legal pluralism does no such thing. It is a discourse of conceptual continuity which does not shatter the conventional framework, especially not the core concepts of law, constitutionalism, international law, sovereignty etc through which we have been accustomed to grasp and understand the law. It is also, at least to a certain extent, a discourse of practical continuity. The state, as the primary locus of any individual's socialisation, can thus retain its traditionally important role in legal and overall political affairs. There is just no need to call for its withering away, let alone for arguing or pretending that that process is already irreversibly

---

[124] Dworkin (n 116) 186.

[125] ibid 185.

[126] Compare with P Eleftheriadis, 'Pluralism and Integrity' (2010) 23 *Ratio Juris* 365, who, however, argues that pluralism is incompatible with integrity as conceived by him.

[127] See Walker (n 42) 347, who observes that pluralism offers an accurate understanding of the world which is a normative value on its own.

[128] According to K Mannheim, *Ideology and Utopia: An Introduction to the Sociology of Knowledge* (Eastford, Martino Fine Books, 2015), false consciousness stands for a distorted mental structure, for one that either has not yet caught up with the present or has moved beyond it prematurely.

[129] This critique applies, in particular, to the use of the constitutional narrative as well as to the language of sovereignty.

in motion.[130] Simultaneously, pluralism leaves no room for perpetuating the alleged monopoly of the statist paradigm and its exclusivity in the making and imagining of the law. Rather, it reveals the many other sources of law-making in and beyond the state that have long been in the latter's shadow. The conceptual and practical continuity of pluralism is thus combined with the integration of the new,[131] making thus pluralism a forward-looking rather than a conservative, even reactionary approach. This is also what ultimately gives pluralism an advantage in terms of descriptive accuracy and explanatory power.

Besides the just-discussed epistemic, descriptive and explanatory advantages, the legal pluralism advocated here is also normatively attractive. It is an inclusive theory, a theory that tries to integrate the claims of all the entities and actors involved, maximising their interests within the perspective of a common pluralist whole. Furthermore, in philosophical terms, pluralism presents a *via media* between the universal and the particular, between the global and the local.[132] For each entity of the plurality, it recognises its distinctiveness, its right to remain different and its own understanding even of the most fundamental values, but simultaneously inhibits them from falling prey to conceitedness, self-sufficiency and isolationism, which could lead to excessive unilateralism and eventually conflicts, both internal and external.

Principled legal pluralism is therefore about the ethos of a dialectically open self.[133] In this quality, in which nothing other than equal human dignity is taken for granted, and everything is open to questioning and constant search for a better, more fitting and more inclusive reflective equilibrium, the legal (as a well as a broader sociopolitical) world is open to adaptation.[134] The latter, as rightly noted by Krisch, is both a product as well as a precondition of a fruitful contestation that pluralism by way of recognition of plurality leaves ample scope for.[135] In turn, contestation and adaptation are the products of a learning process for which

---

[130] Other authors have insisted on this point too. See, for example, S Sassen, 'Neither Global nor National: Novel Assemblages of Territory, Authority and Rights' (2008) 1 *Ethics and Global Politics* 62; G Shaffer, 'A Transnational Take on Krisch's Pluralist Postnational Law' (2012) 23 *European Journal of International Law* 565, 579, who argues that: 'The legal ordering that we see is transnational because it implicates multiple states and constituencies within them, but it is not post-national in that states remain central to the creation, implementation, and contestation of transnational legal ordering.'

[131] RM Unger, *Free Trade Reimagined: The World Division of Labor and Method of Economics* (Princeton, Princeton University Press, 2007) 111: 'The new will have to be combined with the old.'

[132] This normative ambition is also shared by Berman's 'cosmopolitan pluralism'; see Berman (n 40) 141 ff.

[133] On the question of openness in constitutionalism and pluralism, see G Martinico, 'Constitutionalism, Resistance, and Openness: Comparative Law Reflections on Constitutionalism in Postnational Governance' (2016) 35 *Yearbook of European Law* 318.

[134] Krisch (n 50) 228–30.

[135] ibid 230–38.

pluralism provides a platform.[136] Similarly, the very recognition of plurality of legal entities engaged in contestation following pluralist normative underpinnings creates a virtuous circle of checks and balances, which contribute to the order of disorder that can be sounder, more balanced and less prone to excesses and even abuses than that controlled by one single dominant power (monism).

Principled legal pluralism is also a measure of legitimacy of the exercise of legal authority by the entities forming a plurality. Drawing on the concept of a relative authority developed by Roughan,[137] the legitimacy of the exercise of authority of singular entities in a pluralist setting depends on the quality of their engagement with other entities,[138] to the extent that they are faithful to the normative spirit of pluralism and are able to exhibit the dialectic self-openness in the above-described transversal sense. Simultaneously, of course, there is also the other side of the coin: the exercise of authorities in a pluralist setting in a non-pluralist way is illegitimate. As a result, pluralism is not only a measure of legitimacy, but is also its guarantee.

In other words, this dialectic self-openness, if genuinely shared by all, or at least by most of the participants in practice, is conducive to a harmonious environment. Paradoxically, pluralism is therefore not about creating non-order,[139] but is about achieving order through the recognition of disorder. In sharp contrast, the approaches which stress the universality of values, the uniformity of rules, the need for order etc come across as a threat to plurality. They provoke defensive reactions on behalf of the threatened entities, the atmosphere becomes filled with distrust and anxiety, pressing down on the dialectic openness and adding to the construction of a vicious circle of strained and uneasy relationships, eventually turning pluralism into a mere plurality or, even worse, to a singular monolith controlled by a dominant power.

Finally, principled legal pluralism is best suited for the legal realisation of the paramount value of human dignity. This is done through the recognition of

---

[136] ibid 229. Practical operationalisation of this is the so-called experimentalist governance. See F Sabel and J Zeitlin, 'Experimentalism in the EU: Common Ground and Persistent Difference' (2012) 6 *Regulation and Governance* 410, 422: 'What is fundamental is that mechanisms for forming common understanding from the interpretation of difference build mutual trust or confidence and reduce, though they hardly eliminate, requirements for a common cultural starting point.'

[137] N Roughan, *Authorities: Conflicts, Co-operation and Transnational Legal Theory* (Oxford, Oxford University Press, 2013).

[138] ibid 149: 'The foregoing account of relative authority explains authority as a power that is plural and relative rather than singular and exclusive; and entwines the conditions of plural authorities' legitimacy for their subjects, so that each can be legitimate only if they coordinate, cooperate or tolerate one another as the particular balance of procedural and substantive reasons requires.' However, Roughan appears to be putting authority before plurality, while it seems that the opposite is true, namely that the concept of a relative authority is only meaningful and necessary if plurality exists. Furthermore, the openness and interaction between the plurality of authorities could be, probably, better described and furthered through the concept of a relational, rather than relative authority.

[139] Walker (n 2).

plurality as an expression of autonomy, both individual and collective, of the right to do things in one's own chosen way.[140] The autonomy thus stands for the right to self-fulfilment within the ambit of the equal rights of others, which is the right that is derived from the core value of equal human dignity. Respecting plurality, as pluralism does, means heeding individual and collective, private and public autonomy[141] and, in so doing, protecting equal human dignity. But the opposite is also true: detours from pluralism signal disrespect for plurality, which undermines the conditions for autonomy and consequently impacts negatively on the flourishing of human dignity.

---

[140] Compare with Krisch (n 50) 249, who has similarly related the core advantage of pluralism to the furtherance of public autonomy, conceived of as an expression of a right to self-legislation.
[141] ibid.

3

A Pluralist Conception of the EU

I. INTRODUCTION

I N THE PREVIOUS chapter we identified the main elements of the theory of principled legal pluralism. We learned that principled legal pluralism is a theory of law describing, explaining and normatively guiding the situation of plurality of legal orders. Its starting point is a recognition of legal plurality: the existence of multiple legal orders which are recognised *qua* legal orders since they are intelligible to the other, foremost statist legal orders, as legal orders. Second, the principled legal pluralism requires the identified legal plurality to be connected into a common whole without exhausting the autonomous standing of its constitutive legal orders. To do so, it is necessary to develop a normative spirit of pluralism, which necessitates a double commitment: to the plurality and to the common whole, both at the same time. However, as this commitment is subject to inherent epistemic differences in the legal orders involved, the potential conflicts over the divergent formal and substantive claims to authority cannot always be resolved, but their resolution must always be attempted in a principled legal manner in line with the substantive and formal transcontextual legal principles of human dignity and integrity.

The purpose of this chapter is to identify or to develop a conception of the EU which ensues from the chosen theory of principled legal pluralism. It will proceed in two steps. First, we will outline the established conceptions of the EU to test their fit with the theory of principled legal pluralism. We will demonstrate that such a fit is predominantly lacking, which in turn calls for a new conception of the EU. It will be suggested that a pluralist conception of the EU can be provided by the constitutional form of a union. The latter will be rescued from the historically emerged binary trap of contemporary federal thought and will be applied to the EU as it presently stands.

II. THE MANY CONCEPTIONS OF THE EU

There is neither descriptive nor normative consensus about the present conceptual status of the EU. Jacques Delors stressed this more than 30 years ago, warning against the EU becoming some sort of an unidentified political object.[1] Nevertheless, this is not to argue that there is a lack of theories setting out the conceptions of the EU, determining its legal and political identity. On the contrary, there are many and they avoid any easy classification and straightforward demarcation. However, one way of presenting them is by spreading them along a continuum between two opposites: the international organisation and the statist conception of the EU on either end, with an ample space in-between, occupied by the *sui generis* conceptions.

Pursuant to the conventional international law conception of the EU,[2] the EU is an atypical, more centralised[3] and deepened, but still international organisation.[4] Its evolution and present functioning can be best explained through the plethora of international law instruments.[5] Its central actors are its Member States, which act as the masters of the treaties, the bearers of sovereignty and, in legal terms, as the holders of complete and autonomous legal orders. As a corollary—and as is typical of international law—EU law is merely a dependent[6] and at best a partial legal order,[7] which cannot be characterised as autonomous, either in the way used by the CJEU or, or even less, in the traditional statist manner. While this conception descriptively fails to do justice to the present functioning of the EU, it is equally incompatible with the theory of principled legal pluralism, most importantly since it declines to recognise the existence of legal plurality by not regarding EU law as its own autonomous legal order. The conventional international conception of EU law is thus monist rather than pluralist.

The same conclusion applies to the statist conception of EU law pursuant to which the EU is already a state[8] or ought to develop into one.[9] In so doing,

---

[1] Speech by Jacques Delors (Luxembourg, 9 September 1985) www.cvce.eu/content/publication/2001/10/19/423d6913-b4e2-4395-9157-fe70b3ca8521/publishable_en.pdf, at 2.

[2] As there are many conceptions of the EU in general, there is also not just one international law conception of it, but many. The adjective 'conventional' described the most established international law conception of the EU.

[3] C Leben, 'A propos de la nature juridique des Communautés Européennes' (1991) 14 *Droits* 61, 64.

[4] B De Witte, 'Direct Effect, Supremacy, and the Nature of the Legal Order' in P Craig and G de Búrca (eds), *The Evolution of EU Law* (Oxford, Oxford University Press, 1999) 208–10.

[5] T Schilling, 'Who in the Law is the Ultimate Umpire of European Community Law?' *Jean Monnet Working Paper* http://www.jeanmonnetprogram.org/archive/papers/96/9610.html; A Pellet, 'Les fondement juridique internationaux du droit communautaire' in Academy of European Law Staff (eds), *Collected Courses of the Academy of European Law*, vol V, Book 2 (The Hague, Kluwer Law International 1997) 204.

[6] TC Hartley, 'The Constitutional Foundations of the European Union' (2011) 117 *Law Quarterly Review* 225, 235.

[7] Pellet (n 5) 235.

[8] W Hallstein, *Der Unvollendete Bundesstaat* (Dusseldorf, Econ Verlag, 1969). For a recent defence of this approach, see J Baquero Cruz, 'The Legacy of Maastricht-Urteil and the Pluralist Movement' (2008) 14 *European Law Journal* 389; see also, albeit less strong, Nico Krisch, 'Europe's Constitutional Monstrosity' (2005) 25 *Oxford Journal of Legal Studies* 321; L Friedmann-Goldstein, *Constituting Federal Sovereignty: The European Union in Comparative Perspective* (Baltimore, John Hopkins University Press, 2001).

[9] G Morgan, *The Idea of a European Superstate* (Princeton, Princeton University Press, 2005).

sovereignty would travel from the national to the supranational level, which would, in legal terms, constitute itself as a single hierarchical legal order with the CJEU acting as the supreme court. If the international law conception is motivated by the preservation of the Member States, the statist conception replaces the nation state with a supranational state. In either case, the solution is statist and hence monist. There is little or even no room for the preservation and recognition of legal plurality. There can be just one legal order properly so called: either national or supranational.

The *sui generis* conceptions of the EU have tried to eschew this binary closure deriving from the essentially statist legal mindset. However, irrespectively of the exact version of a *sui generis* conception, be it supranational (ordoliberal,[10] functionalist-regulatory[11] or solidarity-based)[12] or constitutional,[13] the eventual conceptual outcome has not been persuasive. It has either fallen back on one of the two default monist statist positions described above or it has remained conceptually inconclusive, stating that the EU is neither a state nor an international organisation, but something in-between, without specifying any further what this 'in-between-ness' conceptually amounts to. From the perspective of our theory of principled legal pluralism, the existing conceptions of the EU are thus marked by two shortcomings: either they, sooner or later, reveal an essentially monist character; or they remain underdefined and hence conceptually undernourished. We will attempt to close this gap by proposing the concept of union and its underlying theory.[14]

III. THE UNION IN AN HISTORICAL PERSPECTIVE

The theory of union endorses a union as a constitutional form. In so doing, it draws from a long history of federal thought and praxis. The union has thus never

---

[10] For an overview, see C Joerges, 'European Economic Law, the Nation-State and the Maastricht Treaty' in R Dehousse (ed), *Europe after Maastricht: An Even Closer Union?* (Munich, Beck, 1994); as well as C Joerges, '"Economic Order"—"Technical Realization"—"The Hour of the Executive": Some Legal Historical Observations on the Commission White Paper on European Governance' (2001) 6 *Jean Monnet Working Paper*, Symposium: Mountain or Molehill? A Critical Appraisal of the Commission White Paper on Governance, www.jeanmonnetprogram.org/archive/papers/01/012201.html.

[11] H-P Ipsen, 'Europaische Verfassung—Nationale Verfassung' (1987) *Europarecht* 195; see also G Majone, 'The European Community as a Regulatory State' in Academy of European Law Staff (eds), *Collected Courses of the Academy of European Law* (Leiden, Martin Nijhoff, 1996); G Majone, 'Regulatory Legitimacy' in G Majone (ed), *Regulating Europe* (London, Routledge, 1996) 287; F Scharpf, 'The Joint-Decision Trap: Lessons from German Federalism and European Integration' (1988) 66 *Public Administration* 239.

[12] P Pescatore, 'Aspects judiciaires de l'acquis communautaire' (1981) 17 *Revue trimestrielle de droit europeen* 617, 623.

[13] JHH Weiler, 'European Neo-constitutionalism: In Search of Foundations for the European Constitutional Order' (1996) 44 *Political Studies* 517. For an overview, see M Avbelj, 'Questioning EU Constitutionalisms' (2008) 9 *German Law Journal* 1.

[14] This draws heavily on M Avbelj, 'Theory of European Union' (2011) 36 *European Law Review* 818.

been just an imagined, ideational concept. On the contrary, as Walker has put it succinctly: 'the idea of a union makes a historical and politico-sociological point to reinforce the basic conceptual one'.[15] The union is thus a historical fact, a constitutional form whose elements can be traced back to the modern non-unitary state building from the sixteenth century onwards. The examples of unionist constitutional structure are the sixteenth-century Dutch Bund, the British Union State,[16] the nineteenth-century Deutscher Bund (1815–66), the Norddeutscher Bund (1866/67–71) and the Deutsche Reich (1871–1918).[17] In particular, the United Provinces of the Netherlands reportedly directly and indirectly influenced the development of enlightenment thought in the seventeenth century, and hence had a strong resonance in the process of establishing the US.[18] It was there that the union was first fully institutionalised. However, and simultaneously, it is also due to the specific development of American federalism that the union as a constitutional form has almost completely disappeared from our contemporary theoretical awareness. This is how.

As Murray Forsyth has argued:

[T]he constitution drafted in the Philadelphia Convention ... is the most important single landmark in the history of federalism. Definitions of the nature of federal regimes depend to a quite remarkable degree on the way in which this particular constitution is interpreted ... The answer given has had far reaching consequences in terms of the conceptualization and categorization of federal governments.[19]

Thanks to the American state-building, the contemporary meaning of federalism is not just essentially different from the original one, it is also importantly reduced. Federalism had initially stood for all those models of government whereby the decisions were taken not by a single centre; rather, they were framed, adopted and executed in a whole range of possible relationships between the core and the periphery, albeit within the common framework of the whole.[20] However, since the end of the American Civil War, federalism has been narrowed down to a distinction between a federation and a confederacy, the former denoting a federal state founded upon a federal constitution and the latter representing a loose relationship between sovereign states under international law.

---

[15] N Walker, *Final Appellate Jurisdiction in the Scottish Legal System* (Edinburgh, 2010) 15.

[16] C Kidd, *Union and Unionism: Political Thought in Scotland 1500–2000* (Cambridge, Cambridge University Press, 2008).

[17] See S Leibfried, K van Elderen, '"And They Shall Beat their Swords into Plowshares"—The Dutch Genesis of a European Icon and the German Fate of the Treaty of Lisbon' (2012) 10 *German Law Journal* 1297, 1306.

[18] RD Congleton, 'America's (Neglected) Debt to the Dutch: An Institutional Perspective' (2008) 19 *Constitutional Political Economy* 35; see also WH Riker, 'Dutch and American Federalism' (1957) 18 *Journal of the History of Ideas* 495.

[19] M Forsyth, *Unions of States: The Theory and Practice of Confederation* (Leicester, Leicester University Press, 1981) 60.

[20] DJ Elazar, 'Introduction' in DJ Elazar (ed), *Federalism and Political Integration* (Ramat Gan, Turtledove Publishing, 1979) 3.

However, this distinction between a confederacy and a federation, so typical of the contemporary understanding of federalism, was not yet present at the time of the adoption of the American Constitution.[21] As the Articles of Confederation had been replaced by a Constitution, the US was not established as a federal state, which did not even exist as a concept. What we presently associate with a federal state was back then known as a national model of government. Yet the US was not that either. The Founding Fathers claimed to have established a compound, mixed model of government which was neither federal (confederal in the present language) nor national (federal in the present language), but a composition of both. While in public life the US was long after the adoption of the Constitution known as 'confederated states', external observers, most notably de Tocqueville, noted that the US was established as:

> [A] new form of government [that calls for] a new [at the time still inexistent] word, which will one day designate this novel invention.[22]

There were at least six features that marked the specificity of the antebellum US: the nature of the founding act; the institutional structure; the scope of the institutions' powers and the effect of their act(ion)s; the status of the federated states and the ultimate source of legitimacy.[23]

In contrast to contemporary confederal regimes, the founding act of the US was a constitution, which despite its name retained certain appreciable elements of a treaty and was therefore regarded as a mixed constitution[24] or even as a constitutional compact.[25] The institutional structure—the Congress, the Executive and the Judiciary—clearly emulated that of the state and differed markedly from the much more limited institutional set-up in the confederacy, where practically all powers were concentrated in the Continental Congress. The scope of powers of the federal institutions exceeded that of the confederacy as they were for the first time authorised to address issues relating to general welfare.[26] Perhaps even more importantly, the acts of federal institutions were recognised as having direct effect. The acts of federal institutions could therefore directly, unlike in a confederation, address the citizens of the federated states which no longer served as an intermediary.

The federated states retained their sovereignty, while the federal level acquired its own sovereignty too. Hence, as Hamilton argued, the US featured two equal co-existing sovereign levels, which concurrently exercised their own share of

---

[21] M Diamond, 'The Federalist on Federalism: "Neither a National nor a Federal Constitution, But a Composition of Both"' (1977) 6 *Yale Law Journal* 1273, 1274.

[22] A de Tocqueville, *Democracy in America* (New York, Penguin Classics, 2003) 138.

[23] Forsyth (n 19) 64–68.

[24] ibid 107, referring to Madison.

[25] ibid 130, referring to Calhoun.

[26] ibid 68.

sovereignty, without one being supreme over the other.[27] In Akhil Amar's words, the US was envisaged as a harmoniously functioning Newtonian solar system:

> [I]n which individual states ought to be preserved as distinct spheres, each with its own mass and pull, maintained in their proper orbit by the gravitational force of a common central body.[28]

Finally, the source of legitimacy of this new form of government was dual: the people of the US as a whole and the peoples of the federated states. This was reflected in the preamble to the Constitution and in the ratification process. While the preamble refers to the people rather than peoples of the US, the Constitution had to be ratified not by the state legislatures, but by 'special conventions in which the people, the constituent power of the various states, could pronounce their verdict'.[29]

All of these unique features were, of course, disputed, initially in theory, but then (which was eventually fatal) also in practice. The divisions ran between the proponents of two contrasting, in themselves essentially opposing visions of government: the centrifugal state-based vision and the centripetal federal government-based vision.[30] The disputes broke out early on. As time passed, however, the unique form of American government came under increasing strain. The rivalries grew stronger. From competing visions,[31] they moved to emerging political conflicts that ever more frequently called for an epilogue before the courts.[32] As is well known, eventually this situation exploded into the Civil War, in which the advocates of the federal government—as they were now known—prevailed over the supporters of the states' rights—the confederates.

This came with two consequences: one for the American model of federalism and the other for the meaning of federalism as such. The distinctive American compound system of government was lost. America was turned into a federal state as we presently know it. The federal level succeeded in securing its legal supremacy, which the Constitution—even if this was contested[33]—had conferred on it

---

[27] ibid 108, referring to Hamilton's work.

[28] AR Amar, 'Of Sovereignty and Federalism' (1987) 96 *Yale Law Journal* 1425, 1449.

[29] Forsyth (n 19) 65.

[30] Diamond (n 21) 1273. The notion of 'federal government' was reportedly authored by the most ardent supporter of the states' rights, John Calhoun, in his Discourse on the Constitution and Government of the United States.

[31] The two first examples were the Kentucky and Virginia Resolutions. Being passed against the Alien and Sedition Acts, they declared that the Constitution was a 'compact'—an agreement among the states, which entailed that the federal government had no right to exercise powers not specifically delegated to it. Should it do so, its acts under them would be declared void by the states. Years later, this 'compact' theory was used in support of South Carolina's nullification of the federal tariffs. See P Brest et al, *Process of Constitutional Decision-Making* (New York, Aspen Law & Business, 2000) 65–70.

[32] The landmark, but simultaneously divisive, cases were *McCulloch v Maryland* 17 US 306 (1819) and *Martin v Hunter's Lessee* 14 US 304 (1816), culminating in the (indirect) Civil War trigger case *Dred Scott v Sandford* 60 US 393 (1857).

[33] For an overview, see Amar (n 28); *The Ableman v Booth* 62 US 506 (1858) was the first case before the Supreme Court in which the state court asserted its own supremacy over the federal courts. The decision was reversed.

from the beginning. Its political supremacy has also been secured.[34] Since then, the model of the American federal state has been treated as a paradigmatic, in some circles even exclusive, example of a federal system of government.[35] Consequently, the old more all-encompassing meaning of federalism was gradually replaced by the presently existing dichotomy between a federal state, which is regarded as a federal structure properly so called, and a confederation, which is merely an entity under international law.[36] Moreover, echoing the power struggles between the ultimately victorious federals and the defeated confederates that marked the evolution of American federalism, the dichotomy has subsequently been accentuated and presented almost as an exclusive choice between order, efficiency and success guaranteed by a federal state[37] and instability, conflicts and failure of the confederal regimes.[38]

Federal thought has thus travelled 'a long journey through time in quest of a meaning'.[39] Before the outbreak of the American Civil War,[40] federalism had been understood and practised as an inclusive theory of state-building, which embraced a whole range of possible relationships between the core and the periphery within the common framework of the federal whole.[41] Under the influence of the American but later also German state-building,[42] the meaning of federalism has been reduced down to a binary distinction between a federation, denoting

[34] However, this does not mean that it has never since been contested. The intervention of the federal army in Arkansas against the state guard, which was necessary to ensure the implementation of the landmark disaggregation case *Brown v Board of Education* 347 US 483 (1958), is one example.

[35] See Diamond (n 21) 1273, who argues that 'most contemporary definitions of federalism are little more than generalized descriptions of the way Americans divide governing power between the states and the central government'.

[36] M Burgess, *Federalism and European Union: The Building of Europe* (London, Routledge, 2000) 259.

[37] The authors conjoined under the name Publius were Alexander Hamilton, John Jay and James Madison. For the purposes of this chapter, the most relevant Federalist papers are: No IX: Union a Safeguard against Faction and Insurrection, No X: The Numerous Advantages of the Union, No XV: Legislative Defects of the Confederation, all available in D Karmis and W Norman (eds), *Theories of Federalism* (New York, Palgrave Macmillan, 2005) 104–33.

[38] Confederation as 'a sovereign over sovereigns, a government over governments, a legislation for communities, as contradistinguished from individuals' was in the Federalist No 20 held to be absurd in theory and counterproductive in practice; see P King, *Federalism and Federation* (London, Croom Helm, 1982) 25; see also S Fabbrini, 'Is the EU Exceptional? The EU and the US in Comparative Perspective' in S Fabbrini (ed), *Democracy and Federalism in the European Union and the United States* (London, Routledge, 2005), referring to Hamilton's writing in the Federalist No 15. Since then, a confederal form of government has attracted a negative evaluation. See also RL Watts, 'Federalism, Federal Political Systems and Federation' (1998) 1 *Annual Review of Political Science* 117, 122.

[39] SR Davis, *The Federal Principle: A Journey through Time in Quest of a Meaning* (Berkeley, University of California Press, 1978), referred to in R Schütze, *From Dual to Cooperative Federalism* (Oxford, Oxford University Press, 2009) 14, who provides a very good overview of the development of a federal idea.

[40] LC Backer, 'The Extra-national State: American Confederate Federalism and the European Union' (2001) 7 *Columbia Journal of European Law* 173.

[41] Elazar (n 20) 3.

[42] Diamond (n 21); Amar (n 28); A Nicolson, *A Sketch of the German Constitution and the Events in Germany from 1815 to 1871* (Longmans, Green and Co, 1875).

a federal constitutional state, and a confederacy, standing for a loose alliance of sovereign states under international law. Thereafter, the relationships between sovereign states have largely been constrained to two alternatives only.[43] The concept of a union, occupying the space between the two extremes, and its underlying theory have thus slipped into oblivion. We will bring it back to life in what follows.

A. The Theory of Union

Drawing on authors as different as Kant[44] and Schmitt,[45] we will focus on six basic features of the union: (1) the founding of the union; (2) its constitutional structure; (3) the modalities of its internal and external functioning; (4) the preconditions for its viability; (5) its objectives and (6) its overall legal and political character. Starting off with its founding, the union is created on the basis of a free agreement by the participating states,[46] which has a special legal status. It is neither a treaty nor a constitution; rather, it combines the features of both, standing for a constitutional treaty.[47] The latter originates from the constitution-making authority of the participating states, but once adopted, it becomes a constitutional charter of a thereby created supranational level, which also affects the constitutional orders of the participating states[48] and of a union as a whole.

The union's constitutional structure is pluralist. It is distinctly composed of three constitutive elements: the Member States, the supranational level—also the union *stricto sensu*—and the common whole—the union *sensu lato*.[49] It is this three-layered structure that complies with the requirements of the theory of principled legal pluralism and makes a union markedly different from federal and confederal regimes.[50] The latter two are both eventually monist constitutional

---

[43] Of course, there have always existed strong academic voices which have opposed this binary reduction of federalism. See, in particular, CJ Friedrich, 'Federal Constitutional Theory and Emergent Proposals' in AW MacMahon (ed), *Federalism: Mature and Emergent* (New York, Doubleday, 1955) 510.

[44] I Kant, *Perpetual Peace* (London, George Allen & Unwin, 1917).

[45] Carl Schmitt, *Verfassungslehre* (Berlin, Duncker & Humblot, 1993).

[46] In that way, the union differs from an empire, which is in principle a non-voluntary association of (conquered) states. See O Beaud, 'Fédéralisme et souveraineté, Notes pour une théorie constitutionnelle de la Fédération' (1998) 114 *RDP* 100.

[47] Schmitt ((n 45) 368) speaks of 'ein Vertrag besonderer Art: ein Verfassungsvertrag'. In the EU context, however, it was Eric Stein who first used the concept of 'Treaty Constitution' to describe the then Community founding acts; see E Stein 'Toward Supremacy of Treaty Constitution by Judicial Fiat: On the Margin of the Costa Case' (1964) 63 *Michigan Law Review* 491.

[48] Schmitt (n 45) 368.

[49] C Schönberger, 'Die Europäische Union als Bund, Zugleich ein Beitrag zur Verabschiedung des Staatenbund-Bundesstaat-Schema' (2005) 129 *Archiv des öffentlichen Rechts* 81, 87; see also Beaud (n 46) 108.

[50] Schmitt (n 45) 371. A problem in Schmitt's definition of the union is that he appears to be identifying the union—as a common legal and political whole—with a supranational level (*Bundesebene*). This inconsistency is removed by Schönberger, who distinguishes between the supranational level and the union that stands for a legal and political common whole composed of two different entities: the

forms. A federation is a two-layered structure, as the common whole is exhausted by the federal level, which is supreme over the federated level of the Member States. Ultimately, in a federation there is just one, eg, federal legal (and political) order, which includes the relatively dependent legal orders of the federated states. In a confederacy, on the other hand, there is no common whole, but only separate states with their autonomous legal orders bound by a loose treaty regime, which is not given an autonomous, independent legal status. A federal state thus represents monism under constitutional law, whereas a confederacy stands for monism under international law.

In contrast, a union exists as a pluralist legal and political entity. It is composed of and continuously presupposes the co-existence of sovereign Member States and of an equally autonomous supranational level. This means that the Member States, by way of their entry into a union, do not waive their sovereignty,[51] either in legal or in political terms. Instead, they keep it within all those spheres of competences that have not been transferred on a newly created supranational level. However, this is also sovereign, precisely within the scope of the competences conferred upon it. It follows from the pluralist internal structure of a union that it features a plurality of autonomous legal orders, a plurality of sociopolitical spaces (polities) and therefore a plurality of sovereigns. In contrast to the federal or confederal monistic solutions with a single locus of sovereignty, either on a federal level or a national level, in a union, both levels are sovereign and must be so preserved. As stressed by one commentator, the question of sovereignty is the ultimate question of the very existence of the individual member states and of the union as a whole.[52] Under normal conditions, this should not arise, but this does not render it irrelevant.[53] It is quintessential for any union that the question of sovereignty remains open and unresolved as long as a union should exist.[54] For once the question of sovereignty was decided either in favour of the participating states or in favour of the supranational level, a union would dissolve.[55]

Inside the particular pluralist common whole of a union, the Member States and the supranational level thus retain or, respectively, acquire their legal and

member states and the supranational level. See also Beaud (n 46) 141, who out of the same concerns for clarity insists on the identical tripartite definition of a federation, consisting of *Federation*, standing for the common whole, *federation*, meaning the federal level, and of the federal constituent entities—the states. We espouse this tripartite definition as well.

[51] Whereby sovereignty is, following Walker, understood as a plausible claim to the ultimate legal and political authority. See N Walker, 'Late Sovereignty in the European Union' in N Walker (ed), *Sovereignty in Transition* (Oxford, Hart Publishing, 2003) 18.

[52] Schmitt (n 45) 371.

[53] This is, in particular, the position of Beaud (n 46) 89: 'La federation ne peut être définie par la notion de souveraineté.' The same conclusion might also be inferred from Schönberger (n 49) 109, who argues that with the help of the concept of sovereignty, the essence of the union cannot be captured, even though both levels: supranational and the member states describe themselves like that: 'Aber diese Souveränitätsformeln können den Bund in seiner Eigenart gerade nicht erfassen.'

[54] Schmitt (n 45) 373.

[55] ibid.

political autonomy, but they do not exist in mutual isolation. Fully in line with the theory of principled legal pluralism, there is no absence of relations between them, but these are heterarchical rather than hierarchical. In contrast to a federation, whose internal structure is marked by the supremacy of a federal level and the subordination of federated states, inside a union the rapport between the national and the supranational level is relational and coordinative. This is perhaps best reflected in the event of conflict between the national and supranational law. While in a federal state it is in fact federal law that invalidates the conflicting municipal law, in a union the supranational law only takes precedence in application before the municipal law of the participating states.[56]

In the more concrete terms of the union's internal and external functioning, a union requires a significant change in the legal and political status of the member states.[57] As it follows from the classics of the theory of a union,[58] membership in the union usually requires a change in the participating states' constitutions.[59] They must allow a supranational legal and political intervention and oversight over their territories.[60] Simultaneously, they must waive a right to self-help against other member states and must submit all their conflicts to a peaceful resolution on the basis of the judicial mechanisms provided for in the founding act of a union. The member states thus lose their internal *ius belli*, whereas externally they can keep it alongside with a union that must have its own capacity to wage war too.[61] Finally, while each member state is free to enter a union, it can neither renounce it individually nor at will.[62] The union, on the other hand, has a duty to defend an independent political existence of all the participating states against external as well as internal destabilising forces.[63]

This is closely related to the main objective of a union: perpetual peace.[64] Following Kant, this should be achieved by way of preserving the sovereignty of the participating states, as a guarantee against the emergence of cultural and social uniformity,[65] which would deprive the citizens of an independent national community of their substantive ethical freedom.[66] Simultaneously, the autonomy of the supranational level must be respected and preserved too, and its relationship with the national level must be conducted in a way that secures the viability of the union as a whole. The objectives of the union are thus threefold: establishing a lasting peace within a viable unionist common whole; securing the autonomous

---

[56] ibid 381.
[57] ibid 366.
[58] ibid 363.
[59] ibid 366.
[60] ibid 370.
[61] ibid.
[62] ibid 367.
[63] ibid 368.
[64] ibid 369.
[65] Jurgen Habermas, *The Divided West* (Cambridge, Polity Press, 2006) 128.
[66] ibid 127.

and functional supranational level; and preserving the distinctiveness of the participating states as a means of protecting the freedom of an individual as part of his or her communitarian self. Incidentally, the insistence on the protection of the ethical freedom of an individual of course reflects the normative expectations stemming from the transcontextual principle of human dignity, which lies at the heart of the theory of principled legal pluralism.

The constitutional form of a union thus reflects several building blocks of the theory of principled legal pluralism: legal plurality, its recognition, transcontextual principles and also, as we shall see in turn, the prerequisite for connecting plurality: the normative spirit of pluralism. The latter is indispensable for the viability of the union whose constitutional structure is deprived of a kind of comforting, *ex ante* stability that the federal or confederal unitary, hierarchical constitutional framework can furnish. Unlike the monistic framework, the grand structure of a union is in a constant and permanent search for the best coordinative equilibrium between the independent participating states and the self-standing supranational level. In this way, as some commentators have noted, the union is condemned to a continuous state of 'in-between' (*ein Zwischen*), marked by inherent dynamics, instability, conflicting objectives[67] and antinomies.[68]

Furthermore, the union also lacks a sense of social homogeneity, which typically performs as a cohesive factor in (federal) states, ensuring their viability. Interestingly, both Kant[69] and Schmitt[70] were convinced that homogeneity is an existential requirement for the union too. Schmitt, unsurprisingly, even went as far as claiming that in the absence of homogeneity, a union is nothing but a void, a deceiving and a fictitious act.[71] It is submitted that he erred in saying this. As envisaged by the theory of principled legal pluralism, the constitutive units of the union are different epistemic sites, marked by an overall social diversity which ought to be preserved. The union as a pluralist constitutional form serves precisely this objective. Its pluralist internal structure is best and uniquely tailored to the integration of states, which are heterogeneous and diverse in many ways, which want to preserve this diversity as part of their identity and as a reflection of their autonomous, independent existence, but which simultaneously strive for an efficient and workable alliance with the other states in order to achieve the objectives that they have in common for the ultimate maximisation of the wellbeing of all their citizens.[72]

---

[67] See Schönberger (n 49) 87, 109.

[68] Schmitt (n 45) 370.

[69] Kant (n 44), for example, insisted that the civil constitution of each participating state should be republican.

[70] Schmitt ((n 45) 376–79) argued that the constituent entities of a union, the member states, have to be substantively similar in terms of their religious, civilisational, social or class-based features, and in terms of their political organisation, but most importantly, they have to be ethnically homogeneous.

[71] ibid 379.

[72] For a similar position, see Beaud (n 46) 96.

In the absence of a monist constitutional structure and substantive homogeneity, the viability of the union is thus ensured through the normative spirit of pluralism as a connecting factor of legal plurality.[73] All constituent entities of a union—the Member States and the supranational level—must recognise each other as unique bearers of distinct schemes of justice, of substantive commitments that each of them as distinct polities adhere to and that should be therefore preserved, but they must simultaneously commit to seeing each other and acting as part of a common pluralist whole: the union as a whole. This double commitment, if genuine, encourages the constituent entities that the pursuit of a common whole will not result in their decline or encroach upon their substantive commitments, which in turn generates mutual trust between them and provides for a cohesive fabric that strengthens the union as a whole. It is on this basis that a union creates commonality from plurality and diversity, while preserving the two, without insisting on any pre-existing essential homogeneity of fundamental values or pre-given substantive, or even civic, unity. And in so doing, it ensures its own viability.

On the basis of the above-mentioned features of a union, its legal and political nature could be defined as a non-statist, three-layered federal pluralist constitutional form, which must be distinguished from a confederacy, as a treaty regime under international law, as well as from the state, both unitary and federal.[74]

IV. THE EU AS A UNION

Having outlined the constitutional form of a union, does the EU, as it presently stands, exhibit any of its six key features identified above? Beginning with its overall legal and political nature, this has traditionally been defined as *sui generis*, meaning that the EU is neither a federal state nor a confederacy. However, recently this empty *sui generis* character has started being filled by academics and institutional actors alike with the characteristics of a union. In his 2012 State of the Union speech, the then President of the European Commission, Jose Manuel Barroso, thus openly called for 'a federation of nation states'. Not a superstate, he hastened to add, but:

> [A] democratic federation of nation states that can tackle our common problems, through the sharing of sovereignty in a way that each country and each citizen are better equipped to control their own destiny.[75]

---

[73] The idea of normative spirit of pluralism is close to what Michel Rosenfeld has called 'comprehensive pluralism'; see M Rosenfeld, 'Habermas' Call for Cosmopolitan Constitutional Patriotism in an Age of Global Terror: A Pluralist Appraisal' (2007) 14 *Constellations* 159.

[74] This resonates with Kant ((n 44) 129–34), who has defined his Union of Peace as a union of states, which is more than a mere peace treaty, but less than a state.

[75] 'Plenary Session of the European Parliament' (Strasbourg, 12 September 2012) europa.eu/rapid/press-release_SPEECH-12-596_en.htm.

He argued in favour of 'a Union with the Member States, not against the Member States',[76] calling for a federation, different from that of the US, following 'a specifically European model'.[77]

That Europe is 'inventing a new political form: something more than a confederation but less than a federation'[78] has also been recognised by prominent scholars, including Jürgen Habermas. Noting that the binary alternative between a federal state (*Bundestaat*) and a confederacy (*Staatenbund*) is a false one and an upshot of the German nineteenth-century *Staatsrechtsdiskussion*,[79] he has explicitly advocated the building of a transnational democratic political union. This should preserve the Member States and simultaneously build a strong supranational level, and through a unique concept of shared sovereignty draw on two sources of legitimacy: the peoples of the Member States and the EU citizens.[80]

As the unionist legal and political nature of the EU is thus increasingly being recognised, both among institutional and academic stakeholders, other traits of the constitutional form of the union can be identified in the EU too. In terms of its creation, of course, the EU was not established as a union, but as an international organisation. It came into being between sovereign states by way of freely agreed international law treaties, two of which have been concluded for an unlimited period of time.[81] The goal of the integration had been made clear before in the Schuman declaration—it was to make war between the integrating states not merely unthinkable, but materially impossible.[82] Integration has been put in service of a lasting peace. Its goal thus coalesced with the paramount objective of a union, and so has the fact that it was established for an unlimited period of time, voluntarily by the independent states, which could not exit the process unilaterally, but only by following a clearly prescribed procedure.[83] Yet the founding acts of the integration were international law treaties and such was its overall legal and political character too. As I have described at great length elsewhere,[84] in order to be regarded as a union, the integration's legal and political nature had to undergo a considerable transformation.

Its chief initiator was the CJEU, which in a series of landmark cases claimed the existence of the EU's own supranational autonomous legal order, whose supreme and exclusive umpire was the CJEU itself. The Court sought to distinguish the supranational legal order from those of the Member States and, in particular,

---

[76] ibid.

[77] 'Speech by President Barroso at the Brussels Think Tank Dialogue' (Strasbourg, 22 April 2013) europa.eu/rapid/press-release_SPEECH-13-346_en.htm.

[78] Jürgen Habermas, 'Why Europe Needs a Constitution' (2000) 11 *New Left Review* 5.

[79] Jürgen Habermas, *Im Sog der Technokratie* (Berlin, Suhrkamp Verlag, 2013) 94.

[80] Jürgen Habermas, *The Crisis of the European Union* (Cambridge, Polity Press, 2012) 12–52.

[81] The Coal and Steel Community expired 50 years after its creation.

[82] R Schuman, 'Declaration of May 9, 1950', europa.eu/abc/symbols/9-may/decl_en.htm.

[83] This was laid down only in the Treaty of Lisbon [2007] OJ C306; see also Consolidated Version of the Treaty on European Union [2016] OJ C202, art 50.

[84] Avbelj (n 14).

from international law.[85] For this reason, it also converted the nature of the EU's founding acts. It argued that not only did the treaties create obligations between the contracting states,[86] they also related directly to the people as the bearers of rights and duties under EU law. The treaties were soon thereafter pronounced a constitutional charter of the EU[87]—a Treaty Constitution.[88] Their original international law character has been constitutionalised.[89] From the Court's claims, and stemming from the practice of other EU institutions, a distinct supranational level began to emerge, purportedly with its own autonomous legal order and sociopolitical identity.[90] Similarly, the founding act started to reflect a hybrid treaty-constitution character,[91] just like in a union.

This legal transformation has, in turn, been sanctioned by the Member States, in particular by their highest courts.[92] Admittedly, they have not acquiesced to the autonomy of the supranational legal order all at once[93] and with the same enthusiasm,[94] but eventually even the most reticent national jurisdictions came to terms with the autonomy of the EU legal order,[95] if not necessarily with all the legal consequences that stem from it.[96] Importantly, the recognition of the

---

[85]   Case C-26/62 *Van Gend en Loos v Nederlandse Administratie der Belastingen* [1963] ECR I; Case C-6/64 *Costa v Enel* [1964] ECR I; Case C-402/05 *Kadi v Commission* [2008] ECR I-6351.

[86]   *Van Gend en Loos* (n 85).

[87]   Case 294/83 *Les Verts v Parliament* [1986] ECR 1339.

[88]   Stein (n 47); see also Eric Stein, 'Lawyers, Judges and the Making of Transnational Constitution' (1981) 75 *American Journal of International Law* 1.

[89]   K Lenaerts, 'Constitutionalism and the Many Faces of Federalism' (1990) 38 *American Journal of Comparative Law* 210.

[90]   For a more recent and also critical research on the role of the CJEU and European lawyers in general in constructing the EU, see A Vauchez and B de Witte (eds), *Lawyering Europe: European Law as a Transnational Social Field* (Oxford, Hart Publishing, 2013); M Rasmussen, 'Revolutionizing European Law: A History of the *Van Gend en Loos* Judgment' (2014) 12 *International Journal of Constitutional Law* 136.

[91]   The Italian Constitutional Court thus declared the Treaty of Rome as *lo statuto fondamentale* (the constitution) of the Community legal order; see Case 183/1973 *Frontini v Amministrazione delle finanze dello Stato* [1974] GU 2.

[92]   K Alter, *Establishing the Supremacy of European Law: The Making of an International Rule of Law in Europe* (Oxford, Oxford University Press, 2001); A Stone Sweet, *The Judicial Construction of Europe* (Oxford, Oxford University Press, 2004).

[93]   The German Constitutional Court in its first EU law-related case in the early 1960s thus held that the EU is neither part of international law nor of national law. It recognised it as an independent legal order, which flows from an autonomous legal source. Similar positions were adopted by the French Cour de Cassation (*Administration des douanes v Societe Cafes Jacques Vabre and Weigel et Compagnie* May 1975: 'In virtue of Article 55 of the French Constitution the Treaty of Rome has a greater authority than the statutes and it is instituting a separate legal order integrated … with that of the member states. It is because of its separateness that thus created legal order is directly applicable to the nationals of those States and binding on their courts') and the Italian Constitutional Court (*Soc Acciaierie San Michele SpA v High Authority* (1967) Common Market Law Review 160).

[94]   See, for example, B Davies, *Resisting the ECJ: Germany's Confrontation with European Law, 1949–1979* (Cambridge, Cambridge University Press, 2012).

[95]   Polish Constitutional Court 'The Accession Treaty' judgment of 11 May 2005, K 18/04, www.trybunal.gov.pl/eng/summaries/documents/K_18_04_GB.pdf, para 12.

[96]   ibid para 333. 'The European instruments have assigned the interpretation of primary and of secondary law to their own European jurisdiction.'

supranational legal autonomy has not been limited to national judicial pronunciations only, but has found resonance with other institutions too. The national legislatures have thus repeatedly and successively amended their constitutions and/or domestic constitutional practices[97] in order to bring national law into conformity with the requirements of EU law. In so doing, the latter's special nature has been recognised by the highest legal acts of the municipal legal orders.[98]

Following the above-mentioned legal and political practices of the supranational and national institutions, the EU has gradually emerged as a pluralist constitutional entity, uniquely composed of three constitutive layers. The first and original layer is a national one. The EU has not been created to replace and supplant its Member States; it has been established to rescue them,[99] to ensure their ongoing existence immediately after the Second World War and in particular later in the era of globalisation, when it became evident that a self-sufficient, isolationist, fully sovereign nation state is not only unsustainable, but that in fact it has never existed or functioned as such in practice at any point in time. The Member States in the EU thus remain Member States with their autonomous legal orders and retain their character of autonomous polities that exist as a powerful but not exclusive source of democratic legitimation of the functioning of the EU as a whole.[100] In short, in line with the unionist constitutional form, the Member States in the EU are not required and have not been willing to waive their status of a state, be it in a legal, political or cultural sense. They, after all, remain sovereign, provided that sovereignty is understood in a refined, pluralist way.[101]

Following this understanding, the EU *stricto sensu*, namely at the supranational level, which has emerged through the treaty-making power of the Member States and thanks to their readiness to transfer the exercise of an increasing amount of their sovereign rights to the institutions in Brussels, is a sovereign entity too. Obviously, the supranational EU is not sovereign in a statist sense, but it is a functionally sovereign entity. It boasts its own autonomous legal order backed up with an emerging and distinct autonomous supranational polity, whereby the legally constructed and incrementally socially internalised EU citizenship plays an important role. The national level and the complementary supranational level thus build an internally plural EU structure, which is made pluralist through an intense and dynamic relationship between the national and the supranational level on the one hand and through the existence of a third unionist level—the EU *sensu lato*—on the other hand.

---

[97] Which was best reflected in the British *Factortame* saga; see Case 213/89 *Factortame Ltd v Secretary of State for Transportation* [1990] ECR I-2433.

[98] For a comprehensive analysis of national constitutional amendments in relation to EU law, see M Claes, 'Constitutionalizing Europe at its Source: The "European Clauses" in the National Constitutions: Evolution and Typology' (2005) 24 *Yearbook of European Law* 81.

[99] AS Milward, *The European Rescue of the Nation State* (London, Routledge, 2000).

[100] This is even something that the German Constitutional Court, perceived by many as a Eurosceptic court, would be willing to concede to.

[101] M Avbelj, 'Theorizing Sovereignty and European Integration' (2014) 27 *Ratio Juris* 344.

The relationship between the national and the supranational levels is heterar-chical rather than hierarchical. Neither the national nor the supranational level is superior to the other. In legal terms, this is best reflected in a relationship between the national and supranational legal orders. This relationship, which is differ-ent from that in a federal state, is not governed by the principle of supremacy, whereby the federal law is the law of the land and consequently prevails uncon-ditionally over the laws of the federated states. Instead, in the EU, the potential conflicts between the supranational and national legal orders are resolved on the basis of the principle of primacy. This is a relational trans-systemic principle of a conflict resolution, which requires the application of EU law and, as a corol-lary, the disapplication of the national laws when the two clash.[102] However, the principle of primacy is neither absolute nor unconditional. As is well known, the national constitutional courts have conditioned it by the EU's respect for the prin-ciples of the conferral of powers, the rule of law, democracy and human rights protection.[103] The CJEU too, while insisting strongly on the unbounded character of primacy, has generally subjected it to three conditions. The duty to disapply the national provision arises only when there is a conflict with a provision of EU law, which is directly effective and adopted within the scope of EU competences. Furthermore, the CJEU has also allowed for other more specific exceptions to primacy, so that, for example, the principle of primacy does not require national courts to interpret national provisions *contra legem*[104] or to infringe human rights of individuals.[105]

However, the heterarchical relationship between the national and supranational legal orders does not hinge exclusively on the principle of primacy, but rests on a sophisticated network of other structural principles too. The principle of loyalty ranks among the more important ones and requires from the EU's constituent entities sincere co-operation towards the achievement of the agreed EU objectives as well as respect for the continuing distinct national constitutional identities of the Member States. However, like the principle of primacy, the principle of loy-alty is not unconditional either, as the very existence of distinct national legal and political sites requires that their distinctiveness is to be preserved. It is here where the EU reflects the broader idea of principled legal pluralism, which admits that different legal and political sites are first and foremost also different epistemic sites, with their unique and irreducible epistemic cores. If the EU is to remain

---

[102] M Avbelj, 'Supremacy or Primacy of EU Law: (Why) Does it Matter?' (2012) 6 *European Law Journal* 744, 750.

[103] ibid.

[104] Cases C-334/92 *Wagner Miret* [1993] ECR I-6911; Case C-91/92 *Faccini Dori* [1994] ECR I-3325; Case C-192/94 *El Corte Ingles* [1996] ECR I-1281; Case C-81/98 *Alcatel Austria* [1999] ECR I-7671; Case C-111/97 *EvoBus Austria v Növog* [1998] ECR I-5411. In these cases, the Court recognised that national law could not be interpreted in full compliance with EU law. A similar prohibition of *contra legem* interpretation was recently stressed in Case C-105/03 *Pupino* [2005] ECR I-5285, para 47.

[105] Case C-105/14 *Taricco*, para 53.

both a plural and a pluralist entity, these have to be preserved, but in so doing, they inevitably stand in the way of unlimited loyalty and/or unconditional primacy. As these limits are an inbuilt structural feature of any union, the EU included, they have to be reckoned with and managed through the development of a normative spirit of pluralism as the source of the union's viability.

The normative spirit of pluralism, which consists of a double commitment to both the plurality and to the common whole at the same time, can be identified in the normative structure of the EU, as well as in the actual institutional practices: legal, political and administrative at the national and supranational levels. These normative commitments and practices make up a third level of the EU: the EU *sensu lato*, or the common whole. This is more than the sum of its national and supranational parts, which are simultaneously preserved. The normative spirit of pluralism is prescribed in the preambles of the founding treaties and takes a form of legal obligation under the title of the principle of sincere co-operation discussed above. The normative spirit of pluralism has been part and parcel of many supranational declarations and other normative programmes.[106] It is dictated by the texts of several national constitutions and reinforced through their construction by the national highest judicial authorities. Even those national courts that have been found by many to be the most reticent towards EU integration, have insisted on the *Europarechtfreundlichkeit*,[107] they praised mutual confidence[108] and have, in general, exercised self-restraint in their defence of the core of their respective national legal orders.[109]

---

[106] See, for example, the Declaration on the Occasion of the 50th Anniversary of the Signature of the Treaties of Rome—the so-called Berlin Declaration: 'We have a unique way of living and working together in the European Union. This is expressed through the democratic interaction of the Member States and the European institutions. The European Union is founded on equal rights and mutually supportive cooperation. This enables us to strike a fair balance between Member States' interests. We preserve in the European Union the identities and diverse traditions of its Member States. We are enriched by open borders and a lively variety of languages, cultures and regions. There are many goals which we cannot achieve on our own, but only in concert. Tasks are shared between the European Union, the Member States and their regions and local authorities ... For we know, Europe is our common future.'

[107] Case 2 BvE 2/08, 2 BvE 5/08, 2 BvR 1010/08, 2 BvR 1022/08, 2 BvR 1259/08, 2 BvR 182/09 Lisbon [2009], BVerfGE 32 at [225]: 'The Basic Law wants European integration and an international peaceful order. Therefore not only the principle of openness towards international law, but also the principle of openness towards European law [Europarechtsfreundlichkeit] applies.'

[108] See, for example, the decision of the Czech Constitutional Court in the Arrest Warrant case, Pl US/04, 5.3. 2006: 'As a general matter, the requirement of dual criminality can be dispensed with, as a safeguard, in relations among the Member States of the EU, which have a sufficient level of value approximation and mutual confidence that they are all states as having democratic regimes that adhere to the rule of law and are bound by the obligation to observe this principle. It is precisely the situation, where the level of approximation among the 25 EU Member States has arrived at such a degree of mutual confidence, that they no longer feel the need to cling to the principle of dual criminality.'

[109] See, for example, decision of the Spanish Constitutional Court, 'Opinion 1/2004, Tribunal Constitucional on the Treaty Establishing a Constitution for Europe, December 2004' (2005) 42 CMLR 1169, 1176, which argued that the unwritten substantive limits to the principle of primacy of EU law set by the Spanish Constitution should not be construed broadly as a different, 'inadequate understanding

However, the expression of the normative spirit of pluralism is not limited exclusively to the courts, but it can be also identified in the political practices. The European Council in particular, as an amalgam of the highest supranational and national interests, is best suited to represent not only the Member States or the EU *stricto sensu*, but indeed the EU as a common whole. At the same time, the European Council, especially in times of crisis, as the following chapter will show, is under the greatest risk of institutionally collapsing into a mere aggregate of conflicting national interests, typical of intergovernmental structures of inter-national organisations. Similar conclusions, but on a lower political ministerial level, apply to the functioning of the Council. The European Commission, as a supranational institution par excellence, is simultaneously charged with the pur-suit of the common EU interest, which is again more than the sum of its national and supranational parts. The European Parliament, which is a political representa-tive body of the supranational level and hence of the EU *stricto sensu*, also to a certain extent plays this double or hybrid common whole political role. This is facilitated through the co-option of the national parliaments in the EU legislative proceedings through the operationalisation of the principle of subsidiarity. The latter leads to a vertical integration of the national parliaments into EU affairs, as well as to horizontal co-operation between them (COSAC). All this results in a specific common whole, which is more than the sum of its insular national and supranational parts. In symbolically legitimating terms of belonging, the hybrid status of the individuals in the EU, who are simultaneously national and suprana-tional citizens, contributes to this effect too.

Finally, the least obvious (since it is also relatively hidden) source of the nor-mative spirit of pluralism and of the EU common whole is its growing body of administrative law and practices taking place within the EU-specific fora of comi-tology and EU agencies. These bodies, endowed with consultative, executive and regulatory competences in administering EU law, are uniquely composed both of national and supranational representatives, which makes them neither national nor supranational, but representatives and formants of the common whole. It is through their practices that the awareness and commitments to the common whole grow in sociological terms and are awarded with concrete legal bite, since their actions often result in binding legal instruments.

In short, there are thus three actors of the EU common whole, which ensure its distinctively pluralist three-level viability. First, there are the national and supra-national courts, which through their judicial pronouncements construct the legal frame(work) of the EU. They provide for the constitutional dimension of the EU *sensu lato*. Second, there are the political institutions of the EU, which drawing on

---

of Article 93 and of its integrationist substance could impede the existence of the EU legal order, especially its necessary instruments for guaranteeing the compliance with law'. See, also the Lisbon Treaty decision of the German Constitutional Court BVerfG: 2 BvE 2/08, 30 June 2009 and a OMT ruling BVerfG, Judgment of the Second Senate of 21 June 2016—2 BvR 2728/13—paras (1–220).

the citizens, both national and supranational, provide for the political and symbolical dimensions of the union *sensu lato*. Third, there is the administrative network, which makes possible the de facto existence of the common whole, through the unique national-supranational administrative practices that ensure the simultaneous legitimate creation of EU rules (with a national and scientific input), their efficient implementation and, perhaps, most importantly, the development of a unionist administrative, bureaucratic ethos that provides for a concrete institutional foundation of the common whole. As the courts' role is limited, for they only rule in cases and controversies, the systemic institutional expression of normative spirit of pluralism, which ensures the viability of the pluralist EU, is thus to a great extent dependent on the quotidian political and administrative practices of the respective supranational and national actors.

4

Transnational Law and the Rule of Law in the EU

I. INTRODUCTION

CHAPTER 3 MARKED off the conclusion of the first, theoretical part of the book. This developed a map of transnational law, expounded the essential elements of our theory of principled legal pluralism and offered a conception of the EU that ensues from this theory. The present chapter opens the second, applicative part of the book. It will contain four case studies of the relationship between EU law and transnational law, focusing on the impact of transnational law on the rule of law, democracy, human rights and justice in the EU. Through the specific case studies, each chapter will examine the nature of the relationship between EU and transnational law. We will, in particular, be interested in the extent to which this relationship presently complies with the requirements of the theory of principled legal pluralism. To the extent that this fit will already be found lacking in descriptive and explanatory terms, we will provide normative prescriptions as to how the relationship could be structured in a pluralist way to better meet the objectives of the rule of law, democracy, human rights protection and justice. With regard to each of the four foundational values of the EU a different type of transnational law will be focused on to test whether the modalities of the relationship between EU law and transnational law depend on the category of transnational law involved.

We will begin by studying the impact of transnational law on the rule of law in the EU by focusing on international law as an example of public transnational law. Our point of departure is the evolution of international law over the last two decades in the context of the global fight against terrorism. As is well known, international law has been classically conceived of as the law governing the relationships between sovereign states subject to their consensus.[1] While much of this classical doctrine still remains valid today, especially after the fall of the Berlin Wall, many of the classical tenets of international law have nevertheless been fundamentally

---

[1] For an overview, see B Fassbender and A Peters (eds), *The Oxford Handbook of the History of International Law* (Oxford, Oxford University Press, 2012).

reshaped.[2] However, the most radical transformation has taken place with regard to the relationship between international law and individuals. Historically, the latter have not been the objects, let alone the subjects of international law. This has changed. With the growth and deepening of international human rights regimes, landmark rulings of the International Court of Justice (ICJ),[3] the proliferation of international NGOs and in particular the international fight against criminal impunity and terrorist threats, individuals have started to occupy an increasingly central (both active and passive) role under transnational law.[4] Individuals, as heads of states or other high-ranking statist officials, have gradually become objects of international law, in particular its criminal arm, and have been rendered responsible for crimes against humanity. However, with the global fight against terrorism, international law's direct impact or sanctioning capacity has been extended to encompass not just individuals as officials, but indeed anyone suspected of engaging in terrorist activities.

The UN regime of so-called targeted sanctions is a paradigmatic example of the described evolution of international law. The regime, which was established on the basis of the Security Council Resolutions in 1999 and 2000, provided for the immediate freezing of all funds and other financial assets as well as for a travel ban of all individuals, natural and legal persons, associated with Osama bin Laden and Al-Qaida.[5] The individuals have been identified by a special expert-based sanctioning committee, which has then proposed the list for the approval to the Security Council. The hence-imposed sanctions had to be effectuated by the UN Member States. As the EU has implemented the sanctions on behalf of its Member States, not only have the listed individuals been negatively affected, but the rule of law as such has been undermined. The notorious *Kadi* case,[6] upon which this chapter will focus, is the most paradigmatic example of the erosion of the rule of law in the EU as a result of the impact of public transnational law.

The importance of preventing the erosion of the rule of law in the EU from the outside, when internally the latter has been undergoing one of its major rule of law crisis,[7] cannot be overstated. The EU simply cannot afford adding more external fuel to the internal rule of law fire that has been burning increasingly intensely. This is why this chapter is going to demonstrate how, on the basis of the theory

[2] In response, Dworkin has proposed a new philosophy of international law. See R Dworkin, 'A New Philosophy for International Law' (2013) 41 *Philosophy and Public Affairs* 2.

[3] See *LaGrand, Germany v United States* [2001] ICJ Rep 466, which ruled that individuals can draw on the Vienna Convention on Consular Relations (VCCR) as a source of their rights.

[4] See, in particular, A Peters, *Beyond Human Rights: The Legal Status of the Individual in International Law* (Cambridge, Cambridge University Press, 2016).

[5] SC Resolution 1267 (1999); SC Resolution 1333 (19 December 2000), art 8.

[6] Joined Cases C-584/10 P, C-593/10 P and C-595/10 P *European Commission and Others v Yassin Abdullah Kadi* [2013] ECR I-0000; for an in-depth analysis of the case, see M Avbelj, F Fontanelli and G Martinico (eds), *Kadi on Trial: A Multifaceted Analysis of the Kadi Trial* (London, Routledge, 2014).

[7] For an overview, see C Closa and D Kochenov (eds), *Reinforcing Rule of Law Oversight in the European Union* (Cambridge, Cambridge University Press, 2016).

of principled legal pluralism, the relationship between EU law and transnational law could be better organised to secure the highest protection of the rule of law both inside the EU as well as transnationally. With this objective in mind, it will first explain the meaning and practical role of the rule of law in the EU and will then show how the cases like that involving Mr Kadi have led to a deterioration in the rule of law conditions inside the EU. Finally, it will outline to what extent the EU institutions, and in particular the CJEU, have already engaged with its international counterparts in the UN following the normative prescriptions of principled legal pluralism. To the extent that this has failed to be the case, this chapter will propose possible improvements.

II. THE RULE OF LAW IN THE EU

The rule of law is a constitutive value of the EU.[8] It is listed in Article 2 of the Treaty on the Functioning of the EU (TFEU), which provides that:

> [T]he Union is founded on the values of respect for human dignity, freedom, democracy, equality, the rule of law and respect for human rights, including the rights of persons belonging to minorities.[9]

These values are not distinctively EU values, but are common to the Member States and are even, as many have been willing to argue, universal. However, despite a widespread, or at least rhetorical, approval of the importance of the rule of law, both in the EU and beyond, it remains contested what the commitment to the rule of law, both theoretically and practically, actually entails. To appreciate the extent of the challenge that transnational law poses to the rule of law in the EU as well as to reflect on the potential solutions to it, it is thus indispensable to understand the meaning of the rule of law first.

There is obviously no single correct meaning of the rule of law. The rule of law is a social concept and has no essence,[10] no conceptual DNA,[11] apart from the meaning that has been conferred on it by the interpretations of its practical usages. The plethora of different and often conflicting interpretations has broadly led to two approaches to the rule of law. A more sceptical approach holds that the rule of law is an essentially contested concept,[12] which is perhaps

---

[8] Consolidated Version of the Treaty on the Functioning of the European Union [2012] OJ C326, art 2.

[9] ibid.

[10] Brian Tamanaha makes this argument with regard to legal pluralism, but it can be extended to the rule of law too. See BZ Tamanaha, 'A Non-essentialist Version of Legal Pluralism' (2000) 27 *Journal of Law and Society* 296.

[11] This echoes Dworkin's argument with regard to the concept of law; see R Dworkin, 'Hart's Postscript and the Character of Political Philosophy' (2004) 24 *Oxford Journal of Legal Studies* 1.

[12] J Waldron, 'Is the Rule of Law an Essentially Contested Concept (in Florida?)' (2002) 21 *Law and Philosophy* 137.

even vacuous[13] and consequently of little practical relevance.[14] On the other hand, a constructive approach finds the rule of law to be an important concept, but the authors here fail to unite on which of its elements—the formal,[15] the substantive[16] or the sociological[17]—ought to be privileged. This chapter bridges the gap between these theoretical disagreements by opting for an integral approach to the rule of law by connecting all of its three dimensions into a single holistic concept.[18]

The formal dimension of the rule of law is concerned with the formal qualities of a legal order. It requires that a legal order is constituted of non-conflicting hierarchically ordered rules of general application. The rules must be precise, definite, of prospective validity and, of course, published. According to Krygier, the main objective of the formal dimension is to prevent arbitrary treatment.[19] The substantive dimension adds the requirement of justice to the rule of law. The means to this substantive end is the protection of human rights. The rule of law can only exist if the human rights and, in particular the human dignity, of each and every individual are protected.[20] Finally, the sociological dimension requires that the rule of law, both in its formal and substantive dimensions, exists in practice as a real-life category. The protection of the rule of law must thus be actual rather than just hypothetical. This depends on the degree of institutionalisation of the rule of law. The actual implementation of the rule of law in practice requires robust institutions staffed with individuals hired on the basis of meritocratic criteria and their overall personal integrity. The latter is a necessary ethical requirement for a genuine commitment to the rule of law.

The normative commitment to the rule of law in the EU is beyond doubt. After all, as the proponents of the classical supranational vision of the then European Communities have argued since the very outset of the integration process: the EU is a community of law.[21] The rule of law is thus the fundamental value of the EU

---

[13] MJ Trebilcock and RJ Daniels, *Rule of Law Reform and Development: Charting the Fragile Path of Progress* (Cheltenham, Edward Elgar, 2008) 13.

[14] S Holovaty, 'Rule of Law in Action' in Venice Commission, *The Rule of Law as a Practical Concept—Reports* (Venice, 2012) 17.

[15] J Raz, 'The Rule of Law and its Virtue' in J Raz (ed), *The Authority of Law: Essays on Law and Morality* (Oxford, Clarendon Press, 1979) 210; L Fuller, *The Morality of Law* (New Haven, Yale University Press, 1964).

[16] R Dworkin, *Law's Empire* (Cambridge, MA, Harvard University Press, 1986).

[17] Krygier notes that 'some of the central questions about the rule of law are sociological ones'. See M Krygier, 'The Rule of Law: Legality, Teleology, Sociology' (2007) 65 *University of New South Wales Faculty of Law Research Series* 1.

[18] M Avbelj, 'Central Europe as a Legal Phenomenon', (2015) 7 *European Perspectives* 53.

[19] M Krygier, 'Four Puzzles about the Rule of Law: Why, What, Where? And Who Cares?' (2010) 22 *UNSW Law Research Paper* 1, 14.

[20] Paul Craig, 'Formal and Substantive Conceptions of the Rule of Law: An Analytical Framework' (1997) 16 *Public Law* 467.

[21] W Hallstein, 'Die EWG—Eine Rechtsgemeinschaft: Rede anlässlich der Ehrenpromotion' in T Opperman (ed), *Europäische Reden* (Stuttgart, Deutsche Verlags-Anstalt, 1979) 341.

and part of the accession *acquis* as well as a condition for granting aid or developmental incentives to third countries.[22] In several steps the CJEU has developed an elaborated jurisprudence that has attempted to entrench the rule of law in all of its dimensions.[23] Initially the Court laboured mostly on the formal dimension of the rule of law. It was striving to subject all the acts of the EU institutions to judicial review[24] and to ensure that the EU and its Member States, when acting within the scope of EU law, respect the principles of legality,[25] legal certainty,[26] legitimate legal expectations[27] and the principle of proportionality.[28] As noted by von Danwitz, the Court has also developed several procedural guarantees in administrative and judicial proceedings, such as the right to defence,[29] the right to be heard,[30] the right to access to file[31] and the right to reasoned decisions.[32] More

---

[22] See, the decision of the CJEU in Case T-340/14 *Klyuyev v Council of the European Union* [2015] ECLI:EU:T:2016:496, para 87: 'In that regard, it must be recalled that respect for the rule of law is one of the primary values on which the European Union is founded, as is stated in Article 2 TEU, and in the preambles of the EU Treaty and of the Charter of Fundamental Rights. Respect for the rule of law constitutes, moreover, a prerequisite of accession to the European Union, pursuant to Article 49 TEU. The concept of the rule of law is also enshrined in the preamble of the Convention for the Protection of Human Rights and Fundamental Freedoms, signed in Rome on 4 November 1950.'

[23] For an excellent overview, see Thomas von Danwitz, 'The Rule of Law in the Recent Jurisprudence of the ECJ' (2014) 35 *Fordham International Law Journal* 1311.

[24] Case 294/83 *Les Verts v Parliament* [1986] ECR I-1339.

[25] See, for example, Case 500/99 *Conserve Italia v Commission* [2002] ECR I-905, para 90. See also the case law relating to the principle of the legality of criminal offences and penalties: Case 60/02 *X* [2004] ECR I-665, para 63; Case 303/05 *Advocaten voor de Wereld v Leden van de Ministerraad* [2007] ECR I-3672, paras 49–50.

[26] See, for example, Case 110/03 *Belgium v Commission* [2005] ECR I-2829, para 30; Case 550/07 *Akzo Nobel Chemicals Ltd and Acros Chemicals Ltd v European Commission* [2010] ECR I-8301, para 100.

[27] See, for example, Case 62/00 *Marks & Spencer plc v Commissioners of Customs & Excise* [2002] ECR I-6348, paras 44–45; Case 681/11 *Bundeswettbewerbsbehörde and Bundeskartellanwalt v Schenker & Co AG and Others* [2013] ECR I-0000, para 41; Case 362/12 *Test Claimants in the Franked Investment Income Group Litigation v Commissioners of Inland Revenue and Commissioners for Her Majesty's Revenue and Customs* [2013] ECR I-0, paras 44–45.

[28] See, for example, Case 3/09 *Afton Chemical v Secretary of State for Transport* [2010] ECR I-7027, para 45; Joined Cases 581/10 and 629/10 *Nelson and Others v Deutsche Lufthansa AG & TUI Travel plc and Others v Civil Aviation Authority* [2012] 1; Case 283/1 *Sky Österreich v Österreichischer Rundfunk* [2013] ECR I-0000, para 50.

[29] See, for example, Case 550/07 *Akzo Nobel Chemicals Ltd and Acros Chemicals Ltd v European Commission* [2010] ECR I-8301, para 92.

[30] See, for example, Case 349/07 *Sopropé-Organizações de Calçado Lda v Fazenda Pública* [2008] ECR I-10369, paras 36–37; Case 27/09 P *France v People's Mojahedin Organisation of Iran* [2011] ECR I-7051, paras 65–66; Case 383/13 PPU *MG and NR v Staatssecretaris van Veiligheid en Justitie* [2013] ECR I-0000, para 32 and the case law cited therein.

[31] See, for example, Joined Cases 238, 244, 245, 247, 250–52 and 254/99 P *Limburgse Vinyl Maatschappij and Others v Commission* [2002] ECR I-8618, paras 315–16; Case 204/00 P *Aalborg Portland and Others v Commission* [2004] ECR I-403, para 68; Case 407/08 P *Knauf Gips KG v Commission* [2010] ECR I-6375, para 22.

[32] See, for example, Case 310/04 *Spain v Council* [2006] ECR I-731857; Case 41/00 P *Interporc v Commission* 2003] ECR I-2156, para 55; Case 521/09 P *Elf Aquitaine v Commission* [2011] ECR I-8947, para 14; Case 547/10 P *Confédération suisse v Commission* [2013] ECR I-0000, para 67.

recently the Court has also built the standards for effective judicial protection in the EU, in particular the right to trial within a reasonable timeframe.[33] It has also reviewed the boundaries between different EU institutions within the EU's own system of checks and balances.[34]

Along with the formal dimension, the CJEU has also gradually developed the substantive standards of the rule of law. The challenge here was particularly acute since the Court faced the task of developing fundamental human rights protection entirely in the absence of any Treaty basis. As is well known,[35] human rights protection in the EU has evolved through five stages. The Court, sticking to the language of the Treaty, first denied that human rights protection forms part of EU law.[36] Under pressure from the Member States' highest judicial authorities, which threatened to undermine the principle of primacy of EU law, the Court, second, inaugurated the EU's own standards of human rights protection in form of the so-called general principles of EU law.[37] Then, in a third step, it extended personal and material scope of the EU standard of human rights protection to encompass not just the acts of EU institutions, but also those of Member States when they implement or derogate from EU law.[38] It was only in stage four that the Member States endorsed the fundamental rights jurisprudence by the Court, first in piecemeal Treaty amendments[39] and then by declaring and finally adopting the EU's own catalogue of fundamental rights contained in the Charter of Fundamental Rights and Fundamental Freedoms.[40] Finally, fundamental rights protection in the EU ought to be completed by the EU's accession to the European Convention for the Protection of Fundamental Rights and Fundamental Freedoms.[41]

---

[33] See, for example, Case 40/12 *Gascogne Sack Deutschland v Commission* [2013] ECR I-0000; Case 50/12 P *Kendrion NV v Commission* [2013] ECR I-0000; Case 58/12 P *Groupe Gascogne SA v Commission* [2013] ECR I-0000.

[34] See, for example, Case 127/07 *Société Arcelor Atlantique et Lorraine and Others v Premier Ministre, Ministre de l'Écologie et du Développement Durable and Ministre de l'Économie, des Finances et de l'Industrie* [2008] ECR I-9895, para 57; Case 344/04 *International Air Transport Association and European Low Fares Airline Association v Department for Transport* [2006] ECR I-403, para 80; Case 37/83 *Rewe-Zentrale v Direktor der Landwirtschaftskammer Rheinland* [1984] ECR I-1229, para 20; Case 63/89 *Assurances du Crédit v Council and Commission* [1991] ECR I-1799, para 11; Case 233/94 *Germany v Parliament & Council* [1997] ECR I-2405, para 43.

[35] For an overview, see M Avbelj, 'European Court of Justice and the Question of Value Choices' (2004) 6 *Jean Monnet Working Paper* 1.

[36] Case 1/58 *Stork & Co v High Authority of the European Coal and Steel Community* [1959] ECR 17.

[37] Case 29/69 *Stauder* [1969] ECR 419; Case 11/70 *Internationale Handelshesellschaft* [1970] ECR 1125; Case 4/73 *J Nold, Kohlen-und Baustoffgrosshandlung v Commission* [1974] ECR 491, 507.

[38] Case 5/88 *Wachauf v Germany* [1989] ECR 2609; Case 260/89 *Elliniki Radiofonia Tileorasi—Anonimi Etairia (ERT-AE) v Dimotiki Etairia Pliroforissis* [1993] ECR I-2925.

[39] Article F/2 Treaty of Maastricht; Consolidated Version of the Treaty on European Union [2016] OJ C202, art 6.

[40] The Charter was solemnly declared at the adoption of the Treaty of Nice, but was only made binding in Treaty of Lisbon.

[41] Consolidated Version of the Treaty on European Union Art 50 [2016] OJ C202, art 6: 'The Union shall accede to the European Convention for the Protection of Human Rights and Fundamental Freedoms.'

However, following the Court's finding of the incompatibility of the Accession Agreement with the EU Treaties, this stage is facing an impasse.[42] Its potentially negative effects have so far been limited thanks to the CJEU jurisprudence which has made the ECHR unilaterally binding on the institutions of the EU.

The formal and substantive dimension of the rule of law in the EU is thus relatively well established. However, the same cannot be said about the sociological dimension. The discrepancy between the rule of law in theory and in actual practice has become most notable in EU Member States whose political and legal evolution over the last few years has earned them the status of constitutionally backsliding countries.[43] Hungary has played a pivotal role in the systemic deconstruction of the rule of law through the constitutional capture of the state, the weakening of the system of checks and balances, formal departure from the normative adherence to liberal democracy and the informal building of a powerful political and economic network of party loyalists, narrowing the scope for social, political and economic pluralism as a *conditio sine qua non* for the veritable existence of the rule of law and democracy.[44] A lukewarm reaction by the EU has turned Hungary, also thanks to the unfavourable conditions caused by the migration crisis, into a role model for other EU Member States, most notably Poland.[45] As a result, due to a growingly unstable political situation, marked by the rise of populist political parties whose agenda is *en bloc* irreconcilable with constitutional democracy,[46] the rule of law across the EU is under systemic internal threat. Adding the unfavourable external developments to it, to which we will turn next, fails to paint a positive picture of the rule of law inside the EU.

III. THE EROSION OF THE RULE OF LAW UNDER TRANSNATIONAL LAW

The international fight against the rise in terrorist threats has resulted in a new role for the individual under international law. As described above, the invention of the so-called smart sanctions has led to situations in which the international law targets individuals directly. The international organisations, most notably

---

[42] Opinion 2/13 of the European Court of Justice on the Accession of the EU to the ECHR.

[43] For an overview, see A Jakab and D Kochenov, *The Enforcement of EU Law and Values: Ensuring Member States' Compliance* (Oxford, Oxford University Press, 2017).

[44] JW Müller, 'The Hungarian Tragedy' (2011) *Dissent Magazine* 1, 5; M Dawson and E Muir, 'Hungary and the Indirect Protection of EU Fundamental Rights and the Rule of Law' (2013) 14 *German Law Journal* 1959; B Bugarič, 'Protecting Democracy and the Rule of Law in the European Union: The Hungarian Challenge' (2014) 79 *LSE 'Europe in Question' Discussion Paper Series* 1; A von Bogdandy and P Sonnevend (eds), *Constitutional Crisis in the European Constitutional Area* (Oxford, Hart Publishing, 2015).

[45] See, for example, TT Koncewicz, 'Of Institutions, Democracy, Constitutional Self-Defence and the Rule of Law: The Judgments of the Polish Constitutional Tribunal in Cases K 34/15, K 35/15 and beyond' (2016) 53(6) *Common Market Law Review* 1753.

[46] JW Muller, *What is Populism?* (Philadelphia, University of Pennsylvania Press, 2016).

the UN, of course rely on its constitutive member states to make the sanctions work in practice. Thus, the implementation of targeted sanctions always relies on a triangle of relationships between the sanctioning international organisation, the implementing member state and the affected individual.[47] In case of the pluralist EU, the complexity is deepened yet further, as the implementation in fact involves two types of actors: the supranational institutions adopting the rules of general application and the national institutions charged with the execution of these rules. The relationship at hand is thus not just one of multilevel governance—it is a relationship between multiple legal orders (international, supranational and national), as well as a relationship between several public authorities and a private individual. It is thus little wonder that cases like that involving Mr Kadi have ignited a vigorous debate on the implications of the targeted sanctioning regime for international law[48] and for the EU,[49] as well as for the affected individual's rights.[50] While concerns have been raised about the further fragmentation of international law, about the undermining of the autonomy of EU law and the flagrant lack of protection of individuals' rights, much less has been written and said about the objective treatment of the rule of law in this triangle—objective in the sense that the impact of the targeted sanctions on the rule of law would be examined specifically and separately as a value in and of itself. In what follows we will turn to this task.

The UN sanctioning regime was established on the basis of Security Council Resolutions 1267 (1999) and 1330 (2000). It has since been revised and amended several times.[51] In the EU, the sanctions were implemented by Regulations

---

[47] See also K Ziegler, 'The Relationship between EU Law and International Law' (2015) 15 *University of Leicester School of Law Research Paper* 1, 2.

[48] KS Ziegler, 'Strengthening the Rule of Law, But Fragmenting International Law: The *Kadi* Decision of the ECJ from the Perspective of Human Rights' (2009) 9 *Human Rights Law Review* 288; G de Búrca, 'The European Court of Justice and the International Legal Order after *Kadi*' (2010) 51 *Harvard International Law Journal* 1; B Fassbender, 'Triepel in Luxemburg—Die dualistische Sicht des Verhältnisses zwischen Europa- und Völkerrecht in der Kadi-Rechtsprechung des EuGH als Problem des Selbstverständnisses der Europäischen Union' (2010) 63 *DÖV* 333; G de Búrca, 'The Road Not Taken: The European Union as a Global Human Rights Actor' (2011) 105 *American Journal of International Law* 649.

[49] D Halberstam and E Stein, 'The United Nations, the European Union and the King of Sweden' (2009) 46 *Common Market Law Review* 64; L Ginsborg and M Scheinin, 'You Can't Always Get What You Want: The *Kadi II* Conundrum and the Security Council 1267 Terrorist Sanctions Regime' (2011) 8 *Essex Human Rights Review* 7; N Lavranos, 'Protecting European Law from International Law' (2010) 15 *European Foreign Affairs Review* 265; G Martinico, 'The Autonomy of EU Law' in Avbelj, Fontanelli and Martinico (n 6).

[50] E de Wet, 'From *Kadi* to *Nada*: Judicial Techniques Favouring Human Rights over United Nations Security Council Sanctions' (2013) 12 *Chinese Journal of International Law* 787; M Payandeh, 'Rechtskontrolle des UN- Sicherheitsrats durch staatliche und überstaatliche Gerichte' (2006) 66 *ZaöRV* 41; A Rosas, 'Counter-terrorism and the Rule of Law: Issues of Judicial Control' in A-M Salinas de Frias, K Samuel and N White, (eds) *Counter-terrorism: International Law and Practice* (Oxford, Oxford University Press, 2012) 83.

[51] For an overview, see F Fontanelli, 'Kadieu: Connecting the Dots—from Resolution 1267 to Judgment C-584/10 P' in Avbelj, Fontanelli and Martinico (n 6).

467/2001 and 2062/2001. They, inter alia, also listed Mr Kadi's name, which caused by way of their direct applicability that all his funds on the territory of the Member States were frozen. It was undisputed that the interference with Mr Kadi's rights to private property took place on the basis of *in camera* decision of the Security Council, in the absence of any judicial review and without any procedural safeguards, such as the right to be heard and the right to defence. Several of Mr Kadi's human rights were thus openly violated and it was consequently left to the EU judiciary to also protect them as a part of a substantive dimension of the EU rule of law.

As is well known, at least initially the EU judiciary was not up to the task of ensuring that the rule of law was efficiently protected. This was the case for several reasons, but mainly because international law posed a challenge not only to the substantive but also to the formal dimension of the rule of law. As explained above, in formal terms the rule of law requires that legal rules of general application form a non-conflicting hierarchical whole. The then Community Court of First Instance (CFI, now the General Court) was at pains to decide how to ensure this rule of law expectation when two legal orders—that of international law and that of the EU—compete for hierarchical prevalence. In trying to square the circle, the CFI ruled in favour of the supremacy of the Security Council Resolutions and hence of international law over EU law,[52] except if the former is incompatible with *jus cogens*. This led the CFI to limit the judicial review of the Resolutions, but also of the EU implementing acts, for their compliance with *jus cogens*.[53] Putting the bar so high, but especially in the context of this case, in which it was clear that no violation of *jus cogens* had taken place, the CFI effectively rendered the targeted sanctions immune to judicial review.

In so doing, the EU ran short of the central rule of law requirement that all acts of the EU institutions are subject to judicial review. Since the targeted sanctions were derived from international law that the CFI declared supreme, no judicial protection was ensured at any level of governance. There was no judicial protection on the level of international law, since there is no court open for the redress of individual. There was no judicial protection on the supranational level, since its judiciary substantively declined the jurisdiction. And finally, there was no judicial protection on the national level, since national courts are proscribed from reviewing the validity of the acts of the EU, such as the implementing regulations in this case. The formal rule of law, in the form of a guaranteed judicial protection which is fair and hence involves the right to defence, the right to be heard, the right to access to file and the right to reasoned decision, thus remained a dead letter. It was guaranteed on paper, but not in practice. The sociological dimension of the rule of law in the EU was thus plainly undermined too.

---

[52] Case T-315/01 *Kadi v Council and Commission* [2005] ECR II-3649.
[53] ibid.

Upon appeal, the CJEU reversed this decision.[54] By referring back to its landmark *Les Verts* ruling,[55] it recalled that the EU is based on the rule of law so that:

[N]either its Member States nor its institutions can avoid review of the conformity of their acts with the basic constitutional charter, the EC Treaty, which established a complete system of legal remedies and procedures designed to enable the Court of Justice to review the legality of acts of the institutions.[56]

As a result, the EU regulations, despite the fact that they were implementing the Security Council Resolutions, in principle ought to have been subject to a full review in light of the EU fundamental rights.[57] Having conducted such a review, the Court found that Mr Kadi's rights to property and to a fair trial were violated, and the regulations were ordered null and void.[58] In so doing and by staying faithful to its own established jurisprudence, the Court thus safeguarded the formal and the substantive dimensions of the rule of law, but left the sociological dimension unimplemented. The effects of the Court's ruling did not extend beyond the paper on which the judgment was scribbled. All the rights of Mr Kadi, which were correctly found to be violated, continued to remain unprotected, as the Court suspended the effects of its ruling for three more months in order to permit the EU legislature to rectify the identified legal shortcomings. As the EU legislature quickly moved on to provide a new legal basis for the targeted sanctions, Mr Kadi, despite winning the case, failed to obtain a remedy and was forced to initiate a new round of judicial proceedings.

Like Mr Kadi's rights, the rule of law—pending further judicial decisions—remained in a state of practical suspense too. The CJEU's formal rather than practical reinstatement of the rule of law demonstrates that both the rights of the individual and the rule of law played a secondary role in this case. Rather than safeguarding the rule of law, the Court's central concern appeared to be to ensure the constitutional autonomy of the EU legal order against international law:[59]

[T]he review by the Court of the validity of any Community measure in the light of fundamental rights must be considered to be the expression, in a community based on the rule of law, of a constitutional guarantee stemming from the EC Treaty as an autonomous legal system which is not to be prejudiced by an international agreement.[60]

---

[54] Joined Cases C-402/05 P and C-415/05 *Kadi and Al Barakaat v Council* [2008] ECR I-6351, para 327.
[55] Case 294/83 *Les Verts v Parliament* [1986] ECR 1339 para 23.
[56] *Kadi and Al Barakaat v Council* (n 54) para 281.
[57] ibid para 326.
[58] ibid.
[59] See also Martinico (n 49) 162.
[60] *Kadi and Al Barakaat v Council* (n 54) para 316.

By any means, this was the effect of the case. While the CJEU made clear that not even the Security Council Resolutions, despite the supremacy claim of the UN Charter, could detract from the autonomy of EU law, the targeted sanctions, which were clearly, both by way of their creation and implementation, incompatible with the EU rule of law, remained in place until 2012. They were eventually removed not as an outcome of the judicial proceedings in the EU, but as a consequence of the Security Council's political decision to have Mr Kadi delisted. In this way, again, the CJEU did not deliver to Mr Kadi what it had proclaimed to be the essence of judicial protection, namely:

> [T]hat it should enable the person concerned to obtain a declaration from a court, by means of a judgment ordering annulment whereby the contested measure is retroactively erased from the legal order and is deemed never to have existed, that the listing of his name, or the continued listing of his name, on the list concerned was vitiated by illegality, the recognition of which may re-establish the reputation of that person or constitute for him a form of reparation for the non-material harm he has suffered.[61]

None of the EU courts, despite Mr Kadi's repeated victories, directly contributed to safeguarding his rights, or to the actual upholding of the rule of law in the EU. Instead, the CJEU and the General Court, following its lead, primarily engaged in an overly self-referential defence of the autonomy of the EU legal order against the international law and the UN at its apex.[62] In so doing, the EU judiciary also failed to take into account the rule of law improvements in the Security Council targeted sanctions regime[63] and hence missed the opportunity to enhance the rule of law not just in the EU but also transnationally.

Last but certainly not least, protecting Mr Kadi's rights formally, but de facto not protecting them, is not just a sign of the rule of law's hypothetical rather than actual existence in the EU—it can also be read as an act of arbitrariness. In this case we are dealing with an individual who was deprived of his fundamental right to property and was subject to a travel ban, first, in the absence of any justification at all[64] and throughout the case without any sufficient justification.[65] As his rights were eventually restored by a sheer act of political discretion, still no compelling justification was produced to render a decade of Kafkaesque proceedings comprehensible to him. Ten years on, the law affecting Mr Kadi's rights remained 'intractably unknowable'.[66] The rule of law regime, which permits such an outcome, of course defies its main objective: the reduction of arbitrariness.[67]

---

[61] *European Commission and Others* (n 6) para 134.

[62] M Avbelj and D Roth-Isigkeit, 'The UN, the EU, and the *Kadi* Case: A New Appeal for Genuine Institutional Cooperation' (2016) 17 *German Law Journal* 153, 164.

[63] ibid 164 ff.

[64] *Kadi and Al Barakaat v Council* (n 54) para 353.

[65] *European Commission and Others* (n 6) para 163.

[66] See L Mason, 'The Intractably Unknowable Nature of Law: *Kadi*, Kafka, and the Law's Competing Claims to Authority' in Avbelj, Fontanelli and Martinico (n 6) 77.

[67] Krygier (n 17).

Political, geostrategic and security considerations, not the rule of law, have had the first and the final say in the case of Mr Kadi. An individual was thus left in the hands of the powerful, defying the constraints of the rule of law, which has failed to penetrate inside the intricate relationship between transnational and EU law, as well inside the pluralist unionist structure of the EU.

The latter too, while rarely in scholarly focus, added its share to the complexity and unsatisfactory rule of law outcome inside the EU. Mr Kadi was deprived of his assets in Sweden, but there was no legal way of claiming them back from this Member State. The Swedish authorities were acting under the mandate of primary and directly applicable EU law that they were required to execute unconditionally. While it was Sweden that violated Mr Kadi's rights in practice, the fact of doing that on the basis of directly applicable EU law deprived Mr Kadi of judicial protection in Sweden. The pluralist structure of the EU, due to which Mr Kadi had to turn to the EU courts to have his rights protected, in fact allowed the Member State that caused the violation to eschew responsibility for ensuring that the imposition of sanctions complied with the rule of law. A pluralist structure of the EU thus provides quite some room for passing the hot potato to another, more remote level of jurisdiction, and transnational law, as we have seen, first formally and then at least de facto, can contribute to all competent authorities effectively escaping the confines of the rule of law. Under such a scenario, the rule of law is everywhere formally protected, but it can be, when really needed, ensured in practice nowhere.

IV. UPHOLDING THE RULE OF LAW IN THE EU UNDER TRANSNATIONAL LAW

Having demonstrated that transnational law, in this case public international law, can worsen the rule of law conditions inside the EU and that these negative effects can also be exacerbated further due to the EU pluralist structure, this section examines how the rule of law in such cases could be better protected following our theory of principled legal pluralism. To recall, the theory of principled legal pluralism is founded on four key elements: (1) the factual existence of a legal plurality; (2) recognition and continuous commitment to its preservation; (3) a dialectic open-self entailing a reflexive attitude in and among the entities forming up a plurality; and finally (4) a commitment to the common pluralist whole. It will be argued that since in Mr Kadi's case the important pluralist elements were absent or were merely rhetorically present, the rule of law was also ensured more poorly.

To begin with, international law and EU law are obviously elements of transnational legal plurality. While some still question whether international law is really law, others lament its fragmentation. Between the two extremes, the fact remains that international law is a relatively coherent body of legal norms whose source of validity can be at least indirectly traced back to the UN Charter. This is confirmed by the Charter's supremacy clause, according to which:

> [I]n the event of a conflict between the obligations of the Members of the United Nations under the present Charter and their obligations under any other international agreement, their obligations under the present Charter shall prevail.[68]

Furthermore, the Statute of the International Court of Justice, established by the Charter, stipulates the substance of international legal order, which consists of: international conventions, whether general or particular, establishing rules expressly recognised by the contesting states;[69] international custom, as evidence of a general practice accepted as law;[70] the general principles of law recognised by civilised nations;[71] and of a number of persuasive authorities to be used as subsidiary means for the determination of rules of law.[72] International law thus certainly represents its own body of law. Pursuant to the criterion of intelligibility introduced in Chapter 2, international law as a normative system has been intelligible to other legal systems as a legal system. International law has been recognised as law, which forms part of the transnational legal plurality, not just by the states, but also by the EU.

The existence of legal plurality, being formed by international law and the EU, cannot be put into question, especially since the law of the EU (as has been discussed at great length in the previous chapter) has also emerged as an autonomous legal order. Its autonomy derives from the claim of the Court of Justice of the European Union (CJEU), which has been directed both at the Member States as well as at the international law. The judicial, institutional and political practices of the Member States and of the EU have rendered the CJEU's autonomy claim plausible, but never entirely uncontested. The autonomy of EU law, as a non-territorial functional legal order, permanently remains somewhat precarious. There is thus a constant need on the side of the CJEU to remain vigilant and to defend the autonomy of its legal order, whenever necessary and proportionate to the perceived challenge or even threat to it. In the case of Mr Kadi, the Court seized the opportunity to pronounce on the substantive limits of its own autonomous legal order against international law. This is something which is recognised by the theory of principled legal pluralism as part of each legal order's irreducible epistemic core. The latter does not consist only of the formal hierarchical structure,[73] but also of the substantive content that this hierarchical structure is there to shield. The protection of the

---

[68] Charter of the United Nations, art 103.

[69] ibid art 38/1a.

[70] ibid art 38/1b.

[71] ibid art 38/1c.

[72] ibid art 38/1d. Examples are judicial decisions and the teachings of the most highly qualified publicists of the various nations.

[73] See the Mox Plant Case 459/03 *Commission v Ireland* [2006] ECR I-04653, para 123: 'an international agreement cannot affect the allocation of responsibilites defined in the Treaties'.

principles of liberty, democracy, and respect for human rights and fundamental freedoms represent a foundation of the EU.[74] They form an untouchable nucleus of principles,[75] which not even the UN Charter sitting at the apex of international law can be allowed to prejudice.[76]

While the CJEU is thus fully entitled to defend the autonomy of EU legal order, the theory of principled legal pluralism requires that this is done in order to respect the remaining three elements a pluralist relationship. First, a legal order needs to recognise the existing plurality and commit to it. With regard to EU law, the recognition of international law's autonomous existence is fairly uncontested. Not only has the CJEU recognised the existence of international law *qua* law, it has also insisted on a friendly approach to it, embedded in the judicial doctrine of a (relative) openness to international law.[77] The latter is already dictated by the Treaty itself. This, inter alia, requires that that the EU shall contribute to 'the strict observance of and the development of international law, including respect for the principles of the United Nations Charter'.[78] On the side of EU law and its institutions, there is thus not just a clear recognition of international law, but also a commitment to its protection and preservation.

Nevertheless, this commitment is not entirely unequivocal or unconditional. Instead, it is still subject to change and gradual evolution. While since the early 1970s the international law has been construed as forming an integral part of EU law[79] so that the relationship between EU law and international law has even been conceptualised in monist terms,[80] in recent years scholars have argued that the CJEU has been pushing this relationship into a dualist direction.[81] The effects of international law in the EU, but not its validity, thus depend on the EU's willingness to provide for it. The case of Mr Kadi is a paradigmatic example of this alleged shift not just towards dualism, but excessive self-referentiality and unwillingness to engage with international law.

The latter is required by a third element of principled legal pluralism: the requirement of a dialectic open-self entailing a reflexive attitude in and among the entities forming a plurality. This also finds expression and confirmation in the EU

---

[74] *Kadi and Al Barakaat v Council* (n 54) para 303.

[75] Martinico (n 49) 165.

[76] *Kadi and Al Barakaat v Council* (n 54) para 285: 'It follows from all those considerations that the obligations imposed by an international agreement cannot have the effect of prejudicing the constitutional principles of the EC Treaty, which include the principle that all Community acts must respect fundamental rights, that respect constituting a condition of their lawfulness which it is for the Court to review in the framework of the complete system of legal remedies established by the Treaty.'

[77] Ziegler (n 47) 4–5.

[78] Consolidated Version of the Treaty on European Union [2016] OJ C202, art 3(5); see also art 21(1).

[79] Case 181/73 *Haegeman v Belgium* [1974] ECR 449, para 5.

[80] RA Wessel, 'Reconsidering the Relationship between International and EU Law: Towards a Content-Based Approach' in E Cannizzaro, P Palchetti and RA Wessel (eds), *International Law as Law of the European Union* (Leiden, Martinus Nijhoff, 2011) 16.

[81] See de Búrca (n 48) 2, who notes that the CJEU in *Kadi* adopted 'a sharply dualist tone'.

law itself. While the above invoked Treaty articles establish a general requirement of the EU's openness towards international law, Article 220 TFEU[82] establishes an explicit legal obligation to engage with international law in general and the UN in particular:[83] 'The Union shall establish all appropriate forms of co-operation with the organs of the United Nations and its specialized agencies.'[84] The EU is thus, as a matter of its own law, legally bound to full co-operation with the UN. This conclusion is reiterated by Article 351 TFEU, which ring-fences the international obligations incurred by Member States prior to their membership of the EU from the influence of EU law.[85] As the UN Charter is doubtlessly among such international obligations, it shall thus enjoy a special, perhaps even legally privileged status with regard to EU law, not because of the UN Charter's alleged supremacy, but due to the EU law itself. Even the Court's jurisprudence before *Kadi* confirms this by requiring consistent interpretation of EU law with international law, and in particular with the Security Council Resolutions.[86]

In this vein, Advocate General Maduro also reminded the Court that it:

> [S]hould be mindful of the international context in which it operates and conscious of its limitations. It should be aware of the impact its rulings may have outside the confines of the Community.[87]

In other words, the CJEU must be institutionally cognitively open. It must be self-reflexive and be able to see the bigger picture in which it participates. It must be committed to ensuring the viability of this bigger picture—of the common whole, as it follows from the fourth element of the theory of principled legal pluralism.

Acting as part of transnational legal plurality, composed of many legal orders, in this case national, supranational and international, which do not and cannot exist as self-contained entities in mutual isolation, each of these legal orders should promote the attitude of a dialectic open-self within the framework of the common whole. This requires, as again Advocate General Maduro was correct to stress, that:

> [T]he Court cannot always assert a monopoly on determining how certain fundamental interests ought to be reconciled. It must, where possible, recognize the authority of institutions, such as the Security Council, that are established under a different legal order than its own and that are sometimes better placed to weigh those fundamental interests.[88]

---

[82] Consolidated Version of the Treaty on the Functioning of the European Union [2012] OJ C326, art 220.

[83] The following two pages draw on Avbelj and Roth-Isigkeit (n 62).

[84] Consolidated Version of the Treaty on the Functioning of the European Union [2012] OJ C326, art 220.

[85] ibid art 351.

[86] See, in particular, Case 84/95 *Bosphorus v Minister for Transport* [1996] ECR I-3953, para 13.

[87] Opinion of Advocate General Maduro in *Kadi and Al Barakaat v Council* (n 54) (16 January and 23 January 2008), para 44.

[88] ibid.

However, the normative expectations of the theory of principled legal pluralism, despite their legal basis in EU law and as reflected in the Advocate General's calls,[89] did not find support in the EU judiciary. On the one hand, the CFI judgment was excessively open. In fact, it was mechanical and formalist, simply crediting the formal hierarchy of international law irrespective of the substantive protection of the rule law in the two legal orders. On the other hand, the CJEU stance was much more exclusionary toward international law. This holds in particular for its *Kadi I* ruling.[90] There the requirements of self-reflexivity, of a dialectic open-self and the commitment to the common whole, were clearly outweighed by the Court's overarching concern for the autonomy of EU legal order.[91]

The latter is understandable to some extent. The EU legal order is still relatively immature and is non-statist. Its autonomy thus needs much more protection than that of a well-entrenched statist legal order. Furthermore, the protection of the autonomy is particularly pertinent against international law. The very distinctiveness of the present EU law lurks in its strategic and deliberate divorce from international law.[92] If EU law were now assimilated under the general international law, all other constitutional doctrines that have developed separately, even in denial of the EU law's original international law status, could come under attack not by the international actors, but by the Member States. Somewhat counterintuitively, in cases like Mr Kadi's, but also in others, such as the protracted (non-)accession to the ECHR,[93] the need to safeguard the autonomy of EU law was, in fact, not directed against international law, but against the Member States.[94] Had the EU not vigorously protected its own autonomy against international law so as to insist that it is up to its judiciary to have a final say and to conduct a full review of EU legal acts implementing the international measures, the Member States could have taken the matter into their own hands by questioning the primacy of EU law under the *Solange* scenario.[95] Thus, the EU legal order under the external pressure would eventually be undermined from the inside.

However, it is submitted that the Court in its protection of the autonomy of EU law has gone beyond what is necessary and has succumbed to excessive

---

[89] Advocate General Bot has thus stressed, inter alia, that the CJEU should tailor its review more to the international context; see Opinion of Advocate General Bot in *Commission and Others* (n 6) para 70.

[90] In *Kadi II*, as has been noted, the Court did soften its self-referential stance a little and demonstrated more openness towards international law. See, for example, N Lavranos and M Vatsov, '*Kadi II*: Backtracking from *Kadi I*' in Avbelj, Fontanelli and Martinico (n 6) 108–20.

[91] Martinico (n 49) 164.

[92] For an excellent analysis of the EU's 'quantitative change of such a magnitude that it is qualitative in nature', eg, for its transformation from international to constitutional polity, see JHH Weiler, 'The Transformation of Europe' (1991) 100 *Yale Law Journal* 2403, 2418.

[93] Opinion 2/13 of the European Court of Justice on the Accession of the EU to the ECHR.

[94] For a similar argument, see C Eckes, 'International Law as Law of the EU: The Role of the Court of Justice' (2010) 6 *CLEER Working Papers* 1, 22.

[95] For a similar argument, see J Kokott and C Sobotta, 'The *Kadi* Case—Constitutional Core Values and International Law—Finding the Balance' (2012) 23 *European Journal of International Law* 1015, 1019.

self-referentiality, with negative effects for the EU's relationship with international law and for the rule of law itself. The relationship between EU law and transnational law has become more antagonistic.[96] The UN claim to supremacy accentuated the EU concerns for autonomy and strengthened its self-referentiality. This has increased the chances of detracting from the long-claimed supremacy of the UN Charter, whose preservation would, as a corollary, require even more insistence on supremacy. The antagonistic competition between the two legal orders would feed the extremes, pushing EU law and international law further apart, rather than facilitating the achievement of their shared objectives: the collective security and the rule of law.

With regard to the latter, several critical observers have already pointed out that the Court failed to sufficiently acknowledge, let alone engage with the significant rule of law improvements on the side of the UN Security Council sanctioning mechanism.[97] Neither in *Kadi I* nor in *Kadi II* did the Court pay much attention to the fact that the procedural rule of law guarantees to the targeted individuals inside the Security Council have evolved over the last decade precisely because of the actions of the EU judiciary. The narrative summary to the listed individuals was introduced first[98] and the states incrementally had to provide more detailed information on the individual target.[99] The sufficiency of the information, the justification for enlistment and communication with an affected individual were taken over by the focal point responsible for individual delisting requests.[100] The focal point has eventually been replaced by the Ombudsperson, whose powers have gradually been increased.[101] While her role has always remained merely informal, her initially exclusively mediating powers were in due course of the *Kadi II* litigation upgraded to the right to recommend delisting, which could only be reversed in the event of consensus in the Sanctioning Committee.[102] Since this is hard to achieve, the Ombudsperson's formally informal status has in practice been turned into an informally formal one. While according to Advocate General Bot this provided sufficient rule of law guarantees to the affected person, the Court did not even address it.[103]

---

[96] Ziegler (n 47) 10.

[97] Avbelj and Roth-Isigkeit (n 62) 164 ff; see also P Margulies, 'Aftermath of an Unwise Decision: The UN Terrorist Sanctions Regime after *Kadi II*' (2014) 6 *Amsterdam Law Forum* 51, 59: 'The ECJ did not deign to explain how more formality would improve on the ECJ's own faulty inferences, enhance the Ombudsperson's valuable efforts, or pry loose sensitive information from wary states. A responsible decision would have at least attempted to answer these questions.'

[98] Case T-85/09 *Kadi v Commission* [2010] ECR II-5177, paras 49–54; for a discussion, see K Lenaerts, 'The *Kadi* Saga and the Rule of Law within the EU' (2014) 67 *Southern Methodist University Law Review* 707, 712.

[99] UN Security Council Resolution 1735 (2006) and UN Security Council Resolution 1822 (June 2008).

[100] UN Security Council Resolution 1730 (2006).

[101] UN Security Council Resolution 1904 (December 2009).

[102] UN Security Council Resolution 1989 (17 June 2011).

[103] As Advocate General Bot has stressed in his opinion ((n 117) para 68).

This has certainly been a missed opportunity, most likely resulting from a misconception that safeguarding the rule of law at the level of the EU is not just a necessary but also a sufficient condition for the protection of the rule of law. However, the opposite is true. In a situation of transnational legal plurality, it is impossible to ensure either collective security or the rule of law within the exclusive confines of a single legal order. As all activities (and not just those carried out by terrorists) increasingly tend to take place across several (legal) domains, so that collective security can only be achieved through a comprehensive involvement of all these systems,[104] the same applies to the rule of law. Even if the EU built an ideal system of the rule of law, which of course (still) has not been the case, this would be under a constant pressure of the external rule of law undernourished legal orders with which the EU would formally or de facto need to co-operate for the achievement of joint objectives. Achieving the rule of law in one legal order, which is no longer self-contained, thus necessarily depends on the rule of law quality of other legal orders with which this legal order interacts.

More concretely, if on the level of the Security Council the rule of law falls short of the comparable standards ensured in the EU legal order, the latter should engage proactively with the former in order to stimulate the development of rule of law standards in international law. Once these were sufficiently developed, the EU could exercise more substantive deference to international law and would consequently need to invest less into the policing of formal boundaries of its legal order. Better protection of the rule of law on the international plane would mean less pressure on the autonomy of the EU legal order and hence improved conditions for the joint co-operation of the two legal systems in the pursuit of collective security. However, the EU reaction in Mr Kadi's case was the opposite. Under the banner of autonomy, it fully invested in the rule of law in the EU, but this investment was exclusively formal, as in practice the rule of law concerns yielded to the interests of collective security.[105] This has created two worlds: a world of rhetoric, in which the rule of law of the EU prevailed, and a practical world, in which the collective security of the UN Security Council reigned at the expense of the actual rule of law. Saying one thing but doing another is a sign of a lack of integrity, which undermines the credibility of both legal orders, as well as the objectives of the collective security and the rule of law they wanted to pursue.

V. IMPROVING THE RULE OF LAW IN THE EU–INTERNATIONAL LAW RELATIONSHIP

The preceding discussion has demonstrated that the rule of law both in the EU and transnationally could be better protected had the relationship between EU

---

[104] See also Avbelj and Roth-Isigkeit (n 62) 168.
[105] ibid.

law and international law followed more closely the normative requirements of principled legal pluralism. What should be strengthened, in particular, is the dialectic open self, self-reflexivity and the commitment to the common whole. The three requirements are closely related. Since in the situation of a transnational legal plurality, the rule of law can only be effectively protected in a holistic perspective, the achievement of the latter requires a dialectic openness to other legal orders, which is, in turn, only possible by virtue of self-reflexivity. Conversely, being self-referential leads to a cognitive closure, an absence of any dialectics and a consequent inability to effectively protect the rule of law within a transnational common whole.

In practice, and to steer away from the overly abstract approach, the normative requirements of principled legal pluralism could be achieved through a closer and more genuine institutional co-operation between the respective legal orders. This should begin by recognising that the objectives of the EU and the UN are shared to an important degree and that they can only be achieved through co-operation rather than antagonism or even strategic power play.[106] This co-operation should, as has been noted by Yang, foremost assume an administrative form.[107] The administration is better placed than the courts to negotiate continuously and strategically.[108] As has been stressed by the new governance literature, the administrative actors *sensu lato*, not limited to the statist administrative bodies, can profit from less formalist, and hence more informal, dialogical and flexible modes of interaction.[109] In pursuit of other interests, such as collective security, they are at least to a certain degree permitted to act under a cloud of secrecy, provided that this is in compliance with the rule of law. However, neither the Council nor the Commission engaged in such continuous administrative co-operation with the UN; rather, they acted through a Member State as its contact point at the UN.[110] Had it been different, they might have produced the evidence that could justify Mr Kadi's continuous placement on the sanctioning list and, simultaneously, enable him to refute the potentially unfounded allegations against him.

This administrative engagement could have also encouraged more systemic positive developments. Since the courts rule in the actual cases and controversies, the court-focused approach is always case-specific. The judicial achievements are thus typically limited to individual cases, in which they offer remedies or not, as we have seen in the *Kadi* case. However, the proof of a lack of a systemic effect in the *Kadi* case can also be found at the level of the Security Council. The latter was, admittedly, under pressure from the EU judiciary to improve its rule of law

---

[106] ibid 156.

[107] Nele Yang, 'Constitutional Dimension of Administrative Co-operation: Potentials for Reorientation in *Kadi II*' in Avbelj, Fontanelli and Martinico (n 6) 172.

[108] ibid 178, referring to K Banks, 'Trade, Labor and International Governance' (2011) 32 *Berkeley Journal of Employment and Labor Law* 45, 113.

[109] Margulies (n 97) 57.

[110] Yang (n 107) 178.

guarantees in the (de-)listing procedures, but the effects of this improvement have been strategically limited. While there are currently 12 smart sanctions regimes in place at the UN,[111] only one of them provides individuals with some due process elements—the one that has been subject to EU judicial review.[112] Taking the rule of law seriously in the EU would mandate that the EU institutions insist in their administrative engagement that the rule of law improvements are extended over the international sanctioning regime as a whole.

In so doing, the UN Security Council would also be more concretely pressed to ensure the rule of law rather than just paying lip service to it, and using it instrumentally to quell the EU rule of law concerns and save its sanctioning mechanism. In other words, it was not just the EU but also the UN that turned the rule of law into a subsidiary mechanism for the achievement of other goals. This is also proven by the procedural deceptions at the Security Council. In the *Jim'ale* case, an individual who had been removed from the EU list was immediately put on the Somali list that was not subject to any rule of law guarantees at the UN level. In this way, the procedural safeguards of the rule of law were circumvented by the Security Council.[113] Such actions are clearly incompatible with the rule of law and they equally do not meet the expectations of the principled legal pluralism. Under the just-described scenario, the EU is not perceived as part of the common whole, but more as an irritant in the way towards the efficient achievement of the UN's objectives. Thus, the systemic closure, self-referentiality and absence of a holistic perspective might be even more pronounced at the level of the UN than at the EU level.

By way of conclusion and turning our focus away from trans-systemic and principled solutions, what else could be done on the side of EU law even more concretely to enhance the rule of law as well as to contribute to the collective security, which is a chief concern of the Security Council? If what is called for is a reflexive, sincere dialogical co-operation between the two legal orders in practice, then the UN Security Council, when its Resolutions are at stake, should have a direct role in the EU judicial procedure.[114] As has already been suggested,[115] in these cases the EU judiciary would be obliged to grant the Security Council the right to intervention. The legal basis for this is already in place,[116] but it should be strengthened

---

[111] A list of the sanction regimes is available at www.un.org/sc/suborg/en/sanctions/information. One of the sanction regimes is for Lebanon, which authorises individual sanctions, but the Security Council has not yet named anyone.

[112] Avbelj and Roth-Isigkeit (n 62) 170–71.

[113] ibid 170, referring to the case of *Jim'ale*; see UN Security Council, 'Security Council Committee on Somalia and Eritrea Adds One Individual to List of Individuals and Entities', Press Release SC/10545 (17 February 2012).

[114] ibid 176.

[115] The following two paragraphs draw on Roth-Isigkeit and Avbelj (n 62) 176.

[116] Statute of the Court of Justice of the European Union, containing the consolidated version of Protocol No 3, annexed to the Treaties, as amended by Regulation No 741/2012 OJ L228, art 40: 'Member States and institutions of the Union may intervene in cases before the Court of Justice. The same right shall be open to the bodies, offices and agencies of the Union and to any other person which can establish an interest in the result of a case submitted to the Court.'

so that in cases like *Kadi*, the Court of Justice would need, on its own motion, to invite the Security Council to intervene. Qualifying the UN as a possible intervener would be an appropriate means to engender reflexive and sincere co-operation between the CJEU and the Security Council. In fact, there is no better way of ensuring sincere co-operation between the institutions of the EU and the UN than by involving them directly and on equal footing in concrete judicial proceedings. It might be only in this way that a meaningful dialogue becomes possible. Until now, the position of the Security Council was available to the CJEU only indirectly through written evidence or it was mediated through the EU institutions and the intervening Member States. Even if they could be seen as making a direct case for the Security Council, this view would be mistaken. The intervening EU Member States are indeed simultaneously Member States of the UN, but the UN is—as an international organisation—more than the sum of its parts and therefore not only deserves but also clearly requires its own representation in front of the Court.

Moreover, the direct inclusion of the Security Council by way of intervention would not only facilitate in procedural terms the desired reflexive and sincere co-operation, but would also contribute to the merits of the case—potentially to the satisfaction of both parties involved. It should be recalled that the contested regulation was, inter alia, invalidated because of the violation of Mr Kadi's right to defence. Due to the lack of sufficient evidence and information produced by the Sanctions Committee, the CJEU could not find the reasons for listing to be well founded.[117] However, had the Sanctions Committee chosen to intervene in the case, it would have had a chance to substantiate its grounds for the listing. The latter would get an opportunity to respond in his defence and the Court could, after the right to defence had been heeded, have decided on the merits being more fully informed. Thus, justice would be ideally done to Mr Kadi and the Sanctions Committee, depending on the amount of evidence that either of the sides could produce. Simultaneously, the objectives of the fight against global terrorism and of ensuring a high degree of collective security would not be threatened by these judicial proceedings, as they could also take place behind closed doors.[118]

In conclusion, the smart sanctions regime pioneered by international law in the absence of any rule of law guarantees at the UN level caused a deterioration in the rule of law conditions in the implementing EU. The latter's judiciary privileged the protection of its own legal order's autonomy over the actual protection of the rule of law and the rights of individuals. This chapter argued that had the relationship between EU law and international law been conducted more in the spirit of principled legal pluralism, all the interests at stake—the rule of law, collective security, the autonomy of legal orders involved and the protection of individual's

---

[117] Opinion of Advocate General Bot (n 117) para 137; *European Commission and Others* (n 6).

[118] Statute of the Court of Justice of the European Union, containing the consolidated version of Protocol No 3, annexed to the Treaties, as amended by Regulation No 741/2012 OJ L228, art 31: 'The hearing in court shall be public, unless the Court of Justice, of its own motion or on application by the parties, decides otherwise for serious reasons.'

rights—would be better ensured. In a situation of legal plurality, the pursuit of the selected interests cannot be limited to singular legal orders. Their achievement depends on the capacity of all the participating actors to see themselves as acting in a common whole, of course proceeding from their own epistemic premises, but opening up to others as well as to the common whole.

EU law and international law provide for several legal, political and administrative mechanisms to make this pluralist engagement possible. This chapter has shown the extent to which they have already been relied upon, as well as how they could still be better used in the future. In addition to merely pointing out principled, abstract potentials for a pluralist engagement, it has also outlined some concrete institutional proposals. As the focus has rested on a single, but very important ruling of systemic proportions, the debate has still, admittedly, been centred on the improvements that could be implemented on the side of the EU judiciary. However—as has been stressed, although it merits repeating it once more—the actual systemic implementation of the principled legal pluralism in the relationship between EU law and international law in particular requires an enhanced and continuous engagement of administrative and political branches. They are, after all, constitutive of quotidian practices. The courts, by and large, perform only curative functions, bringing the practices back on (the rule of law) track once they have steered too much from it. The relationship between EU law and transnational law thus already exhibits several traits of our theory of principled legal pluralism, but, as this chapter has shown, there is still plenty of room for improvement. This is there not just for pluralism's own sake, but for the values, such as the rule of law, that the trans-systemic relationships are more conducive to when conducted in a pluralist manner.

5

Transnational Law and Democracy in the EU

I. INTRODUCTION

HAVING ANALYSED THE influence of public transnational law on the rule of law in the EU, this chapter moves on to examine the challenges of transnational law for democracy in the EU during the (recent) economic crisis. Much has already been written about the ills and virtues of EU democracy. The so-called democratic deficit has been treated, if not exhaustively, then to the exhaustion of its audience. Making little progress, one should add, the debate has boiled down to entrenched opinions on the very existence or non-existence of an actual democratic deficit. To avoid this limbo, our focus on EU democracy here will be much more specific. We will concentrate exclusively on democratic developments in the EU in the context of the ongoing financial and economic crisis. In so doing, two distinct and yet related democracy-affecting processes will be investigated. The first process is internal to the EU. It results from the EU's own response to the economic crisis in the context of its specific constitutional structure.[1] The second process is external to the EU and essentially concerns its Member States' access to credits offered by global financial markets. As the accessibility of funds in global financial markets depends heavily on the sovereign bond ratings provided by credit rating agencies (CRAs), the external impact of these transnational actors on national and supranational democracy in the EU will also be studied.

Both democracy-affecting processes under investigation here are underpinned by an assumption that democracy is about self-determination.[2] A democratic polity is one in which its members decide together on the resolution of collective problems, issues and challenges in procedurally predetermined ways. However, a real and meaningful democracy only exists in a polity in which self-determination

---

[1] M Avbelj, 'Theory of European Union' (2011) 36 *European Law Review* 818.

[2] The idea goes back to Kant and Rousseau, who have insisted that the addressees of the laws must also understand themselves as their authors, which is the expression and a proof of their political autonomy. See, for example, J Habermas, 'Constitutional Democracy: A Paradoxical Union of Contradictory Principles?' (2001) 29 *Political Theory* 766.

is actual and not merely hypothetical. This means that the decision makers in such a polity possess actual means for deciding on major issues of genuine and concrete relevance to the polity. The former stands for economic and the latter for political sovereignty. In other words, a democratic polity must possess sufficient economic resources (economic sovereignty) to be able to exercise competencies over the key aspects of its sociopolitical existence (political sovereignty). Of course, both terms—sufficient economic resources and key competencies— are relative, context-dependent and a question of degree, making it hard, if not impossible, to argue *in abstracto* when a polity runs out of its economic and political sovereignty.

However, irrespective of the exact point of the drying out of economic and political sovereignty, I argue that a meaningful democracy is in close correlation with them. If a polity is bankrupt or at least heavily indebted, then it is obvious that the democratic process of self-determination in such a polity has no means available to it to influence the sociopolitical world to any tangible extent. A polity without economic resources is practically dysfunctional, a failed polity, but also democratically emptied. Its democracy might still exist formally, on paper, but not in practice. The outcome is similar if a polity, even if it has economic funds available, has refrained from exercising its key competencies. Also, in such a polity, democracy as self-determination might exist as a formal, yet practically empty, shell.

The argument of this chapter is therefore structured as follows. The concept of democracy will be fleshed out first. This will be followed by a two-pronged study of the internal and external democracy-affecting processes described above, taken separately as well as jointly, and of their impact on democracy in the EU. Finally, some normative proposals, embedded in the theory of principled legal pluralism, to improve the state of EU democracy in the present unfavourable internal and transnational environment will be offered in the conclusion.

II. ON THE CONCEPT OF DEMOCRACY

There are many conceptions of democracy out there. Eleftheriadis broadly distinguishes three competing theories of democracy: the collective theory, the procedural theory and the substantive theory.[3] The collective theory conceives of democracy as the self-government of a sovereign people.[4] The procedural theory defines democracy as a fair procedure for participation in deliberation and

---

[3] P Eleftheriadis, 'Democratic Accountability for a Monetary Union' in R Bellamy and U Steiger (eds), *The Eurozone Crisis and the Democratic Deficit* (Florence, European University Institute, 2013) 1, 5–7.

[4] ibid 5.

decision making,[5] while the substantive theory postulates the equal treatment of every individual as a paramount substantive value of democracy.[6] Rather than seeing these theories in competition, this chapter too, like in the case of the rule of law, opts for an integral approach so that the concept of democracy defended here is the sum of all these theories. Accordingly, inspired by the work of Fritz Scharpf, I have argued[7] that democracy can best be described as consisting of three elements: input legitimacy, democratic political process and output legitimacy, whereby all of its elements are conducted within the framework of the rule of law.

The starting point of input legitimacy is a free individual whose equal human dignity awards him or her with an unalienable right of self-realisation within the limits set by the equal rights of others. The purpose of democracy is to ensure the flourishing of individuals pursuant to their own chosen conception of a good life. Since there are many different individuals, there are many conceptions of a good life, which means that a free society is inherently pluralist. The essence of democracy is to cherish this plurality and make it work. A prerequisite for democracy is thus a pluralist polity, a polity in which all-encompassing pluralism—political, value, religious, cultural, interest-based and economic pluralism—exists, is ensured and fostered. To limit or even to deny pluralism means curtailing an individual's right to self-fulfilment. The suppression of pluralism always leads to an incursion into an individual's freedom and his or her autonomy and ultimately afflicts his or her human dignity.

The input legitimacy in a democracy must therefore enable the most faithful translation of this societal pluralism possible, composed of individual and collective interests, in the formation of a government. To do so, democracy must be inclusive. This is best ensured by fair elections which comply with the highest constitutional standards,[8] including a free and pluralist media, a vibrant civil society and robust political parties. The latter represent the backbone of democracy as they stand for an institutional link between individuals, civil society and the political process conducted in the parliament.

Directly elected by the people, the parliament enjoys the highest democratic legitimacy and is therefore endowed with the power to select the executive branch. The latter manages the state by proposing new laws and executing the existing ones. The judiciary, as the third independent branch, ensures that the

---

[5] ibid 7. This theory is most closely associated with the works of J Habermas, *Between Facts and Norms* (Cambridge, MA, MIT Press, 1996), but perhaps also of J Waldron, *Law and Disagreement* (Oxford, Oxford University Press, 1999).

[6] Eleftheriadis (n 3). The substantive theory of democracy has been defended by, for example, R Dworkin in *Law's Empire* (Cambridge, MA, Harvard University Press, 1986).

[7] See M Avbelj, 'Crises and Perspectives of Building a European Nation—The Case of Slovenia' in P Jambrek (ed), *Nation's Transitions: Social and Legal Issues of Slovenia's Transitions: 1945–2015* (Brdo, Graduate School of Government and European Studies, European Faculty of Law, 2014).

[8] The elections must be general, equal, direct, secret and, of course, free.

law is observed and that individuals' rights are not violated. From a democratic perspective, it is crucial that the parliament's composition reflects the plurality residing inside the polity and that those elements of the polity that failed to prevail in the elections enjoy all the rights and privileges of the opposition. The latter controls those in power and suggests alternative solutions with an ambition to win the next elections. At the heart of the parliamentary proceedings thus lies a political conflict which, however, must be conducted in dialogical way by striking compromises in view of achieving the polity's common good. The media plays a decisive role here, monitoring the work of both the government coalition and the opposition, enabling the voters to form their political preferences for the next election. This system of checks and balances between different branches of government is sometimes also complemented by popular referenda, which serve as an additional check on the decisions of elected officials, as well as by the constitutional court.

Finally, any government, including a democratic one, is there to achieve certain outcomes. It is on this basis that its outcome legitimacy is measured. In a democracy the outcomes ideally have to benefit as many as possible, but they must simultaneously come into being in accordance with the law. This is important so that democracy remains faithful to its essential commitment to respect the freedom and equal human dignity of every individual, rather than turning into a utilitarian system in which individuals are instrumentalised in the hands of the arbitrary power.

Having said that, what remains to be emphasised is the inherent, intimate link and mutual dependence between democracy and the rule of law. In a democracy, all three of its elements—input and output legitimacy and the political process through which they are connected—have to take place within the framework of the rule of law. Simultaneously, there can be no rule of law if the laws that govern people do not come into being in a democratic manner. Democracy and the rule of law thus presuppose each other, but at the same time their relationship is not entirely symbiotic. There is a dormant democratic threat that a democratic majority trumps the rights of the outvoted minorities. This is what the rule of law is there to prevent. However, this counter-majoritarian problem, as it has come to be known,[9] is only a purported one. If democracy is not understood as a simple rule by the majority, but as a system for the organisation of political power whose central value is the protection of equal human dignity, then the constitutional self-limitation of a democratic majority does not entail the denial of democracy, but is its vindication.[10]

---

[9] The term was first introduced by A Bickel in *The Least Dangerous Branch* (Indianapolis, Bobbs-Merrill, 1962) 16.

[10] This would be again in line with Dworkin's conception of substantive democracy: Dworkin (n 6). For further discussion, see F Michelman, *Brennan and Democracy* (Princeton, Princeton University Press, 1999) ch 1.

III. DEMOCRACY IN THE EU

Having outlined the concept of democracy to be used here, it cannot be overlooked that this concept derives from the statist tradition and is expected to do its work inside a state. Like many, if not even all constitutional concepts, democracy also carries a strong statist imprint.[11] Democracy simply is a statist concept and, when juxtaposing it with the EU, which is not a state, what one finds is not a democratic deficit but a conceptual misfit. As it makes very little sense to argue that pears suffer from an apple deficit because they are not apples but pears, it is equally unproductive to draw up a laundry list of democracy within states, compare it line by line with democracy in the EU, and then because of its missing statist democratic elements declare the EU democratically deficient. This comparative exercise, so typical of EU scholarship, will therefore be eschewed here by simply assuming that the EU as a union is not a state, thereby making any mechanical comparison between intra-state democracy and democracy in the EU inappropriate.

As we have explained in Chapter 3, the supranational level of the EU has developed its own, particular supranational political community.[12] The EU polity is composed of the citizens of the Member States who have been recognised with the complementary status of EU citizens. Through the rights attached to their status, whose essence is equal treatment within the material scope (*ratione materiae*) of EU law, they have been legally acknowledged and constructed as a supranational constituency which can directly inspire the EU political authority via a bottom-up influence. On the one hand, this legally mandated de-alienation effect has paved the way for the gradual sociological emergence of the Community-wide 'we feeling',[13] whereas on the other hand, the EU institutional decision-making structure has been set up in a way to mimic as far as possible the elements of a statist democracy: input legitimacy, a democratic political process and output legitimacy.

The success of this latter strategy has been mixed, presumably because of the very conceptual inappropriateness of translating statist democratic mechanisms to a non-statist entity. For example, since the 1970s, the EU has worked hard to improve its input democratic legitimacy by strengthening the role and powers of the European Parliament. However, with the growing role of the Parliament, which has eventually become an equal co-legislator, we have also paradoxically witnessed growing abstention from elections. The formal attempts to improve

---

[11] N Walker, 'EU Constitutionalism in the State Constitutional Tradition' (2006) 21 *EUI Working Papers—Law Department* 1: 'Although the term constitution, like much of our contemporary political vocabulary—including democracy, republicanism, federation and citizenship—predates the modern state, its mature conventional meaning has emerged from the social and political context of the modern state and bears its imprint.'

[12] ibid.

[13] KW Deutsch, SA Burrell, RA Kann and M Lee, Jr, *Political Community and the North Atlantic Area* (Princeton, Princeton University Press, 1957) 36.

input legitimacy have not been internalised by EU citizens. This is notwithstanding the attempts to make EU elections even more attractive by translating the latter's result directly, in the form of *Spitzenkandidaten*,[14] into the composition of the European Commission, whose by now (at least allegedly) independent, bureaucratic supranational character will inevitably, but also more unpredictably, become politicised. This might also impact on the dynamics of the EU democratic political process, which continues to take place in the more or less vacuous EU public sphere.[15] It is also here in the institutional triangle between the Commission, the Parliament and the Council that the legislative process, characterised by its peculiar absence of ideological divisions between the coalition and the opposition, is conducted. However, the EU has been able to benignly neglect all of these democratic peculiarities as long as it could rely on its traditionally dominant way of democratically legitimising itself through the output legitimacy.[16] The process of EU integration has been about uploading competencies from the national to the supranational level motivated and legitimated by the greater output on both levels. As is well known, the outbreak of the acute financial and economic crisis has decisively put an end to this possibility.

A friend in need is a friend indeed, and it has been only with the emergence of the economic crisis that the true extent of the crisis of democracy in the EU has become apparent. Fritz Scharpf has aptly dubbed this state of affairs the pre-emption of democracy.[17] The pre-emption of democracy in the EU has occurred on both the national and supranational levels across three dimensions: substantive, institutional and economic. The pre-emption of national democracy has mainly occurred under the internal constraints of the EU's specific constitutional structure, whereas the pre-emption of supranational democracy has been caused by external constraints resulting from the actions of transnational actors. We turn next to a more detailed description of this phenomenon, starting with the pre-emption of national democracy first.

---

[14] See, for example, M Kumm, 'What Kind of a Constitutional Crisis is Europe in and What Should Be Done about it?' (2013) 801 *WZB Discussion Paper* 18: 'It is high time to be serious about proposals, endorsed among others by current President of the European Parliament Martin Schulz and by Wolfgang Schäuble, to make the elections for the European Parliament genuine European elections for the choice of the President of the European executive.'

[15] For a more in-depth discussion of this particular problem, see F Perez, *Political Communication in Europe: The Cultural and Structural Limits of the European Public Sphere* (Basingstoke, Palgrave Macmillan, 2013).

[16] See for example, J Habermas, 'Democracy, Solidarity and the European Crisis' (lecture delivered at KU Leuven, 26 April 2013), http://www.pro-europa.eu/index.php/en/at-issue/european-identity/11-j%C3%BCrgen-habermas-democracy,-solidarity-and-the-european-crisis, who stated that: 'The Union legitimized itself in the eyes of the citizens primarily through its outcomes and not so much from the fact that it fulfilled the citizens' political will.'

[17] F Scharpf, 'Monetary Union, Fiscal Crisis and the Preemption of Democracy' (2011) *MPIfG Discussion Paper* 11.

IV. THE PRE-EMPTION OF NATIONAL DEMOCRACY IN THE EU

The pre-emption of national democracy in the EU has occurred across three dimensions: substantive, institutional and economic. The substantive pre-emption of democracy describes the process of reducing the number of competencies preserved by the Member States. The institutional pre-emption of democracy denotes the declining role of national parliaments as a core representative institution of the people, which is simultaneously at the heart of the national democratic political process. Finally, the economic pre-emption of democracy indicates the factual incapacity to exercise competencies due to a lack of economic resources. The three processes are both independent of each other as well as closely intertwined, and together contribute to the hollowing-out of the national democratic process. The substantive pre-emption feeds directly into the declining role of the national parliaments as they are formally left with fewer substantive policy fields in which they can legislate. However, the role of national parliaments can be decreasing even if the scope of the national competencies is left intact, so that other branches, in particular the executive one, take up tasks, sometimes even informally, traditionally belonging to the legislative branch. However, the latter phenomenon is not exclusive to the EU. Most modern democracies have seen the trend of a rising executive, but the EU has added its own special twist to this.[18] Finally, the economic pre-emption of democracy can again happen in the circumstances of the full preservation of both substantive and institutional democracy, when the two cannot be practised simply because the state has run out of money to fund its apparatus and core functions. Several EU Member States, as we shall see below, have found themselves in a similar situation in the economic crisis context due to the transfer of monetary competencies to the EU. The substantive pre-emption of democracy has therefore importantly contributed to the economic pre-emption of democracy. We now turn to a more detailed description of these processes.

The substantive dimension of democracy denotes the material competencies that remain within the domain of the national democratic process. The state has traditionally been considered to have comprehensive control over all social affairs in the public domain. As a sovereign state, it has exercised the entire bundle of competencies in full and to the exclusion of any other non-statist authority in its territory.[19] All political issues *sensu lato*, which encompass everything that is not of

---

[18] D Curtin, 'Challenging Executive Dominance in European Democracy' in C Joerges and C Glinski (eds), *The European Crisis and the Transformation of Transnational Governance* (Oxford, Hart Publishing, 2014) 205. Curtin refers to Peter Mair, who has argued that the EU has been 'deliberately constructed as "a protected sphere" in which policy-making can evade the constraints imposed by representative democracy at national level'. See P Mair, *Ruling the Void: The Hollowing of Western Democracy* (London, Verso, 2013).

[19] Matej Avbelj, 'Theorizing Sovereignty and European Integration' (2014) 27 *Ratio Juris* 344.

an exclusively private concern, have been subject to democratic decision making. The people of the state have thus self-legislated *in toto*. The national democratic process was thereby fully substantiated. Nothing would be beyond its control. Of course, while such a total democratic state has always been just an ideal, perhaps even a fiction, with the co-operation of states under international law and further-more under the impact of processes of supranational integration (such as the EU) and globalisation, the gap between the national democratic ideal and reality has been growing steadily.

In the process of EU supranational integration, the Member States have thus transferred an ever-bigger share of the national bundle of their competencies to the supranational level. The uploading of national competencies to the EU has taken place gradually, through different stages. In the first stage, economic com-petencies were transferred to the EU, closely following the well-known Balassa model of economic integration.[20] In 1968, the Member States formed a customs union, and in 1993 the single market was completed, leading to the creation of the monetary union with the issuance of a single currency in 2001, whose crisis several years later prompted the laying down of the keystone of a nascent fiscal union. In the second, more political stage of integration, competencies beyond economic ones have been transferred, such as justice, security and foreign affairs. The sheer number of competencies transferred to or even taken over by the EU through the proverbial competence creep[21] has been detracting from the substance of the national democratic processes to the extent that theory has started to talk about *Entstaatlichung* (emptying of the state),[22] and the national constitutional courts, in particular the Federal Constitutional Court of Germany (BVerfG), were prompted to draw a line in the sand of what is still acceptable so that a Member State and its democracy can still be meaningfully described as such.[23]

However, the full extent of the substantive pre-emption of national democ-racy can be understood best if our focus is complemented by the pre-emption of democracy in its institutional dimension. The two have been occurring side by side and simultaneously. In national institutional terms, the process of European integration has meant the persistent rise of the executive branch at the expense of the legislative branch. For several decades, the representatives of the national governments were exclusive EU legislators in the Council whose legal acts held, according to the principle of primacy, precedence in application before national laws, as well as the incipient capacity of pre-empting national legislative

---

[20] B Balassa, *The Theory of Economic Integration* (Sydney, Allen & Unwin, 1961).

[21] S Weatherill, 'Competence Creep and Competence Control' (2004) 23 *Yearbook of European Law* 1.

[22] JB Cruz, 'The Legacy of the Maastricht-Urteil and the Pluralist Movement' (2008) 14 *European Law Journal* 389, 392.

[23] See the Lisbon Treaty decision of the BVerfG: 2 BvE 2/08, 30 June 2009.

fields in the domains unified or fully harmonised by the EU legislature.[24] The national parliaments have thus not only become substantively undernourished but also increasingly institutionally sidelined. They have tried to fight back on the national level by increasing control over national governments' actions in the EU legislative process, as well as on the supranational level by involving themselves in scrutiny of the European Commission's respect of the subsidiarity principle.[25] The new approach to harmonisation and other models of the so-called new EU governance[26] designed to leave more room to the national legislature for the autonomous exercise of national regulatory choices have also been attempted.

A. The Substantive and Institutional Pre-emption of National Democracy in an Economic Crisis

The outcome has been modest, but even as such it has been almost entirely offset by substantive and institutional developments in the wake of the EU economic crisis. As is well known, in 2009 the eurozone countries found themselves in a vicious circle of a sovereign debt crisis which threatened not only their individual economies, but also by way of a domino effect the survival of the single currency as such. Almost entirely unprepared for such a scenario and under great pressure, the EU sought the assistance of the International Monetary Fund (IMF) and hastily drew together rescue funds for the most vulnerable economies in need of financial assistance.[27] These so-called bail-out funds have enabled struggling Member States to meet their financial obligations to external and internal creditors and thus escape almost imminent bankruptcy. However, this financial assistance came with strict conditions, mandating comprehensive and not infrequently painful structural reforms, the purpose of which was twofold: to ensure that the credits would be repaid as the reforms take shape and the economy picks up; and to prevent the moral hazard lurking in the possibility of using the money while continuing on the same old economically devastating course.

However, while well motivated, the effect of these conditions has been a de facto substantive and institutional emptying of national democracies in the economically pre-empted Member States. The national parliaments have been turned into

---

[24] See R Schutze, 'Supremacy without Pre-emption? The Very Slowly Emergent Doctrine of Community Preemption' (2006) 43 *Common Market Law Review* 1023, 1032.

[25] D Jancic, 'Representative Democracy across Levels: National Parliaments and EU Constitutionalism' (2012) 8 *Croatian Yearbook of European Law and Policy* 227, 264.

[26] B Eberlein and D Kerwer, 'New Governance in the European Union: A Theoretical Perspective' (2004) 42 *Journal of Common Market Studies* 121.

[27] In particular, Portugal, Ireland, Greece and Spain.

rubber-stamping institutions.[28] The Member States, which have already transferred a significant share of their national competencies to the EU, now find themselves in a dire economic situation, leaving them, in political terms, with a take-it-or-leave-it scenario. This is an example of a 'zero-choice democracy'.[29] They either signed up to the troika conditions or faced a default on their debts, with potentially disastrous and therefore practically unthinkable national and supranational economic and political consequences. As a result, even those limited material competencies that have at least formally remained with the Member States can no longer be de facto self-legislated upon by these countries' peoples in the context of their indebtedness. This confirms a simple truth: while in liberal democratic countries the economy is to enjoy as much autonomy from the political as possible,[30] on the other hand, politics cannot be meaningfully exercised in the absence of sufficient economic funds. In other words, political self-determination is only possible in conditions of economic independence, which as a rule applies to any entity, whether national or supranational.

However, the depth of the crisis suggested that a one-off response to it was insufficient and that a more systemic approach to reforming the EU's economic governance is called for. As we shall see, its implementation has put additional strains on national democratic processes. A systemic shift in EU economic governance was introduced by the Treaty on Stability, Coordination and Governance in the Economic and Monetary Union (hereinafter the Fiscal Compact),[31] together with the so-called 'six-pack'[32] and 'two-pack' legislation.[33] These intended to

---

[28] See, for example, A Hirvonen, 'Reinventing European Democracy: Democratization and the Existential Crisis of the EU' in M Fichera, S Hänninen and K Tuori (eds), *Polity and Crisis* (Farnham, Ashgate, 2014) 154.

[29] C Joerges, 'The Transformations of Europe and the Search for a Way out of its Crisis' in Joerges and Glinski (n 18) 35 fn 30, referring to N Hlepas, 'Supranational Technocracy and Zero Choice Democracy: The Greek Experience' (ms on file with the author).

[30] KH Ladauer, 'Globalization and Public Governance: A Contradiction?' in KH Ladauer (ed), *Public Governance in the Age of Globalization* (Aldershot, Ashgate, 2004) 9.

[31] Treaty on Stability, Coordination and Governance in the Economic and Monetary Union (Fiscal Compact). The Fiscal Compact is not an instrument of EU law; rather, it was concluded as an international treaty among all the EU Member States, other than the UK and the Czech Republic.

[32] Council Regulation (EU) 1173/2011 of 16 November 2011 on the effective enforcement of budgetary surveillance in the euro area [2011] OJ L306/1; Council Regulation (EU) 1174/2011 of 16 November 2011 on enforcement measures to correct excessive macroeconomic imbalances in the euro area [2011] OJ L306/8; Council Regulation (EU) 1175/2011 of 16 November 2011 on the strengthening of the surveillance of budgetary positions and the surveillance and coordination of economic policies [2011] OJ L306/12; Council Regulation (EU) 1176/2011 of 16 November 2011 on the prevention and correction of macroeconomic imbalances [2011] OJ L306/25; Council Regulation (EU) 1177/2011 of 8 November 2011 on speeding up and clarifying the implementation of the excessive deficit procedure [2011] OJ L306/33; Council Directive 2011/85/EU of 8 November 2011 on requirements of budgetary frameworks of the Member States [2011] OJ L306/41.

[33] Council Regulation (EU) 472/2013 of 21 May 2013 on the strengthening of economic and budgetary surveillance of Member States in the euro area experiencing or threatened with serious difficulties with respect to their financial stability [2013] OJ L140/1; Council Regulation (EU) 473/2013 of 21 May 2013 on common provisions for monitoring and assessing draft budgetary plans and ensuring the correction of excessive deficit of the Member States in the euro area [2013] OJ L140/11.

achieve several objectives. First, they reinforced the Stability and Growth Pact[34] as the substantive framework of European economic governance and placed it within a well-defined timeframe known as the European Semester. The substantive framework centres on fiscal and economic policies, such as budgetary control and control of macroeconomic imbalances in the Member States, and consists of so-called preventive and corrective arms. The former's purpose is to ensure that Member States do not deviate from the agreed fiscal and economic criteria, while the latter provides for the measures (including sanctions) necessary to ensure compliance in cases of deviation.

The cycle of a European semester starts in November each year, when the Commission presents its annual growth survey,[35] along with the alert mechanism report in which it singles out for an in-depth review those Member States that exhibit macroeconomic imbalances.[36] Simultaneously, the Member States have to report on their fiscal policy. Their budgetary duty is twofold. First, they are to present a draft annual budget for assessment to the European Commission and the Council, as well as the preparation of the Stability Programme laying down the national mid-term budgetary objectives (MTBOs) for the next three years. The latter is, again, evaluated by the European Commission, both *ex ante* and *ex post* (that is, confirming past and likely future compliance with commitments).[37] Besides the Stability Programme, the Member States also have to present the National Reform Programme in accordance with the Europe 2020 Strategy and the Euro Plus Pact[38] to demonstrate how they intend to meet the latter's economic objectives.

The European Commission integrates its findings on both the fiscal discipline and the national macroeconomic situation into country-specific recommendations, which are finally adopted by the European Council. If a Member State falls short of the prescribed fiscal benchmarks or exhibits an excessive macroeconomic imbalance, the corrective arm of the EU's economic governance is launched, resulting in an excessive deficit procedure (EDP)[39] and/or an excessive imbalance procedure (EIP). The EDP is triggered if a Member State violates the deficit or the debt rule. According to the former, the annual budgetary deficit cannot exceed three per cent of GDP; according to the latter, the national debt must be less than 60 per cent of GDP or, if higher, it must be shrinking at a satisfactory pace.[40]

---

[34] European Commission, 'Stability and Growth Pact', https://ec.europa.eu/economy_finance/economic_governance/sgp/index_en.htm.

[35] European Commission, 'Making it Happen: The European Semester', 7 July 2015, ec.europa.eu/europe2020/making-it-happen/index_en.htm.

[36] ibid.

[37] ibid.

[38] European Central Bank, 'Economic Policy—Economic Reforms', 2015), www.ecb.europa.eu/mopo/eaec/ecopolicy/html/index.en.html.

[39] Consolidated Version of the Treaty on the Functioning of the European Union [2012] OJ C326 Art 126.

[40] The gap between the national debt and the 60 per cent requirement must be diminishing at a rate of five per cent annually.

Following adoption of the Fiscal Compact, the national budgetary positions, such as the Member States' MTBOs, have to be balanced or in surplus. This is achieved if the MTBO deficit does not exceed 0.5 per cent,[41] or one per cent for those Member States whose national debt is significantly less than 60 per cent.[42] If this benchmark is not achieved, other than in cases of exceptionally permitted deviations,[43] an automatic correction mechanism is initiated.[44]

The EDP results in enhanced surveillance of a Member State by the European Commission, the strictness of which varies depending on the gravity of the economic situation in a Member State. Three types of EDP can thus be effectively distinguished: (1) regular enhanced surveillance; (2) enhanced surveillance with precautionary financial assistance; and (3) enhanced surveillance under the macroeconomic adjustment programmes. Once subject to a regular EDP, a Member State must adopt a budgetary and economic partnership programme consisting of a detailed description of the structural reforms required to correct the excessive deficit.[45] In addition, the Commission can request a number of specific measures to implement the enhanced surveillance.[46] The Commission carries out regular review missions together with the European Central Bank (ECB), the European Supervisory Authorities and the IMF.[47] These are reinforced in the case of enhanced surveillance with precautionary financial assistance from the European Stability Mechanism (ESM)[48] and/or European Financial Stability Facility (EFSF)[49] under an Enhanced Conditions Credit Line or a Precautionary Conditioned Credit Line, for which a Member State has to meet specific criteria and policy conditions.[50] Finally, countries in the Macroeconomic Adjustment Programmes[51] are subject to

---

[41] Fiscal Compact (n 31) art 3(b).

[42] ibid art 3(d).

[43] ibid art 3(c).

[44] ibid art 3(e).

[45] ibid art 5.

[46] European Commission, 'The Two-Pack on Economic Governance: Establishing an EU Framework for Dealing with Threats to Financial Stability in Euro Area Member States' (2013) 147 *Occasional Papers* 1, 10: '1) A stress test on banks to be implemented by the ECB/EBA; 2) An assessment of the domestic financial supervisory capacity to be implemented by the ECB/EBA; 3) Any information needed for the monitoring of macro-economic imbalances; 4) A comprehensive independent audit of the public accounts of all sub sectors of the general government; 5) Any information available for the monitoring of the fiscal deficit; 6) Access to disaggregated data on the developments of the financial sector. In addition, Member States must also meet new reporting requirements foreseen for countries under the excessive deficit procedure (EDP) irrespective of the existence of the latter.'

[47] ibid 11.

[48] European Stability Mechanism, www.esm.europa.eu/index.htm.

[49] European Financial Stability Facility, www.efsf.europa.eu/about/index.htm.

[50] European Commission (n 46).

[51] Greece, Ireland, Portugal and Cyprus were subjected to a macroeconomic adjustment programme. Portugal and Ireland have already exited it and are now in the post-programme surveillance phase. Spain was not part of the macroeconomic adjustment programme as it requested financial assistance for the recapitalisation of its financial institutions only: European Commission, Communication from the Commission to the European Parliament, the Council, the European Central Bank, the European Economic and Social Committee and the Committee of the Regions, COM(2014) 905 (28 November 2014) 9.

the strictest surveillance and must ensure full cooperation with the Commission, the ECB and the IMF to prevent the Council interrupting their access to financial assistance.[52]

On the other hand, the EIP imposes on the affected Member State a duty to prepare a corrective action plan, which must be endorsed by the Council and the Commission, the latter also being responsible for closely monitoring the plan's implementation.[53] All of these surveillance measures, in both the preventive and corrective arms of fiscal and macroeconomic control, are supported by the threat of sanctions. These sanctions, depending on the infringement, can be gradually increased from an interest-bearing deposit of up to 0.2 per cent of GDP to a non-interest-bearing deposit of the same size and, finally, a fine of 0.2 per cent of GDP or a maximum 0.5 per cent of GDP.[54]

The thus reformed EU economic governance model has importantly impinged on national democracy in both substantive and institutional ways. In substantive terms, national fiscal powers have been constrained the most, to the extent that two important democracy pre-emptying effects can be spoken of. First, by consti-tutionalising the golden fiscal rule requirement on the national level, a whole set of important economic questions will be removed from the national ordinary demo-cratic process and political contestation.[55] Second, by increasing EU control even over the exercise of national budgetary competencies, the Member States might be giving up the last material brick of national democracy. If anything constitutes the heart of national self-legislation or self-determination, then this is collectively making or at least influencing the decisions on how to spend the money the state collects from its taxpayers. As there should be no taxation without democratic representation, this very representation becomes meaningless if it can no longer decide how and what the collected taxes are to be spent on. If decisions regarding the fiscal burden imposed on citizens and the social conditions in which they will live are effectively taken away from the national electorate,[56] then the national democracy has undergone a systemic substantive pre-emption, not only a tempo-rary one, resulting out of a transient troika conditionality.

---

[52] Council Regulation 472/2013 (n 33) art 7 integrates the previous intergovernmental macroeco-nomic adjustment programmes with the new supranational regulation.

[53] European Commission, 'The EU's Economic Governance Explained', Fact Sheet, 28 November 2014, 4, europa.eu/rapid/press-release_MEMO-14-2180_en.htm.

[54] ibid.

[55] Pursuant to art 3 of the Fiscal Compact (n 31), the national budgets must be balanced or in surplus (art 3(1)), which means that other than in explicitly prescribed exceptional cases (art 3(3)), a lower level of structural deficit cannot exceed 0.5 per cent in GDP at market prices (art 3(1)(b)) or one per cent in case of countries whose general government debt in GDP is significantly lower than 60 per cent (art 3(1)(d)). These rules must be inscribed in the national law of a binding and permanent character, preferably constitutional (art 3(2)).

[56] See M Dawson and F de Witte, 'Constitutional Balance in the EU after the Euro-Crisis' (2013) 76 *Modern Law Review* 817, 823. The authors are alluding to the Lisbon decision of the BVerfG (n 23) paras 256, 259.

This is not to argue that such a point in national democratic development has already been reached, but important steps have indeed been taken in that direction, depending on the economic stature of a given Member State. As we have seen above, the EU economic governance regulation draws an important distinction between Member States with balanced economic figures and those which exhibit either fiscal or even broader macroeconomic imbalances. In the economically balanced states, the EU's material inroads into national democratic processes will be more limited than in the economically imbalanced states. While both groups of Member States face EU legal restrictions on growth in domestic expenditure, which in principle cannot exceed potential growth in GDP, the imbalanced states must also cut their domestic expenditure to compensate for the identified budgetary imbalance.[57] In addition, they must 'ensure rapid convergence' towards a balanced budget.[58] This adjustment path is then subject to the annual assessment of the stability programme of each Member State, which is, as reported by Chalmers, wide-ranging and onerous: 'it assesses not simply their targets, the robustness of their planning, the direction of any reforms and crucially but the socio-economic context and the demands placed on them by this'.[59] It goes without saying that these rules translate directly into how taxes are being decreased or increased; they determine the scope of the governmental investment as well as the depth and breadth of the national welfare state. All of these are issues that national parliamentary elections should be decided on and decide about.

When combining this substantive pre-emption of national democracy in economic governance by the institutional regime, we can see that the position of national parliaments has been further weakened. Their fiscal competencies have, as described above, been substantively limited and also put under a great time constraint due to the timing of EU semesters. After the EU institutions have spoken about the soundness of a proposed national budget, a national parliament is left with very little time and even less room for democratic political manoeuvring. The national parliaments are thus again being turned into rubber-stamping institutions.[60] Things get even worse for the national parliaments of those Member States under enhanced surveillance. The present EU legislation provides only for a limited information flow to them from the EU institutions involved in the surveillance and for so-called economic dialogue, whereby representatives of the Commission may be invited by national parliaments to justify the specific measures to be adopted by that Member State.[61]

---

[57] D Chalmers, 'The European Redistributive State and a European Law of Struggle' (2012) 18 *European Law Journal* 667, 679.

[58] ibid.

[59] ibid.

[60] Dawson and de Witte (n 56) 834: 'The time constraints imposed by the European Semester make it all but impossible for national parliaments to control their own executives.'

[61] See, for example, European Commission (n 46) 17.

Further, at the peak of the economic crisis in 2011, the Member States decided to coordinate on the EU level even those economic policies that had formally remained outside of the scope of EU competencies. The Europe 2020 Strategy and the Euro Plus Pact[62] have been decisive in this regard. They provide for so-called integrated guidelines, combining the broad economic policy guidelines and employment guidelines, covering the macroeconomic, microeconomic and employment policies, which are proposed by the Commission and adopted by the Council. They serve as the common objectives which ought to be achieved in a country-specific way by each Member State through the National Reform Programme. The national parliaments, social partners and civil society are specifically invited to participate in preparation of the Programme. However, this is more to create the impression of the ongoing national ownership of the structural reforms, while the latter are essentially being driven by the Commission, the Council and the European Council.[63] What we are witnessing here is the significant inroads of EU institutions into the formally exclusive national economic competencies through the allegedly nationally 'owned' and controlled open method of coordination.[64] This is an example of a further substantive pre-emption of national democracy without any formal transfer of competencies.

Finally, during the economic crisis, formal and informal institutional shifts, which will be described in more depth below, have taken place in the EU and affected not only supranational but also national democracy. An important formal shift was the introduction of so-called reversed qualified majority voting in the Council, which means that an economic measure proposed by the Commission against a Member State in the EDP and/or EIP is deemed to be adopted unless blocked by a qualified majority of the Member States. This system, again, tips the balance in favour of the supranational institutions, which is all the more apparent, as pointed out by Dawson and de Witte, in smaller Member States, which now face a much harder task of blocking legislation they oppose. This effect is exacerbated by the informal institutional shift taking place at the level of the Council, whose steering and controlling role over the EU decision-making process has expanded substantially,[65] even to the extent that the Council has increasingly assumed the role of a de facto legislative initiator.[66] The combined effect of these institutional

---

[62] European Commission, 'The Euro Plus Pact' (2015) 3 *EPSC Strategic Notes* 1.The purpose of the Euro Plus Pact is to foster competitiveness and employment; contributing further to the sustainability of public finances and reinforcing financial stability: European Central Bank (n 38) 4.

[63] ibid 3.

[64] However, Joerges (n 29) 41 provides a more optimistic view, arguing that the powers of national parliaments remain considerable as long as they retain their so-called 'ownership' of the national contributions to the Semester process. On the other hand, see D Jancic, 'Countering the Debt Crisis: National Parliaments and EU Economic Governance' (2014) 1 *LSE Law: Policy Briefing Papers* 1, who argues that national parliaments are actually the beneficiaries of the euro crisis.

[65] Dawson and de Witte (n 56) 832.

[66] ibid 830; Curtin (n 18) 210.

shifts is an appreciable strengthening of the executive branch in the EU and, in particular, of the most powerful EU Member States with the greatest influence in the Council, at the expense of the national legislative branches as well as of the smaller and economically weaker Member States in general.[67]

B. The Economic Pre-emption of National Democracy in an Economic Crisis

In the course of the development of European integration, but especially in the years following the outbreak of the economic crisis, national democracy has thus come under considerable strain in its substantive and institutional dimensions. The situation has been exacerbated when we add to this the economic dimension. To repeat the simple truth: in practice, there can be no democracy conceived of as self-legislation by the people in the absence of the economic funds required for its exercise. The state can typically rely on three sources of revenue to fund its activities: fiscal resources, monetary resources and foreign loans. The process of European integration has affected all three of them. With the establishment of the single market, a whole range of protectionist measures, including fiscal ones, was eliminated, which initially led to a decline in national fiscal resources that was later compensated for through the positive effects of the economies of scale.[68] The greater yield of the single market thus offset the loss or the capping of many national fiscal measures. This positive economic effect was further increased, although unevenly among the Member States,[69] by establishment of the single currency, although this move meant that the eurozone Member States relinquished their monetary competencies and turned them into an exclusive EU competence under the control of the ECB. These positive economic effects lasted as long as the economic trend also remained positive. As this suffered a downward turn, the Member States found themselves in an uneasy fiscal situation which could no longer be rescued by the traditional resort to the national monetary instruments of currency devaluation intended to pump the necessary money into the domestic economic system and simultaneously improve, albeit artificially, its level of competitiveness in the global economy. The only way out was to raise loans in the global financial markets. However, this option was foreclosed immediately when the markets, also under the impression of the global economic crisis, sensed

---

[67] Dawson and de Witte (n 53) therefore speak about the dismantling of the substantive, institutional and spatial balance so crucial for the EU's legitimate functioning and its overall viability.

[68] It has been estimated that the single market has contributed two to three per cent to the growth of the EU GDP: see, for example, B Straathof, G-J Linders, A Lejour and J Mohlmann, 'The Internal Market and the Dutch Economy' (2008) 168 *CPB Netherlands Bureau for Economic Policy Analysis* 1, 9.

[69] F Mattern, E Windhagen, J Musshoff, H-H Kotz and W Rall, *The Future of the Euro: An Economic Perspective on the Eurozone Crisis* (Berlin, McKinsey & Company, Germany, 2012).

the high risk associated with the troubled countries' national bonds and claimed yields on them that were economically unsustainable.

At the peak of the crisis, the Member States thus found themselves in a triple economic deadlock. Their budgets were deeply in the red, of course in violation of EU law; the monetary competencies to alleviate the situation had gone; and access to the global financial markets was effectively closed. The only way out of the economic collapse was to turn to the EU—but the EU too, as explained above, was completely unprepared. Unlike in a federal state, the EU was legally and practically prevented from assisting its Member States in need in either monetary or fiscal terms. With regard to the former, the EU founding treaties contain a no-bail-out clause[70] and the ECB's power to print money is limited,[71] whereas in fiscal terms the EU budget, as noted by Scharpf, 'is miniscule in comparison to the budget of federal states', largely because 'there are no European taxes and there is no European social policy to alleviate interregional imbalances'.[72] As a result, the economic crisis has threatened to create a domino effect, spilling over from one country to another, to eventually engulf the EU as a whole. Ultimately this would lead to the complete economic pre-emption of democracy not only on the national but also on the supranational level. To prevent this, the Member States and the EU have struggled to regain access to the global financial markets. Yet, in so doing, they have run into external constraints posed by a specific set of transnational actors: the CRAs.

V. THE PRE-EMPTION OF SUPRANATIONAL DEMOCRACY

Having described the pre-emption of democracy at the national level, which has occurred in the process of European integration and in particular under the impact of the economic crisis, it is important to note that these democracy pre-emption effects have not been limited to the Member States, but extend to the EU at a supranational level too. Here, one cannot speak of a substantive pre-emption of democracy, as the material scope of EU competencies has been increasing rather than decreasing. Similarly, in institutional terms at the supranational level, the trend has been one of democracy-enabling rather than one of pre-emption. In order to escape the charge of a democratic deficit, the EU has been doing its best to mimic as far as possible the institutional structure of national democracies. This has translated directly into the constant improvement of the European Parliament's position in the EU institutional constellation, so that it has eventually

---

[70] Consolidated Version of the Treaty on the Functioning of the European Union [2012] OJ C326 Art 125.

[71] However, the ECB has been losing these bounds, especially recently with the so-called quantitative easing programme.

[72] Scharpf (n 17) 34.

become an equal co-legislator. The chain of democratic legitimation from EU citizens to the European Parliament has thus been formally established and made operational, even though it is widely believed that this link has not been appropriately internalised by the EU constituency.[73] In this respect, at least formally, the institutional dimension of EU democracy serves well the requirements of input and representative democracy as described at the beginning of this chapter. Nevertheless, as already intimated above, the EU response to the economic crisis has brought about certain institutional changes that are reversing this established trend.

First of all, several of the crisis mechanisms had to be concluded under international law, so they are intergovernmental rather than supranational in nature. This per se brings them beyond the scope of competencies of the European Parliament, which is thus excluded from their shaping and control. Moreover, even those legislative mechanisms in six-pack and two-pack forms which have been adopted by the European Parliament only provide for a duty of notification and economic dialogue of the European Commission and the Council with the European Parliament. As observed by Dawson and de Witte, with the escape to international law, the core legislative institutional triangle between the Commission, the Council and the European Parliament has been seriously weakened,[74] and the institutional balance has been shifting to the most influential capitals of Europe, as represented in the European Council. In institutional terms, the most important decisions regarding the crisis and post-crisis management are therefore not adopted by democratically representative institutions, but by an intergovernmental forum that many argue leans in favour of the biggest and economically more powerful Member States. These institutional changes clearly detract from the ideal of a supranational democracy: they lend support to the claims of the existence of a democratic deficit and, if nothing else, fuel the impression of the pre-emption of supranational democracy.

However, the most significant impact of the democratic crisis in the EU has been in the latter's economic dimension. For the first time, the EU, or at least the eurozone, has found itself in an economic situation beyond its control, whereby the availability of funds needed for the functioning of both the EU and national democracies hinges on the global financial markets' willingness to make loans available under still acceptable or at least economically sustainable financing conditions. What is also new, and perhaps even unprecedented, is the fact that in determining the lending conditions, the global financial markets have, rather than relying on the actions or assurances of the Member States or even the EU as a

---

[73] This is also confirmed by a declining interest in the EU citizens' initiative: while 49 such initiatives have been launched, only two have been completed, although without any meaningful follow-up by the European Commission. See H Mahoney, 'EU Democracy Tool Hanging in the Balance' *EU Observer* (26 February 2015) https://euobserver.com/political/127808.

[74] Dawson and de Witte (n 56) 828 ff.

whole, followed the sovereign bond ratings of the CRAs. In this way, these agencies have started to act as gatekeepers of the global financial markets, determining the economic and therefore, at least indirectly, also the democratic fate of the EU as a whole. This presents us with an interesting case study of the influence of transnational actors such as CRAs on democracy in the EU.

A. CRAs and the Economic Pre-emption of Democracy in the EU

CRAs form part of the international financial architecture[75] and profoundly influence the ordering of global financial markets.[76] They are typical actors of transnational law. They belong to the field of private administrative transnational law, which, as Chapter 1 has explained, consist of: (1) administrative rules adopted by (2) private transnational actors, which (3) bind or regulate through acceptance (4) the collective practices of numerous entities in designated sectors without their prior assent to these rules.

The designated sector at hand is a global market in sovereign bonds, such as debt securities issued by states to raise money in global financial markets. The three biggest global CRAs—Moody's, Standard & Poor's and Fitch—jointly control around 70 per cent of the overall market[77] and as much as 90 per cent of the sovereign bond market,[78] and are all private companies established in New York with many branches worldwide. Despite national legal anchoring, they are transnational actors because their activities stretch far beyond the US; they perform services for a majority of states and make their products available to the global financial markets.[79] The latter adapt their actions subject to the ratings issued by CRAs. They do so voluntarily, in pursuit of the greater efficiency generated by CRAs, which arguably help reduce the asymmetry of information traditionally existing in the markets.[80]

The products of CRAs in the sovereign bonds market are ratings which assess the credit capacity of a state. These ratings do not have a legal character and are therefore not binding with the force of positive law. Their formal authority stems from the CRAs' expertise, while their practical authority derives from the fact that the produced ratings are followed in practice by the relevant markets. The states which order and pay for their ratings cannot influence the criteria under which

---

[75] A Darbellay, *Regulating Credit Rating Agencies* (Cheltenham, Edward Elgar, 2013) 5.

[76] ibid 6.

[77] G Mattarocci, *The Independence of Credit Rating Agencies* (Amsterdam, Elsevier, 2014) 40, according to the percentage of customers served by the CRA with respect to the overall market: Moody's: 35.8 per cent; Standard & Poor's: 20.25 per cent; and Fitch: 16.05 per cent (2012 figures).

[78] R Abdelal, *Capital Rules: The Construction of Global Finance* (Cambridge, MA, Harvard University Press, 2007) 162.

[79] The main contemporary uses of CRAs have been described as financial information, regulatory tools, contracting tools and monitoring tools: see Darbellay (n 75) 37–41.

[80] ibid 38.

they are developed. They are therefore set unilaterally by the CRAs and are not based on a contract or any other instrument requiring the consent between the CRA and the country ranked. This endows the CRAs' ratings with elements of vertical hierarchy and authority, and hence makes them administrative in their character.

The ratings are thus private administrative norms[81] which, following the criteria chosen by the CRAs, establish the state's credit capacity, which is then followed by the global markets in determining the interest rates to be paid on the national bonds. The CRAs' rating has important direct public and private economic consequences. If the required interest rates are low, loans are more readily available and the state does not find it hard to finance its needs, even in the absence of its own funds. In contrast, if the interest rates are (too) high, the state's access to the global markets becomes limited or even closed, which can (potentially) place huge constraints on the provision of public services. However, the worsening of a sovereign bond rating also negatively affects the private sector due to the so-called sovereign ceiling effect. Private entities cannot normally be ranked higher than the state in which they are established.[82] If a state is downgraded, the ratings of private companies incorporated within them also decrease. Money then also becomes more expensive for those companies, which all translates into a worse overall business environment. In short, the CRAs' ratings directly affect the economic conditions of the public and private sector in a given state and, as such— since modern democracies are fund-dependent—have an important impact on democratic life in that state.

For example, in the above-described situation of an internal economic preemption of national democracies in the conditions of exclusive EU monetary competencies with the concurrent absence of EU fiscal competencies, several EU Member States found themselves on the brink of bankruptcy due to the prohibitive bond yields resulting from the CRAs' ratings. For the first time, the CRAs' systemic importance in global financial markets had become apparent, and the systemic risk for sovereign states and the global economy as a whole that CRAs' ratings can (potentially) bring about had also become obvious. This resulted in several critical reactions.

---

[81] This is confirmed by the European Parliament, Council Regulation (EU) 462/2013 of 21 May 2013 amending Regulation (EC) No 1060/2009 on credit rating agencies [2013] OJ L146/1 (CRA III Regulation), para 8, which makes it explicit: 'Credit ratings, unlike investment research, are not mere opinions about a value of a price for a financial instrument or a financial obligation. Credit rating agencies are not mere financial analysts or investment advisors. Credit ratings have regulatory value for regulated investors, such as credit institutions, insurance companies and other institutional investors. Although the incentives to rely excessively on credit ratings are being reduced, credit ratings still drive investment choices, in particularly because of information asymmetries and for efficiency purposes.'

[82] H Almeida, I Cunha, MA Ferreira and F Restrepo, 'The Real Effects of Sovereign Ratings: The Sovereign Ceiling Channel', 2014, www.business.illinois.edu/halmeida/Ratings.pdf.

The CRAs were attacked for their lack of transparency and accountability in the production of ratings.[83] The arguments that a degree of secrecy and distance from the rated state are necessary to shield the independence and expertise of the CRAs[84] were criticised as falling short of rule-of-law standards. In particular, this is because the rated state (or other entity) basically lacks any means to have its voice heard or to challenge the rating in an appropriate forum. Moreover, the impartiality of the CRAs was contested too.[85] Concerns were raised about potential conflicts of interest due to the issuer-pays model[86] and preferential treatment of the economies of big and strong states over those of smaller and weaker states.[87]

This perception has been reinforced by the fact that the three biggest CRAs are all based in the US. In addition to their American leaning, the CRAs have also been criticised for keeping an oligopoly in the market,[88] which contributes to the homogenisation of information.[89] This has further accentuated the systemic risk, in particular when combined with the pro-cyclical effect of the CRAs' actions.[90] Especially in times of crisis, the CRAs have often been slow to react.[91] They have tended to downgrade a state only when a crisis was already in full swing, but in so doing have intensified the affected state's worsening economic conditions.[92]

As the EU found itself in this situation, it had to react to the CRA challenge as part of its anti-crisis mechanism. Its strategy has been twofold: to strengthen the EU regulatory control over CRAs and simultaneously to undermine the latter's importance. In an attempt to increase its regulatory sway over CRAs, in 2009 the EU adopted a new regulation,[93] which has since been amended twice.[94]

---

[83] D Kerwer, 'Holding Global Regulators Accountable, The Case of Credit Rating Agencies' (2004) 11 *School of Public Policy Working Paper Series* 1, 10.

[84] ibid 10.

[85] Council on Foreign Relations, 'The Credit Rating Controversy', www.cfr.org/financial-crises/credit-rating-controversy/p22328.

[86] See, for example, European Parliament Resolution 2010/2302(INI) on credit rating agencies: future perspectives (23 March 2011).

[87] D Zaidi, 'A New Credit Rating Agency for BRICS' *Economy Watch* (13 February 2015) www.economywatch.com/features/A-New-Credit-Rating-Agency-for-BRICS.02-13-15.html.

[88] O Cramme, 'The EU's War against Credit Rating Agencies is Symptomatic of a New Struggle between Politics and the Market, But it also Lays Bare Growing Tensions in the European Project and Globalisation as a Whole' *LSE Blogs* (19 July 2011) http://eprints.lse.ac.uk/37969/1/blogs_lse_ac_uk-The_EUs_war_against_credit_rating_agencies_is_symptomatic_of_a_new_struggle_between_politics_and_the_.pdf.

[89] Darbellay (n 75) 179 ff.

[90] ibid 186.

[91] J de Haan and F Amtenbrik, 'Credit Rating Agencies' (2011) 278 *DNB Working Paper* 1, 2.

[92] Darbellay (n 75) 188.

[93] Council Regulation (EC) 1060/2009 of 16 September 2009 on credit rating agencies [2009] OJ L302/1.

[94] European Parliament and Council Regulation (EU) 513/2011 of 11 May 2011 amending Regulation (EC) No 10/60/2009 on credit rating agencies [2011] OJ L145/30 (CRA II Regulation). The CRA II Regulation came into force on 1 June 2011. European Parliament Council Regulation (EU) 462/2013 of 21 May 2013 amending Regulation (EC) No 1060/2009 on credit rating agencies [2013] OJ L146/1 (CRA III Regulation). The CRA III Regulation came into force on 20 June 2013.

It has attempted to address the shortcomings of CRAs identified above: the lack of transparency and accountability; the potential conflicts of interest; the unreliability of ratings; and rule-of-law concerns.[95] These objectives were to be achieved through territorialisation. Any CRA that wishes to operate in Europe must register with the European Securities and Market Agency (ESMA). To do so, it must meet a number of demanding material conditions,[96] which are continuously observed by the ESMA. The latter is allowed to impose fines[97] or even to withdraw a registration if a CRA fails to satisfy these conditions.[98] The new legal regulation also provides for a European civil liability regime, enabling the aggrieved parties (investors or issuers) to claim damages from CRAs in case of their malpractice.[99] By tying CRAs back to the EU territory and prescribing detailed material standards for their functioning, the EU is striving to regain regulatory control over their activities at home as well as to spread its normative regulatory influence beyond its confines to the realm of transnational law.

On the other hand, the strategy of undermining the importance of CRAs consists of two main elements: deregulation and pluralisation. Deregulation involves reducing the regulatory reliance, both national and supranational, on the CRAs' ratings. The EU and the US[100] are thus trying to roll back a long-present trend in which they have co-opted CRAs for their specific expertise and have outsourced certain regulatory functions to them, essentially endowing them with the influence they presently have.[101] The regulatory over-reliance ought to be redressed by removing the references to CRA ratings from EU and national law by 2020, and by encouraging practices via ECB and national central banks that will dissuade market actors from mechanistic reliance on CRA ratings.[102] Further, the CRAs are also explicitly prohibited from equipping their sovereign bond ratings with any direct or explicit policy recommendations on the policies of sovereign entities.[103] However, the efforts to diminish the influence of CRAs have not been very successful so far, especially in the absence of a meaningful alternative source of credit ratings.[104]

---

[95] European Parliament, 'The Directorate General for Internal Policies, Credit Rating Agencies: Implementation of Legislation, Study for the Econ Committee', 1, 6, www.europarl.europa.eu/document/activities/cont/201407/20140731ATT87404/20140731ATT87404EN.pdf.

[96] ibid 7. Here, the quality of credit ratings and rating methodologies, the independence of the credit rating process, the disclosure of credit ratings and methodologies, and the corporate governance and organisational arrangements are crucial.

[97] CRA III Regulation (n 81) art 36.

[98] European Parliament (n 95) 7.

[99] CRA III Regulation (n 81) art 35.

[100] The US Dodd-Frank Act of 2010 is reported to have removed all regulatory references to ratings: Darbellay (n 75) 9.

[101] ibid 47: 'Credit ratings are generally used by regulators for two main purposes: determining risk sensitive capital requirements and defining investment restrictions.'

[102] CRA III Regulation (n 81) para 6.

[103] ibid para 45.

[104] European Parliament, 'The Directorate General for Internal Policies, Credit Rating Agencies: Implementation of Legislation', www.europarl.europa.eu/activities/committees/studies.do?language=EN.

With regard to the intended pluralisation, this has combined the objectives of Europeanisation and anti-trust measures. The political heads of Europe[105] as well as the EU legislature[106] have called for the establishment of a European public CRA. Alternatively, it was also suggested that public credit ratings could be issued by the ECB, which has rejected the idea,[107] or that the Commission's reports on the economic situation in Member States should be complemented by an assessment of their creditworthiness.[108] All of these proposals intend to decrease the influence of American CRAs and, simultaneously, by bringing in new regional CRAs, to gradually contribute to a reduction of the presently existing oligopoly. The same objective is pursued by the requirements to rotate CRAs when rating a specific entity and the involvement of smaller CRAs whose market share does not exceed 10 per cent. Smaller CRAs were even considered by the Commission to be financially supported and integrated into a more formal network.[109] However, the Commission's recent follow-up report cast significant doubts on the feasibility of such a plan, especially since it has failed to win the support of smaller CRAs themselves.[110]

VI. ASSESSMENT FROM THE PERSPECTIVE OF PRINCIPLED LEGAL PLURALISM

Having presented the state of national and supranational democracy in the EU and its degree of pre-emption in the substantive, institutional and economic dimensions due to the internal and external constraints under which the EU operates, what can be said about it from the perspective of principled legal pluralism and what, if any, normative prescription can the latter prescribe for it? In answering this question, account shall be taken of an important difference between the internal and the external constraints on democracy in the EU. The internal constraints, which derive from the EU's own constitutional structure, can still be controlled and even removed by the EU and its Member States, whereas the external constraints cannot be. The latter therefore pose a more formidable, and to a certain extent also an unprecedented practical and theoretical challenge. Most of the discussion that follows will therefore be dedicated to addressing the external constraints on EU democracy under transnational law. Nevertheless, a few words should be said about the internal constraints too.

---

[105] Andrew Willis, 'Merkel Backs Creation of European Credit Rating Agency' *EU Observer* (4 May 2010) https://euobserver.com/economic/30001.

[106] CRA III Regulation (n 81) preamble, para 43.

[107] See Ni Tait, 'ECB Cool on Plan for Credit Rating Agency' *Financial Times* (24 February 2011) www.ft.com/cms/s/0/3ffa993a-3f6c-11e0-a1ba-00144feabdc0.html#axzz3TWA3C8rM.

[108] CRA III Regulation (n 81) para 40.

[109] ibid para 50.

[110] European Commission Report on the Feasibility of a Network of Smaller Credit Rating Agencies, COM/2014/0248 final.

Internal constraints have already been subject to an extensive debate within the EU democratic deficit literature.[111] This has also featured the pluralist attempts of remedying the EU democratic deficit. One such alternative has been the constitutional form of a union that comes along with some normative prescriptions for reducing the national and supranational pre-emption of democracy. It requires the EU to walk a fine line between the two opposites: supranational centralisation and national devolution. With regard to the former, it is necessary to acknowledge that the economic objectives have traditionally entailed a transfer of competencies from the national to the supranational level in the EU. This effect increases in times of crisis. The ECB quantitative easing programme[112] is a paradigmatic example, an attempt to quell the crisis by an additional centralisation of powers that might not have even been envisaged in the EU founding treaties. This centralisation admittedly eases the economic situation in the most affected countries. By providing a fresh flow of supranational money, it decreases the national dependence on the external transnational actors, and in so doing it improves at least the economic state of national and EU democracy. But this improvement is only ostensible.

Quantitative easing is already a form—admittedly a very rudimentary one—of a transfer union: from the rich north to the less prosperous south, which requires not only a democratic back-up, but also strong inter-state solidarity. As neither is present in the EU, the push towards a transfer union automatically generates the opposite reaction of a devolution. Rather than internalising the externalities of the economically poorly performing Member States, those Member States that are faring better economically push for a repatriation of competences from the supranational to the national level.[113]

In this case, economic centralism is replaced by national isolationism. Both are, obviously, normatively monistic solutions, not concerned with the preservation of the pluralist balance between the national and the supranational level. Moreover, the national isolationism is clearly economically unfeasible in the context of the globalised economy. Additionally, neither of them is appealing from a democratic perspective. Centralising solutions results in the further substantive and institutional erosion of national democracy, whereas the national devolutionary demands inevitably detract from substantive and institutional supranational democracy. A fine-tuned balance between the national and supranational democratic dimension is therefore necessary. By preserving the ethos of a common pluralist whole,

---

[111] See, for example, A Follesdal and S Hix, 'Why There is a Democratic Deficit in the EU: A Response to Majone and Moravcsik' (2006) 44 *Journal of Common Market Studies* 533.

[112] G Claeys, A Leandro and A Mandra, 'European Central Bank Quantitative Easing: The Detailed Manual' (2015) *Bruegel Policy Contribution* 1, www.bruegel.org/publications/publication-detail/publication/872-european-central-bank-quantitative-easing-the-detailed-manual.

[113] The UK has been the most vocal proponent of this development, which eventually resulted in its decision to leave the EU.

some more flexible institutional and even constitutional solutions that would give a better expression to the diversity of the national and supranational expectations, needs and requirements, and which would therefore also better address the internal constraints on EU democracy, could be attempted.[114]

Having briefly touched upon the internal constraints, let us now look in some more detail at the external ones. Here, we focus on the relationship between the EU and CRAs as transnational actors. To what an extent does this relationship reflect the four elements of the theory of principled legal pluralism: (1) the factual existence of a legal plurality; (2) recognition and continuous commitment to its preservation; (3) a dialectic open-self entailing a reflexive attitude in and among the entities forming up a plurality; and finally (4) a commitment to the common pluralist whole?

The presence of the first element is established. There is the EU with its own pluralist legal order, and CRAs' private transnational legal entities as a source of private transnational administrative law. These two legal entities recognise their individual and separate legal existence as a matter of fact. However, it is far more questionable whether they are committed to preserving this plurality. This shadow of doubt pertains, in particular, to the EU. As CRAs have neither a normative ambition nor a practical capacity to subsume the EU legal order under themselves, we have few reasons to assume that they are not committed to preserving the EU legal order's continuous independent and autonomous existence. Obviously, the same is not true of the EU. Its legislature has explicitly recognised that 'for the time being credit rating agencies are [still] important participants in the financial markets', but this ought to be changed. As we have seen, it has been part of the EU's deliberate strategy to undermine the importance of CRAs; to intervene in their sphere by establishing its own public CRA or to bolster the existing smaller private CRAs; to tie CRAs to its territory and render them subject to its own regulatory regime. This is anything but a commitment to the CRAs' continuous meaningful independent existence. Instead, it exhibits a monist attitude, which however in the absence of a dialectic open-self is detectable on both sides.

In illustration, there are basically no data demonstrating that CRAs in any way take into account the consequences, whether direct or indirect, of their sovereign bond ratings for the rated entities beyond the immediate increase or decrease of the yields on the bonds under review. Even though, as has been illustratively argued, downgrading a state can be compared to 'dropping a bomb' on a country,[115] the CRAs fail to account for the (in)direct implications of their

---

[114] M Avbelj, 'Differentiated Integration: Farewell to the EU-27' (2013) 14 *German Law Journal* 191.

[115] F Partnoy, 'The Siskel and Ebert of Financial Markets?: Two Thumbs Down for the Credit Rating Agencies' (1999) 77 *Washington University Law Quarterly* 619, 620, quoted in Darbellay (n 75) 153: 'there are two superpowers in the world today in my opinion. There's the United States and there's Moody's Bond Rating Service. The United States can destroy you by dropping bombs, and Moody's can destroy you by downgrading your bonds. And believe me, it is not clear sometimes who's more powerful'.

economic ratings on, for example, democracy in a rated entity. The EU, as we have seen, has reacted to this by upgrading and adjusting its economic structure to the challenges posed by the CRAs, but this has undermined its democracy (perhaps unintentionally) even further. The EU's response has also been less dialectically self-reflexive as anticipated by principled legal pluralism. Rather than investing more in reforms of its own constitutional structure, which has provided fertile grounds for an external pre-emption of democracy by CRAs, it has turned its critical edge against the CRAs, attempting to limit them in what they can or cannot do with their ratings. Finally, in the absence of a commitment to plurality, lacking a dialectic open-self, it is also very hard to expect the development of the commitment to the common whole—that is, of the awareness that the actions of CRAs and the EU are mutually interdependent, and that they cannot be treated in isolation as they affect each other as well as cause externalities beyond their own immediate realms.

This brief review demonstrates that the relationship between the EU and CRAs as transnational legal actors has so far not been carried out in legally pluralist terms and that neither the proposed nor implemented EU reforms point in that direction. Simultaneously, these rather monistic reforms in which the EU strives to undermine CRAs, bring them back under its territorial regulatory regime and stretch its regulatory umbrella over the realm of transnational law have so far not worked and are unlikely to do so in the future. The CRAs have simply overgrown not just the national regulatory capacity, but also that of the EU. The global financial markets' habit of obedience to CRAs vindicates their administrative legal character, irrespective of the EU's attempts to limit or undercut them. The monistic aspirations of EU institutions to bring CRAs under their control are therefore doomed to fail. A different approach is therefore called for—not only on the side of the EU, but also on behalf of the CRAs. They must be reminded that with great power comes great responsibility. As their products are not mere opinions or investment research results, but have a regulatory value,[116] the CRAs need to ensure that they meet the procedural and substantive rule-of-law standards and, similarly, they need to be aware of and mitigate the consequences of their ratings beyond the immediate economic ones. This is essentially what our theory of principled legal pluralism requires.

In conclusion, it can thus be stated that had the EU and the CRAs conducted their relationship pursuant to the theory of principled legal pluralism, the circumstances of the economic crisis, its outcome and the consequences for democracy in the EU and its Member States, described above would have been less grave. For the future, it is thus necessary for the CRAs and the EU to develop an epistemic awareness about the common whole they form, out of which the commitment to it will gradually grow. In their actions, they have to develop a reflexive

---

[116] CRA III Regulation (n 81) para 8.

self-openness which, on the side of the CRAs, will require a reform of the key elements of the rating process along the lines of the rule of law and greater accountability, whereas the EU should simultaneously work on its internal democratic constitutional structure and engage externally with the CRAs on co-operative rather than dominating terms. However, this reflexive self-openness should not remain exclusively on the level of aspiration or normative orientation, but should gradually adopt a more concrete institutional form. The key role in the EU should be played by the ESMA, with which the CRAs could engage either individually or through a common representative.

6

EU Law, Transnational Law and Human Rights Protection

The Case of Privacy

I. INTRODUCTION

THIS CHAPTER EXAMINES the relationship between EU law and transnational law with regard to protection of the right to privacy. The question of the relationship between EU law and transnational law will, however, not hone in on transnational law as a whole. Instead, we will focus on two types of transnational law that in recent years have posed the most notable challenges to EU law. The first type of transnational law is *lex sportiva*, more specifically its sub-part which is concerned with the establishment of the world anti-doping regime maintained by the World Anti-Doping Agency (WADA). The second kind of transnational law is *lex informatica*[1] and the transnational law of corporations, in particular the role of the global corporation Google, which is best known for running its eponymous Internet search engine. Pursuant to our classification in Chapter 1, the first type of transnational law belongs to so-called administrative hybrid transnational law, whereas the second is an example of private transnational law created by a global corporation.

We will be interested in whether the difference in the type of transnational law prompts a difference in the response of EU law when it comes to protecting the right to privacy in both regimes. Two case studies, one of WADA and the other of Google, will therefore be conducted to establish the character of the relationship between EU law and transnational law with regard to protecting the human right to privacy. In the conclusion, the chapter will determine to what extent this relationship, as it presently stands, exhibits the normative expectations of principled legal pluralism and, to the extent that these desired features are still lacking, which of them do so and how they could be brought about.

---

[1] JR Reidenberg, 'Lex Informatica: The Formulation of Information Policy Rules through Technology' (1998) 76 *Texas Law Review* 553, 555, who has defined *lex informatica* as 'a set of rules for information flows imposed by technology and communication networks'.

To see what is at stake in practice, imagine yourself, just for a few minutes, as an elite athlete. Not only does this involve hard training, full-time dedication to your profession and disregard of many brighter and lighter sides of life, it might also entail a complete waiver of your privacy. As an elite athlete you have to consent 'to provide a sample at any time and at any place by any Anti-Doping Organization (ADO) with testing authority over [you]'.[2] Moreover, you also have to 'provide accurate and complete information about your whereabouts during the forthcoming quarter, including where you will be living, training and competing during that quarter, and to update those [information] where necessary, so that you will be located for testing during that quarter'.[3] In short, your life is always under scrutiny by ADOs and you can be subject to testing at any moment, including during your night rest as you sleep at home. Should you not comply with these requirements, you are suspended from taking part in competitions, for a long time, sometimes for life.

This has prompted several observers to liken the status of elite athletes to prisoners, incarcerated under the anti-doping rules enforced by non-statist transnational private and hybrid organisations. Even if this point of comparison is exaggerated, the fact remains that these organisations' interference with athletes' right to privacy is subject to fewer and less cumbersome conditions than those that have to be met by the state and its organs. Is this compatible with EU law, where the right to privacy ranks high and is ensured in a number of legal acts of EU secondary law, in the EU Charter of Fundamental Rights, but it also forms part of the general principles of law common to the Member States? This is what the next part of this chapter aims to explain.

Now, change the perspective and step into the shoes of an individual who ran into troubles a few years ago, when they were publicly reported, but which have since been long resolved and are, at least according to the affected individual, completely irrelevant today. However, thanks to modern Internet technology and in particular due to sophisticated search engines like Google, this information keeps popping up on the Internet whenever this individual's name is inserted into the said search engine. Does this individual's right to privacy, as guaranteed in EU law, require the global corporation running that search engine to remove the link to the website containing the unwanted information? Does the individual have the right to be forgotten? If so, how is this to be balanced against Google's right to conduct business and Internet users' freedom of expression, and what do the answers to these questions entail for the right to privacy on the Internet? Here then the question is posed about the relationship between EU law and the private transnational law of global corporations within *lex informatica*. This discussion will form section III of this chapter.

---

[2] World Anti-Doping Agency, *World Anti-Doping Code* (Montreal, WADA, 2015) art 5.2.
[3] World Anti-Doping Agency, *International Standard Testing and Investigations* (Montreal, WADA, 2017) Annex I Code 2.4, 84.

II. THE RIGHT TO PRIVACY BETWEEN *LEX SPORTIVA* AND EU LAW

Before we delve into the practicalities of elite athletes' right to privacy under EU law and *lex sportiva* as anecdotally sketched out in the above paragraphs, let us first define the contours of the applicable legal regimes. The nature of EU law has been extensively discussed in Chapter 3, so we will proceed directly to *lex sportiva* to identify the place of an anti-doping regime within it. In so doing, and even though this view is certainly not shared by everyone,[4] we will draw on the works of those who do recognise the existence of *lex sportiva* or the law of sports as an autonomous legal system of transnational law[5] by virtue of its many characteristics usually associated with a Hartian legal system.[6] Following Duval, *lex sportiva* can be conceptualised as a unity of primary and secondary rules and principles[7] of mainly private, but sometimes also hybrid, transnational law.[8]

The most typical primary rules of *lex sportiva* are the rules of the game (*lex ludica*);[9] the rules regulating the organisation of competitions,[10] the anti-doping rules and the economic rules of sport.[11] But *lex sportiva* also features Hartian secondary rules: rules of change, rules of adjudication and the rule of recognition.[12]

---

[4] See T Davis, 'What is Sports Law?' in R Siekmann and J Soek (eds), *Lex Sportiva: What is Sports Law?* (The Hague, Asser Institute, 2012) 3, who submits that traditionally *lex sportiva* has not been given a status of law. This view has been held, for example, by the following authors: PC Weiler, *Sports and the Law* (Rochester, NY, American Case Book Series, 2010); MJ Cozzillio, MR Dimino, GA Feldman and MS Levinstein, *Sports Law: Cases and Materials* (Durham, NC, Carolina Academic Press, 1997). As reported by L Casini, 'The Making of *Lex Sportiva* by the Court of Arbitration for Sport' (2011) 12 *German Law Journal* 1317, 1319, this view is also defended by some national courts, such as the Frankfurt Oberlandesgericht and the Swiss Bundesgericht.

[5] See, most notably, F Latty, *La lex sportiva—Recherche sur le droit transnational* (Leiden, Martinus Nijhoff Publishers, 2007).

[6] A Duval, '*Lex Sportiva*: A Playground for Transnational Law' (2013) 19 *European Law Journal* 827 ff.

[7] Others have suggested a different classification so as to distinguish between public and private sports law; see, for example, RCR Siekmann, 'What is Sports Law? A Reassessment of Content and Terminology?' in Siekmann and Soek (n 4) 381 ff.

[8] ibid.

[9] K Foster, '*Lex Sportiva* and *Lex Ludica*: The Court of Arbitration for Sport's Jurisprudence' in Siekmann and Soek (n 4) 126 has defined *lex ludica* as encompassing 'two types of rules that are distinctive and unique because of the context of sport in which they occur and are applied. One covers the actual rules of the game and their enforcement by match officials ... The second type is what can be termed the "sporting spirit" and covers those ethical principles of sport that should be followed by sports persons. The concept *lex ludica* thus includes both the formal rules and the equitable principles of sport. They are arguably immune from legal intervention because they are an "internal law" of sport—a private governance that is respected by national courts, and as such is best applied by a specialised forum or system of arbitration by experts'.

[10] Duval (n 6) 828: 'These rules provide a benchmark for the selection of the host country and for the monitoring of the organization.'

[11] ibid 829. These rules have been triggered by 'the economic dimension of sport, enhanced by its progressive profesionalization [and pertain] especially to rules regulating the sporting labor market, such as transfer windows, training compensation, or rules regulating the profession of agent.' One could also add media rights, sport-betting etc.

[12] HLA Hart, *The Concept of Law* (Oxford, Clarendon Press, 1994).

The latter can be identified in the practice of the Court of Arbitration for Sport (CAS), seen as the 'world court of sport',[13] whose initially contested claim to act as an exclusive jurisdiction for sport-related disputes has in recent years been accepted in ever-wider circles.[14] The CAS thus legally unites a great diversity of *leges sportivae*,[15] enacted by a number of sport federations and organisations, which are ultimately at least in terms of substantive compliance, if not necessarily due to the formal organisational scheme, united under the umbrella of the International Olympic Committee (IOC), acting as 'the global sovereign power in sport'.[16]

Having established the existence of *lex sportiva* as an autonomous legal system of transnational law, answering the main questions of this chapter dictates focusing only on one set of its primary rules, namely those concerned with anti-doping regulation. The fight against doping has a long history[17] and has involved a plethora of actors, not exclusively within the private world of sport, but also under the colour of public law literally on all levels of legal regulation: national, supranational and international. This means that the anti-doping legal regime does not exclusively belong to the autonomous *lex sportiva*, but is also created by and constitutes part of other legal orders. At the most general and universal level, anti-doping is regulated under international law by the 2005 UNESCO International Convention against Doping in Sport.[18] On a regional level in Europe, the issue was first regulated even earlier, already in 1989 when the Council of Europe adopted its Anti-Doping Convention.[19] As we shall see, the fight against doping is also recognised by the law of the EU, whereas domestic regulations can vary, in particular with respect to the public and private divide, as long as they stay within the legal limits set by the aforementioned legal orders.[20]

---

[13] Duval (n 6) 830 fn 68, referring to the Swiss Federal Tribunal decision in the *Danilova* case BGE 129 III 445, at 462.

[14] Casini ((n 4) 1321) observes that while in the 1980s the CAS issued only a few decisions a year amid a deliberate obstruction by several of the world's most important sport federations, the trend has been changing since, meaning that the CAS has issued more than 800 decisions in the last decade.

[15] See Latty (n 5) 158.

[16] K Foster, 'Is There a Global Sports Law' in Siekmann and Soek (n 4) 43, drawing on M Beloff, T Kerr and M Demetriou, *Sports Law* (Oxford, Hart Publishing, 1999).

[17] While doping was already perceived as an important problem in sports before the Second World War and this perception intensified in the 1960s and later, the legal battle against doping properly started only in the 1980s under the auspices of the International Olympic Movement, it really took off and proliferated following the doping scandal during the Tour de France in 1998. See, for example, MJ Mitten and H Opie, '"Sports Law": Implications for the International, Comparative and National Law and Global Dispute Resolution' in Siekmann and Soek (n 4) 178–79; see also M Kedzior, 'Effects of the EU Anti-doping Laws and Politics for the International and Domestic Sports Law in Member States' (2007) 1–2 *International Sports Law Journal* 111.

[18] www.unesco.org/new/en/social-and-human-sciences/themes/anti-doping/international-convention-against-doping-in-sport.

[19] Council of Europe, Treaty No 135, Anti-Doping Convention, http://www.coe.int/en/web/conventions/full-list/-/conventions/treaty/135.

[20] See, for example, *The Implementation of the Wada Code in the European Union* (The Hague, TMC Asser Institute, 2010).

The grounds for the present well-organised, systemic, indeed hierarchical legal and institutional structure of the anti-doping regulation in *lex sportiva* were laid in 1999 with the establishment of WADA by the IOC. WADA is the international independent organisation formally established as a private foundation under Swiss law by the IOC. It is a hybrid organisation, equally funded by the sports movement and nation states[21] and endowed with the task of promoting, coordinating and monitoring the fight against doping in sport in all its forms.[22] However, its most important contribution to anti-doping is the development of anti-doping rules, contained in the World Anti-Doping Code (hereinafter the Code),[23] which is implemented and concretised further through five International Standards (IS)[24] that serve to harmonise various technical areas of anti-doping measures and policies.[25] Pursuant to Part III of the Code,[26] both documents are binding on WADA and their signatories: the IOC, the Paralympic IOC, international federations (IF), national Olympic and Paralympic committees, national anti-doping organisations, major event organisers; as well as, of course, athletes and other persons: athlete-support personnel and regional anti-doping organisations.

However, the Code itself is not directly legally binding upon states. Their somehow qualified legal obligation to fight doping is instead derived from the 2005 UNESCO Convention against Doping in Sport. The Code is reproduced in the appendix to the Convention, but its binding legal nature under international law is explicitly excluded. The states are instead 'only' committed to respecting the Code. Further, the Convention is also set up as a legally autonomous instrument which has primacy over other regulations in the same anti-doping functional field.[27] This conflicts with WADA's conception of anti-doping rules in *lex sportiva*, which is equally conceived of as having autonomous and possessing primacy over other rules. Article 24 of the Code thus stipulates that the official text of the Code shall be maintained by WADA[28] and interpreted as an autonomous text, not by reference to the existing law or statutes of the signatories and governments.[29] Furthermore, the parties are prohibited from subjecting and limiting anti-doping rules to and by national requirements.[30] This duty extends to all courts and other

---

[21] ibid.

[22] ibid.

[23] World Anti-Doping Agency (n 2).

[24] World Anti-Doping Agency (n 3).

[25] ibid. These standards concern: prohibited list, testing, laboratories, therapeutic use exemptions and protection of privacy and personal information.

[26] World Anti-Doping Agency (n 3) pt III.

[27] Article 2 of the International Convention against Doping in Sport (Paris, 2005) provides that definitions of the key concepts in the Convention 'are to be understood within the context of the World Anti-doping Code, [but] in case of conflict the provisions of the Convention will prevail'.

[28] World Anti-Doping Agency (n 2) art 24(1).

[29] ibid art 24(3).

[30] ibid introduction.

adjudicating bodies, which are explicitly advised to 'be aware of and respect the distinct nature of the anti-doping rules in the Code'.[31] Of course, this raises a question, as also noted by the EU Anti-doping Expert Group, about the compliance of such a regime with the uniformity of EU law[32] and its fundamental principles of primacy and autonomy.

The role of the EU in the field of sport in general and in the fight against doping in particular has traditionally been quite limited.[33] Sport has fallen within the material scope of EU law as far as it has been regarded as an economic activity by taking the form of gainful employment or of a service for remuneration.[34] In that way, it has been directly or indirectly regulated through the free movement provisions, as construed in the jurisprudence of the CJEU. The Treaty of Lisbon has introduced a new, but narrow, more or less symbolic, legal basis for the EU's own competence to legislate in the field of sport.[35] This includes the fight against doping, as the EU's actions are to be specifically aimed at 'promoting fairness and openness in sporting competitions and ... protecting the physical and moral integrity of sportsmen and sportswomen'.[36] This commitment to anti-doping policy is also stressed in the White Paper on Sport presented by the European Commission.[37] While the EU thus partakes in the objective of fighting doping, it has also been increasingly extending its regulatory reach over various anti-doping measures and mechanisms. The Court has been playing a central role in this. Its *Meca-Medina and Majcen* ruling represented a landmark development in this field.[38]

In this case, the Court has confirmed and applied a two-pronged judicial test for *lex sportiva* and anti-doping rules in particular. *Lex sportiva*, irrespective of the nature of its rules, even when purely sporting in nature[39] (such as anti-doping rules), fall within the *ratione materiae* of the Treaty and can be subject to judicial review either for compliance with the EU free movement provisions or with the EU competition rules. The rules of *lex sportiva* will be subject to the free movement provisions if they emanate from gainful employment or a remunerated service and will be found to be in compliance with EU law if they do not constitute restrictions prohibited by the 'four freedoms' provisions. Alternatively, the rules of *lex sportiva* will be reviewed for compliance with EU competition rules if they emanate from the activity of an undertaking. They will be upheld if this

---

[31] ibid 17.

[32] Expert Group, 'Anti-Doping' (XG AD), EU Contribution to the Revision of the WADA Code, 17 October 2011.

[33] For an overview, see S Weatherill, 'Is There Such a Thing as EU Sports Law?' in Siekmann and Soek (n 4) 302 ff.

[34] Case 36/73 *BNO Walrave and LJN Koch v Association Union cycliste internationale, Koninklijke Nederlandsche Wielren Unie and Federación Española Ciclismo* [1974] ECR 01405.

[35] Consolidated Version of the Treaty on the Functioning of the European Union [2012] OJ C326, art 165.

[36] ibid.

[37] White Paper on Sport COM/2007/0391, 2.2 Joining forces in the fight against doping.

[38] Case 519/04 P *Meca-Medina and Majcen v Commission* [2006] ECR I-06991.

[39] ibid para 27.

undertaking does not restrict competition or abuse its dominant position in a way that would affect trade between Member States.[40] In short, the anti-doping rules of *lex sportiva* come within the material scope of the Treaty and are therefore under the Court's jurisdiction. In this review, the Court will doubtlessly adhere to the principle of autonomy, following which EU law, its meaning and especially its validity can be determined exclusively by the Court, as well as the principle of primacy, according to which EU law has precedence over all other legal regulations, irrespective of their source and hierarchical status, and hence includes anti-doping rules. In principle, there thus exists a notable tension between the autonomous and primary transnational legal order of *lex sportiva* and the equally autonomous and primary EU law. What happens if this tension takes the more concrete shape of a conflict over the adequate protection of the right to privacy at the intersection of these legal orders?

A. Mediating and Resolving the Tensions between *Lex Sportiva* and EU Law with Regard to the Right to Privacy

The problem is both jurisdictional and substantive. An elite athlete who believes that anti-doping rules violate his or her right to privacy can either pursue his or her right through the fora provided by *lex sportiva*, or through the national and EU courts, and potentially also through the European Court of Human Rights. *Lex sportiva*, as we have seen, insists on the exclusivity of its fora. This is an affront to national, EU and ECHR laws that ensure the right to judicial protection to everyone inside their legal jurisdictions. The two legal orders, *lex sportiva* and EU law (to focus on it alone), thus provide for two different and, at least as claimed by *lex sportiva*, mutually exclusive jurisdictions over the same kind of claims and persons.

If someone is unhappy with the outcome in one jurisdiction, he or she can try to obtain a more favourable one in another jurisdiction. The potential plurality of outcomes in the same matter, of course, works to the detriment of the rule of law (legal predictability) and detracts from the autonomy of the affected legal orders. The potential for a clash among jurisdictions due to unequal outcomes in the same case grows if the two jurisdictions do not subscribe to the same substantive standards of a particular human right protection, in our case the right to privacy.

Not unlike the anti-doping rules, the right to privacy is also protected in several legal orders at the national, supranational, (regional) international and transnational levels. It is enshrined in the constitutions of most EU Member States; it is explicitly protected by the EU Charter of Fundamental Rights and a number of legislative acts of the EU; it is safeguarded by Article 8 ECHR; and it is recognised

---

[40] ibid para 30.

by the WADA anti-doping *lex sportiva* rules.[41] However, nominal or principled adherence to the protection of the human right to privacy across these regimes does not mean that they necessarily subscribe to the same privacy protection standard in practice. As these are all distinct, self-proclaimed autonomous legal orders and therefore unique sociopolitical contexts, it can be assumed that they might also strike a different balance in the protection of the fundamental values.[42] In other words, as these legal orders are different sociopolitical, but also epistemic sites, they can subscribe to different substantive standards of protection of privacy, which can lead to tensions between the WADA regime and EU law.

The following three examples can serve as a useful illustration of three concrete tensions between the WADA requirements and EU law. First, WADA's 'whereabouts'[43] rules that require athletes' permanent and constant temporal and spatial availability for testing, including between 11 pm and 6 am,[44] put into question an athlete's right to respect for private and family life, as enshrined in Article 7 of the Charter[45] and in Article 8 ECHR. They are also in tension with the Working Time Directive provisions, which guarantee workers minimum rest periods as well as minimum annual leave.[46]

Second, the WADA rules require mandatory public reporting of identified doping cases at a minimum by placing the required information on the ADO's website for one month or the duration of any period of ineligibility, whichever is longer.[47] This could, especially if used as a sanction,[48] infringe an athlete's right to the protection of his or her personal data, which is ensured in Article 8 of the Charter and concretised further in the Data Protection Directive.[49]

Third, WADA runs the Anti-Doping Administration and Management System (ADAMS), a web-based database management tool registered in Canada for data entry, storage, sharing and reporting,[50] which enables it to act as a central clearing

---

[41] See, in particular, the World Anti-Doping Agency's International Standard for the Protection and Personal Information (ISPPPI, 2014, implemented 2015).

[42] See JHH Weiler, 'Fundamental Rights and Fundamental Boundaries: On Standards and Values in the Protection of Human Rights' in N Neuwahl and A Rosas (eds), *The European Union and Human Rights* (Leiden, Martinus Nijhoff Publishers, 1995).

[43] J Halt, 'Where is the Privacy in WADA's "Whereabouts Rule"?' (2009) 20 *Marquette Sports Law Review* 267.

[44] See World Anti-Doping Agency (n 2) arts 5.2 and 22.1.3; and World Anti-Doping Agency (n 3) art. 4.5.5.

[45] Everyone has the right to respect for his or her private or family life, home and communications.

[46] See Directive 2003/88/EC of the European Parliament and of the Council of 4 November 2003 concerning certain aspects of the organisation of working time [2003] OJ L299, ch 3; see also Halt (n 43) 283 ff.

[47] World Anti-Doping Agency (n 2), art 14.3.2 and 14.3.4. Pursuant to art 14.3.6, this requirement does not apply in case of a minor.

[48] Expert Group (n 32).

[49] Directive 95/46/EC of the European Parliament and of the Council of 24 October 1995 on the protection of individuals with regard to the processing of personal data and on the free movement of such data [1995] OJ L28.

[50] World Anti-Doping Agency (n 2) Appendix 1, Definitions.

house for doping control testing and results.[51] Since the use of the database is compulsory and, as noted by the EU working group on privacy, requires data sharing on a large scale worldwide, between private and public actors and third countries whose adequate level of personal data protection might be difficult to establish, the described WADA rules quite likely conflict with Article 8 of the Charter and, more specifically, with the overall system of personal data protection established by Directive 95/46/EC.[52] The latter, first of all, requires explicit[53] and unambiguous[54] consent for the processing of personal data such as those collected by WADA and, in principle, prohibits their transfer to third countries with an inadequate level of personal data protection.[55] The new regulation, which will enter into force in May 2018, has strengthened the consent requirement further.[56]

However, it is interesting to observe that these tensions have so far largely been dealt with in a dialogical way, relying on persuasive authorities, expert groups and diplomacy rather than taking the form of a direct legal conflict to be mediated through the courts. There has thus been ongoing and constant communication between WADA and the EU regarding the Code and its amendments as well as other anti-doping standards, in particular those involving privacy. For that purpose, the EU has established several working groups.[57] The communication takes place transnationally at the level of experts, both national and supranational, as well as at an administrative level involving national civil servants. It takes the form of claims and counterclaims, insisting on the specificity, autonomy[58] and primacy[59] of each of the systems involved that, however, most frequently end with a conclusion expressing trust in the other party to integrate these claims into the functioning of its system as fully as possible.[60]

---

[51] ibid art 14.5.

[52] Directive 95/46/EC (n 49) art 25(1). For a more in-depth discussion, see Expert Group (n 32).

[53] Directive 95/46/EC (n 49) art 8a.

[54] ibid art 7a.

[55] ibid art 25.

[56] Regulation (EU) 2016/679 of the European Parliament and of the Council of 27 April 2016, in particular art 7.

[57] See, for example, EU Working Group on Anti-doping, replaced by Expert Group on Anti-Doping created by the Council in adopting its Working Plan for 2011–2014, Resolution of the Council and of the Representatives of the Governments of the Member States, meeting within the Council, on a European Work Plan for Sport for 2011–2014 (2011) OJ C162/1, 1–5.

[58] See WADA Comments to the Proposed EU Data Protection Regime 4, which has alluded to the EU's own recognition of the 'specificity of sport' and insisted on strengthening the respects for the sports movement's autonomy.

[59] 0746/09/EN WP 162 Article 29 Data Protection Working Party Second Opinion 4/2009 [2009] 3: 'The Working Party emphasizes that controllers in the EU are responsible for processing personal data in compliance with domestic law and must therefore disregard the World Anti-doping Cope and International Standards insofar as they contradict domestic law.'

[60] ibid 19: 'The Working Party trusts that all ADOs and other actors involved will take up their own respective responsibilities to ensure that the remarks made by the Working Party are fully taken into account, and that full compliance with EU data protection rules will be guaranteed.'

For example, the above-mentioned tensions over the WADA whereabouts rules, the ADAMS database and mandatory reporting have been subject to an intense exchange between WADA[61] and the European Commission, which has relied on expert input by the EU's Article 29 Data Protection Working Party,[62] the EU Working Group on Anti-doping[63] and the Anti-doping Expert Group.[64] In this communication, the parties have often relied on the opinion of external actors using their persuasive authority to bolster their positions.[65] However, the communication has taken the form of a dialogue, leading to a reconsideration of positions, mutual adjustments and amendments to the existing standards.[66]

As much (if not most) of the described tensions between the anti-doping *lex sportiva* and EU law are thus resolved through patient, incremental, expert-based dialogues among the representatives of the two systems, it should not come as a surprise that there have been very few legal cases in which the WADA rules have been explicitly challenged in the CJEU. In fact, no cases have been initiated by EU institutions and only two have been brought by aggrieved individuals, who had failed to succeed with their claims within the *lex sportiva* regime.

The first was the *Meca-Medina and Majcen* case, already discussed above. As we have seen, the case is important because the CJEU laid down three building blocks for the relationship between EU law and anti-doping *lex sportiva*. First, anti-doping *lex sportiva*, even if it consists of rules of a purely sporting nature, fall within the ambit of the material scope of EU law (*ratione materiae*) over which the Court exercises judicial review.[67] Second, anti-doping *lex sportiva*, in principle, promotes objectives which are legitimate and shared by the EU.[68] Third, the compatibility of the anti-doping *lex sportiva* with EU law depends on its compliance with the requirements of the principle of proportionality. In practice, this boils down to a test of whether a concrete anti-doping rule does not go beyond what is necessary to achieve its legitimate end.[69] Here it is important to note that the judicially created principle of proportionality has also been used as a framing

---

[61] World Anti-Doping Agency, 'European Commission Consultation: The Legal Framework for the Fundamental Rights of Personal Data', http://ec.europa.eu/justice/news/consulting_public/0003/contributions/organisations_not_registered/wada_en.pdf.

[62] Article 29 Data Protection Working Party, Opinion 3/2008 on the World Anti-Doping Code Draft International Standard for the Protection of Privacy, http://ec.europa.eu/justice/data-protection/article-29/documentation/opinion-recommendation/files/2008/wp156_en.pdf; see also second opinion 0746/09 EN 2009 (n 59).

[63] European Commission, EU Expert Groups 'Anti-Doping', 'Sport Statistics' and 'Sport, Health and Participation':finalmeetingreports,ec.europa.eu/sport/news/2013/20130823-eu-xpgs-reports_en.htm.

[64] See, in particular, Expert Group (n 32).

[65] WADA's reliance on the former president of the ECtHR, Jean-Paul Costa.

[66] See, for example, EU Commission Press Release IP/09/733 (2009): 'The Commission greets the adoption of the revised Standard as a successful outcome of co-operation between the EU and WADA and is looking forward to continued dialogue and co-operation with WADA over data protection issues.'

[67] *Meca-Medina and Majcen* (n 38) para 23.

[68] ibid para 43.

[69] ibid para 42.

principle of the political and expert dialogue among the two systems described above. It has been the language of proportionality in which the actors of the two systems have attempted to couch their claims to demonstrate and prove the validity of their rules.

The second case was *Canas*.[70] Like the *Meca-Medina and Majcen* case, it was brought by an individual who was unhappy with his legal prospects in *lex sportiva* and therefore tried to seek EU judicial protection, again like *Meca-Medina and Majcen*, through the legal provisions of the Treaty ensuring fair and undistorted competition in the single market.[71] This time around, the EU courts again confirmed their jurisdiction over anti-doping *lex sportiva*, but refused to engage with the merits of the case due to the lack of the applicant's standing since his professional sport activity had already ceased. Read together with the Commission's initial refusal to take up the case of an alleged violation of EU competition rules for the lack of insufficient community interest,[72] this might exhibit the EU judicial as well as general institutional reluctance to interfere with the anti-doping *lex sportiva*. In its decision, the Commission, for example, stressed that the question of doping in sport, the decisions concerning prohibited substances and the object of sport in principle belong to the rule-makers, scientific and sporting communities with specific expertise over these matters.[73] It also indicated its dissatisfaction with the potential forum shopping, reflected in the individual's attempts to use the EU judicial mechanism without fully exhausting that of *lex sportiva*, which had not only acted lawfully but even ruled in favour of the individual's rights.

Both the Commission and the courts have thus demonstrated a considerable degree of self-restraint, paying heed to the relative autonomy of *lex sportiva*:[74] formal jurisdictional and through that also substantive autonomy. This corroborates scholarly observations that the European Commission has taken on a 'hands-off approach to how governing bodies organize their sports'[75] and has 'little appetite'[76] for bringing legal challenges against *lex sportiva*, which confirms that the EU has been 'remarkably generous to sport'.[77] This is, after all, also visible in many EU documents, of both a legal and political nature, in which the EU is called upon to respect the special nature and the autonomy of sport for its importance in society and to 'listen to sports associations when important questions affecting sport are at issue'.[78] However, as a corollary to this deferential stance of the EU, the

---

[70] Case T-508/09 *Cañas v Commission* and Case 269/12 P *Cañas v Commission* [2013] EU:C:2013:415.

[71] ibid.

[72] European Commission, Case Comp/39471, C(2009)7809, para 18.

[73] ibid para 49.

[74] B Kolev, '*Lex Sportiva* and *Lex Mercatoria*' in Siekmann and Soek (n 4) 227.

[75] G Pearson, 'Sporting Justifications under EU Free Movement and Competition Law: The Case of the Football "Transfer System"' (2015) 21 *European Law Journal* 220, 237.

[76] ibid 231.

[77] ibid 232, referring to S Weatherill, 'The Olivier Bernard Case: How, if at All, to Fix Compensation for Training Young Players?' (2010) 6 *International Sports Law Journal* 1, 1–2.

[78] Treaty of Amsterdam, Declaration 29: Declaration on Sport; OJ C340, 10 November 1997; European Commission, The Helsinki Report on Sport, COM(1999) 644.

right to privacy in anti-doping regimes enjoys a correspondingly more lax, less stringent level of protection.

III. THE RIGHT TO PRIVACY BETWEEN
LEX INFORMATICA AND EU LAW

Having examined the right to privacy at the intersection of *lex sportiva* and EU law, let us now focus on protection of the same right in the context of the inter-action between EU law, private transnational law of global corporations and *lex informatica*. A case study of the right to be forgotten as recognised by the CJEU against Internet search engines such as Google will be used to illuminate the rela-tionship between these legal regimes and of the way of striking an appropriate bal-ance between them to safeguard the individual's right to privacy.[79] *Lex informatica sensu lato* is a transnational law of the Internet[80] which consists of a plethora of autonomous technical standards and protocols produced independently of states for the global functioning of the Internet, substantive standards of Internet gov-ernance and of rules governing e-commerce. In comparison with *lex sportiva*, *lex informatica* is still in *statu nascendi* and therefore, unlike *lex sportiva*, cannot yet be labelled an autonomous legal system of transnational law pursuant to the classical Hartian criteria. Its rules and principles are still evolving. While rules of change, although admittedly numerous, are established relatively well, the rule of adjudi-cation and consequently the rule of recognition are still underdeveloped or even absent. On the other hand, the private transnational law of global corporations, as discussed in Chapter 1, encompasses norms which regulate the internal gov-ernance of a corporation as well as the relationships between corporations, their customers and trading partners. It has always been composed of numerous legal orderings, without (an explicit) pretence to form an autonomous private trans-national corporate legal system *sensu lato* of its own. In what follows, pursuant to the necessarily circumscribed focus of this chapter, we are not going to address the relationship between EU law, *lex informatica* and transnational corporate law *in*

---

[79] Following the decision in the *Google Spain* case, another important *lex informatica* ruling was handed down in Case 362/14 *Maximillian Schrems v Data Protection Commissioner* [2015] ECR I-0000, hereinafter the *Facebook* case. While the *Google Spain* case is directly related to our discussion of trans-national administrative hybrid and corporate law, the *Facebook* case has a more inter-statal dimension, bearing less direct relevance to this chapter's discussion. In contrast with the Google case, where the subject under judicial review was the internet corporation itself, in the *Facebook* case the adequacy of the level of protection of personal data in a third state (eg, the US) was examined. It has been discov-ered that for several important reasons, the US failed to ensure the essence of the right to privacy with regard to the protection of personal data, which resulted in the invalidation of the EU Commission's decision granting the so-called system of the safe harbour principle.

[80] Others have used alternative denominations, such as *lex inernetica* and *cyberlex* (*mercatoria*); for an excellent overview of the different usages of the term and the evolution of scholarship, see A Patrikios, 'Resolution of Cross-border E-Business Disputes on the Basis of Transnational Substantive Rules of Law and E-Business Usages: The Emergence of the *Lex Informatica*' (21st Bileta Conference, Malta, 2016).

toto, but only to the extent that they overlap regarding protection of the right to privacy on the Internet.

The central actor in this relationship, besides the EU, is the global corporation Google. The latter is an Internet giant, a mega-project[81] which has, in less than 20 years since it was launched, emerged with a dominant—indeed, monopolist—position among Internet search engines,[82] Internet advertising services, webmail platforms and social networking sites.[83] In so doing, it has belied the beliefs (or hopes) that the Internet is 'a not owned entity',[84] meaning that 'nobody owns the infrastructure of the Internet, not even a single state, nor can any corporation or individual control, maintain, sell, dismiss, rent or even regulate it'.[85] Admittedly, Google does not own the Internet or its infrastructure, but because of its dominant, sometimes even exclusive role on it, it makes literally hundreds of millions of individuals and thousands of companies around the globe dependent on its own policies[86] and standards.[87] The Internet rules by Google are adopted autonomously, and therefore one-sidedly, inside the corporation pursuant to its business model, its conception of the global Internet and following its corporate interests. They are offered to its addressees on the basis of a take-it-or-leave-it approach. As leaving it effectively means excluding yourself from the Internet, taking it simultaneously amounts to consent, which is, in the absence of a meaningful alternative, very often not really freely given.

The question of the right to privacy on the Internet is broad and encompasses all those instances in which individual's personally identified or personally identifiable data[88] could be affected on and by the Internet. In what follows, we will shed light on just one such example that has recently been subject to litigation by way of a preliminary ruling procedure at the CJEU.[89] The case was referred to Luxembourg by a Spanish court (Audencia Nacional) ruling in the dispute between Google Spain and Google Inc and the Spanish Data Protection Agency (the AEDP) and Mr Costeja González. The latter had obtained a decision from the AEPD ordering Google Inc to withdraw personal data relating to him from

---

[81] M Paradiso, 'Google and the Internet: A Mega-project Nesting within Another Mega-project' in SD Brunn (ed), *Engineering Earth* (Berlin, Springer 2011).

[82] Pursuant to ComScore, the US Market Share is 65.6 per cent: https://www.comscore.com/Insights/Rankings/comScore-Releases-February-2015-US-Desktop-Search-Engine-Rankings. In the EU, this figure is even higher—between 90 and 96 per cent: www.mvfglobal.com/europe. The global share is 65.73 per cent: www.netmarketshare.com/search-engine-market-share.aspx?qprid=4&qpcustomd=0.

[83] It has also established itself firmly in the other spheres of global communications, which are, however, not of direct relevance to the present chapter.

[84] Paradiso (n 81) 50.

[85] ibid.

[86] See, for example, Google's Privacy Policy, www.google.com/policies/privacy.

[87] Google's Terms of Service, www.google.com/policies/terms.

[88] For this distinction, see PM Schwartz and DJ Solove, 'The PII Problem: Privacy and a New Concept of Personally Identifiable Information' (2011) 86 *New York University Law Review* 1814, 1817.

[89] Case 131/12 *Google Spain SL and Google Inc v Agencia Española de Protección de Datos (AEPD) and Mario Costeja González* [2014].

Google's index and to prevent access to this data in the future.[90] His complaint was based on the fact that when his name was entered in the Google search engine, this would produce links to two pages of a local newspaper, which in 1998 published information about his real-estate auction connected with attachment proceedings for the recovery of social security debts.[91] He argued that the proceedings had been fully resolved a long time before and the information was thus outdated and now entirely irrelevant.[92] The CJEU ruled in his favour. It did so in several steps by addressing: (1) the material scope (*ratione materiae*); (2) the territorial scope of the Data Protection Directive; (3) the scope of Google's legal obligation deriving from the Directive; and (4) the content of the individual's right to be forgotten.

With regard to the material scope of the Directive, the Court confirmed that the activity of Internet search engines is equal to the processing of personal data within the meaning of the Directive and the operators of the search engine qualify as controllers of personal data within the meaning of the Directive too.[93] The Court also entertained little doubt about the territorial scope of the Directive. It ruled that the activity of a search engine falls under the territorial jurisdiction of the Directive when its operator has established a branch or subsidiary in a Member State, which 'is intended to promote and sell advertising space offered by that engine and which orientates its activity towards the inhabitants of that member state'.[94] It is therefore immaterial that Google Inc is established in California and that it runs its search engine in the absence of any intervention on behalf of Google Spain, which only provides support for Google's advertising activities.[95] Google thus incurred a duty to remove from the list of results obtained by a search made on the basis of a person's name links to third-party webpages containing information about this person. This obligation is independent of the need for the prior or simultaneous removal of this information from the webpages retrieved, as well as of the fact that the information has been published lawfully.[96]

The Court concluded that the thereby established individual's right to be forgotten or delisted[97] as a rule overrides not only the economic interest of the operator

---

[90]   ibid para 2.
[91]   ibid para 14.
[92]   ibid para 15.
[93]   ibid para 100/1.
[94]   ibid para 100/2.
[95]   ibid para 51.
[96]   ibid para 100/3.
[97]   It has been argued that the right to be forgotten is a misnomer and that it would be more correct to speak about the right to be delisted, to appeal against the processing of one's own individual data or as the right to make it more difficult to search for certain personal information in a certain way. See the Advisory Council to Google on the Right to Be Forgotten (6 February 2015) 3 fn 1. See also Christopher Kuner, 'The Court of Justice of the EU Judgment on the Data Protection and Internet Search Engines' (2015) 3 *LSE Law, Society and Economy Working Papers* 11, who suggests rebranding the right to be forgotten as the right of suppression.

of the search engine, but also the interest of the general public in having access to that information upon a search relating to the data subject's name, unless certain particular reasons, such as the individual's role in public life, in accordance with the principle of proportionality dictate the opposite conclusion.[98] In practice, in order to make this right operational, the individual addresses his or her request to be 'delisted' to the operator of a search engine, whose decision can be appealed to the national data protection authority, which can then also be subject to national judicial control.

A. The CJEU's Balance between EU Law, *Lex Informatica* and the Right to Privacy

It follows from the just-presented case that the CJEU has taken a firm stance on protection of the right to privacy against Internet search engines.[99] First of all, it made sweeping jurisdictional claims, both territorial and material. Google Inc, a US corporation, was territorialised to Spain by way of its advertising company, which falls within the 'context of the activities' of a search engine.[100] In material terms, the CJEU did not hesitate to identify Google as a controller of data by opting for a broad definition of personal data, processing of personal data and the controller. In so doing, it brushed away the Advocate General's warnings that an over-inclusive interpretation of the *ratione materiae* of the Data Protection Directive is likely to entail unreasonable and excessive legal consequences.[101] However, the ruling of the Court, which is also not entirely exact about its territorial scope and effects beyond the EU,[102] has been stretched even further by the EU's Article 29 Working Party. It has argued that the ruling applies to all of Google's search domains, not just those of the EU Member States, including the global.com, as well as that the right to be forgotten belongs to everyone, not just EU citizens.[103]

In a similar vein, the Court has decided on a high standard of protection of the right to privacy. Despite the Advocate General's calls to consider the principle of proportionality when striking a balance between privacy and the competing interests of Google and *lex informatica*, the Court has relied on it only nominally and

---

[98] *Google Spain* (n 89) para 100/4.

[99] This trend has been confirmed by *Maximillian Schrems* (n 79), the *Facebook* case.

[100] *Google Spain* (n 89) para 52.

[101] ibid, Opinion of the Advocate General, para 30.

[102] Kuner (n 97).

[103] Article 29 Data Protection Working Party, Guidelines on the Implementation of the Court of Justice of the European Union Judgment on 'Google Spain and inc. V. AEPD and Mario Costeja Gonzalez.' C-131/12, November 2014, http://ec.europa.eu/justice/data-protection/article-29/documentation/opinion-recommendation/files/2014/wp225_en.pdf.

has decided that the right to be forgotten, as a specific emanation of the right to privacy, *as a rule* prevails over the competing economic rights as well as over the freedom of speech of Internet users. The Court has been so much concerned with protecting the right to privacy that it might have simply forgotten that other rights are also applicable.[104] In particular, it has failed to pay due respect to the freedom of expression, which is not even explicitly mentioned. In so doing, the Court appears to be departing from its previous case law, in which it has insisted on a careful balancing between the competing rights and interests of individuals, companies and Internet users.[105] The Court has, eventually, also ruled on the merits, struck a balance between the competing rights, which is something that it typically leaves in the hands of the national courts, and, furthermore, has issued very detailed guidance for implementation of the decision, usually included in the dicta, but now inserted into holding!

In short, the Court has thus firmly advocated the EU's own privacy standards, exporting them transnationally or at least producing appreciable externalities for other legal orders. In so doing, it is making powerful regulatory inroads into the Internet, shaping its developing regulatory content, counteracting the actions and standards of global Internet corporations such as Google, but without paying much or even any regard to their counterweighing values, interests and concerns. Similarly, the Court has failed to consider whether its far-reaching ruling is enforceable at all, given the borderless Internet and literally countless technological means for making delisted search results widely available again.[106]

This has prompted a critique not just from the direct addressee of the ruling, as could have been expected, but also by academic commentators who have again reminded us that the Court has, to paraphrase Weiler, 'withdrawn into its own constitutional cocoon, isolated the international context and ruled entirely on the basis of internal constitutional precepts'.[107] Earlier, de Búrca also observed that the Court has developed a 'self-referential and detached style of judgment; largely unconcerned about the external impact and influence of its rulings'.[108]

---

[104] S Peers, 'The CJEU's *Google Spain* Judgment: Failing to Balance Privacy and Freedom of Expression', 2014, http://eulawanalysis.blogspot.co.uk/2014/05/the-cjeus-google-spain-judgment-failing.html.

[105] Case 238/05 *Asnef-Equifax v Asociación de Usuarios de Servicios Bancarios* [2006] ECR I-11125; Case 73/07 *Tietosuojavaltuutettu v Satakunnan Markkinapörssi Oy and Satamedia Oy* [2008] ECR I-09831; Case 101/01 *Lindqvist* [2003] ECR I-12971.

[106] One such counter-initiative has been Hidden from Google, 'a website which is archiving examples of internet censorship that are taking place under a controversial new law'.

[107] Kuner (n 97) 17, quoting JHH Weiler, 'Editorial: EJIL Vol. 19:5', www.ejiltalk.org/letters-to-the-editor-respond-to-ejil-editorials-vol-195, describing the approach of the CJEU in the *Kadi* judgment (Joined Cases C-402 and 415/05P, *Kadi & and Barakaat International Foundation v Council & Commission* [2008] ECR I-6351).

[108] G de Búrca, 'After the EU Charter of Fundamental Rights: The Court of Justice as a Human Rights Adjudicator' (2013) 20 *Maastricht Journal* 168.

Google's own reaction to the CJEU decision could be described as reserved compliance. The Court's ruling has simultaneously constrained and strengthened its position. Imposing on it the obligations stemming as a corollary from the right to be forgotten, Google had to re-adjust its technological and business model. However, at the same time, it has been endowed with regulatory powers that it did not have before. By virtue of the CJEU decision, Google has been co-opted in the EU regulatory structure, in which it is acting as a first-instance authority deciding on the individual's right to be delisted. To minimise its obligations and to narrow the implications of the CJEU's decision as much as possible, Google assembled an Advisory Council on the Right to be Forgotten composed of top international independent experts in the field. They have attempted to counterbalance, in their view, the EU's over-reaching territorial and material jurisdictional claims, and suggested that the principles of proportionality and practical effectiveness permit Google to limit its delisting obligation only to the EU Member States' search engines, rather than extending it across the globe.[109] In the opposite case, there exists a peril that repressive regimes would 'lock' their users into heavily censored versions of search results around the globe,[110] in accordance with their own laws, but potentially contrary to the laws of other legal orders.[111]

The term 'repressive' was probably used inadvertently, because it also appears to be quite faithfully describing the attempts to limit Google's activities further. The latter is thus, in view of the Article 29 Working Party, prevented from informing the users of its search engines that certain results have been removed, since 'there is no legal basis [for such a communication] under EU data protection law'.[112] But in accordance with the constitutional principle of liberty, Google can do anything which is not prohibited, rather than the other way around. Apparently, the Article 29 Working Party in its zeal to protect the right to privacy got slightly carried away, which also explains why it was generally left unimpressed by Google's Advisory Board's conclusions and insisted on its own expansive understanding of the CJEU, threatening new judicial proceedings if necessary.[113] The EU Commission reportedly reacted to this by calling on stakeholders 'to continue engaging in a constructive dialogue with the enforcement authorities in solutions to comply with the Court ruling'.[114] This dialogue between the Article 29 Working Party and the three biggest search engines has, indeed, been ongoing since 2014.[115]

---

[109] The Advisory Council to Google on the Right to Be Forgotten, https://drive.google.com/file/d/0B1UgZshetMd4cEI3SjlvV0hNbDA/view, 20.

[110] ibid.

[111] ibid 19.

[112] Article 29 Data Protection Working Party (n 103) para 23.

[113] M Ahmed, R Waters and D Robinson, 'Google Risks Legal action over "Right to Be Forgotten" Report' *Financial Times* (5 February 2015), https://www.ft.com/content/3db91400-ae15-11e4-919e-00144feab7de.

[114] ibid.

[115] Kuner (n 97).

IV. THE EU'S RELATIONSHIP TO *LEX SPORTIVA* AND
LEX INFORMATICA COMPARED

Having presented the EU's role in protecting the right to privacy in two distinct transnational legal regimes of sport and the Internet, there are several similarities in the way these two relationships have been structured, but interestingly there are even more differences. The point of departure is certainly the same. From the perspective of the right to privacy, an individual's relationship to Google closely mirrors the relationship between an elite athlete and the anti-doping *lex sportiva*. In both cases, the individuals give up a significant share of their privacy, often by consent, which due to the explicit asymmetry of power is unbalanced and maybe not effectively free. In awareness of this problem, the EU has in both cases made strong jurisdictional claims to establish its own concurrent, indeed primary authority over the substantive issues shared by the legal regimes. But, while with regard to the anti-doping regime of *lex sportiva* the EU's jurisdictional grip has remained at the level of principle only, in the case of Google within *lex informatica*, the EU did not just bark, but it also, as we have seen, bit. In the case of *lex sportiva*, the EU has satisfied itself with the formal existence of its authority. It has established itself as the ultimate gatekeeper for exceptional circumstances. However, beyond that it has shown deference to *lex sportiva*, leaving the disputed issues surrounding privacy in the hands of expert bodies that were to engage in a self-reflexive dialogue to resolve the actual and potential conflicts incrementally, step by step. The EU courts ought to be kept out of this relationship as much possible as the fora of *lex sportiva* are better equipped to rule on these specific issues. Moreover, the EU judicial infrastructure cannot be used to challenge the anti-doping regime simply by everyone around the globe; rather, there should be a clear EU interest involved. Indeed, as has been argued,[116] the EU has adopted a hands-off approach to *lex sportiva*.

This contrasts significantly with the EU's attitude to *lex informatica* and Google inside it. Here the EU has doubtlessly adopted a hands-on approach. While also in this relationship the dialogue among experts of both legal orders plays an important role in settling actual and potential conflicts, the space for dialogue, the room for manoeuvre is much smaller because of the CJEU's judicial intervention. Whereas in the case of *lex sportiva* the Court has always stopped at the jurisdictional level, without going into the merits so as to interfere with the autonomy of the anti-doping regime, in the case of Google, the Court has rendered a powerful, substance pre-empting ruling, defining the fundamentals of the right to privacy on the Internet as conceived of by EU law. The Court has justified this approach by the necessary vigilance about the personal profiling of individuals, which is not only possible, but can also be rendered ubiquitous thanks to search engines

---

[116] S Weatherill, *European Sports Law: Collected Papers* (Berlin, Springer, 2013) 113.

and modern Internet technology.[117] The difference in the approach might have also been motivated by the character of the transnational legal regimes at stake. The case of Google appears at the intersection of private transnational corporate law and *lex informatica*, which is distinctively economic in nature. These purely economic interests, according to the Court, apparently deserve less deference than the sporting objectives of *lex sportiva*, which are in principle shared by EU law and therefore found to be legitimate.

Another reason for the EU's different treatment of the two transnational legal regimes might be located in their maturity and density. As we have seen, *lex sportiva* is a well-developed autonomous system of transnational law. *Lex informatica*, on the other hand, is not and is still in the making. It might have been this novelty, this uncharted terrain, that has prompted the Court to be become more involved in *lex informatica* than would ever be possible in *lex sportiva* in order to influence its development in accordance with the EU's regulatory ambitions and objectives. The CJEU's approach to *lex informatica* can thus be seen a pre-emptive strike, imposing the conditions for the relationship between the two systems as unilaterally as possible and then—and only then—subjecting it to the same softer, dialogical, also political, expert-based requirements underlined by the principle of proportionality. It has been the language of proportionality in which the actors of legal systems have attempted to couch their claims to demonstrate and prove the validity of their rules. The latter thus appears to be the structural principle which mediates the relationship between EU law and other transnational legal regimes. However, in the case of *lex sportiva*, the proportionality review in the EU is subject to a much smaller degree of judicial scrutiny than in the case of *lex informatica*. As a corollary, individuals' right to privacy on the Internet is afforded a higher level of protection than the same right of elite athletes in the anti-doping regime.

V. ASSESSMENT FROM THE PERSPECTIVE OF PRINCIPLED LEGAL PLURALISM

Having examined the relationship between EU law and transnational laws of sport and the Internet, to what extent does this relationship exhibit the normative expectations of the principled legal pluralism? And, to the extent that these desired features are still lacking, which of them and how could they be brought about?

As we know, to speak of legal pluralism, one must first establish the existence of legal plurality. This ought not to be disputed. EU law is an autonomous legal order; *lex sportiva* is an autonomous system of transnational law; Google is part of private corporate transnational law; and *lex informatica* is clearly in *statu nascendi* as a transnational legal regime. Nevertheless, as already noted, the former two legal regimes are much more developed and much more legally stratified than the latter

---

[117] *Google Spain* (n 89) para 100.

ones. This, consequently, translates into a varying degree of presence of the second element of legal pluralism: the recognition of and continuous commitment to the preservation of the legal plurality. In the relationship between EU law and *lex sportiva*, which are both relatively well-established legal orders whose claims to their own legal autonomy have been widely recognised as plausible, this second element is much more present than in the case of transnational private corporate law as it intersects with *lex informatica*. It can be inferred from this that the maturity or robustness of a legal order positively correlates with the recognition and commitment to the legal plurality. The more a given legal order is established, so that its claim to legal autonomy has become recognised in wider legal circles, the more probable it is that an overall sentiment of the recognition of legal plurality and commitment to its preservation will pervade the relationship between itself and other legal orders. If this second element of the legally pluralist relationship, as the EU's treatment of the Google case shows, is still lacking in the EU's attitude to *lex informatica*, this is due to the latter's ongoing rudimentary legal status. Should this evolve further and its legal autonomy be strengthened, the second element would be accordingly reinforced too.

The lesson just learned also extends to the third element of principled legal pluralism: the existence of a dialectic open-self entailing a reflexive attitude in and among the entities forming a plurality. Between EU law and *lex sportiva*, the presence of this element can be traced in numerous dialogical exchanges and meetings between the representatives of the two systems, in particular among experts. While each of the systems in legal terms acts self-referentially and makes claims to its own primacy in the shared domains, these legal claims have never boiled down to a legal conflict because of the self-reflexive, deferential and sometimes even generous attitude to each other among the actors of the legal systems. On the other hand, this inter-systemic generosity has resulted in an insufficient level of protection of the right to privacy of elite athletes. It is, again, different with regard to *lex informatica*, where the EU has seized its privileged legal position against the less developed legal order and has asserted and imposed its own desired standards on private transnational corporate actors as well over the Internet as a whole, irrespective of the national boundaries. Admittedly, here too political and, in particular, expert dialogue has been encouraged and has indeed been taking place among the legal orders, but it has done so under the shadow of a strong judicial precedent in which the EU has, to a greater rather than a lesser degree, already pre-empted much of the discursive scope in a relatively unilateral, non-reflexive way. Furthermore, and similar to its attitude to the CRAs, the EU has launched a process of attempted weakening of the excessively dominant role of transnational private corporations, like Google. A number of anti-trust procedures that the European Commission has launched against Google[118] reveal the EU's ambition to control

---

[118] European Commission, 'Antitrust: Commission Sends Statement of Objections to Google on Comparison Shopping Service' (2015); for an overview, see ec.europa.eu/competition/elojade/isef/index.cfm?fuseaction=dsp_result&case_title=Google.

transnational corporate law and curtail its influence whenever it is found to be harmful to the pursuit of the EU's economic objectives, most notably expressed in the requirement of undistorted competition.[119]

Finally, this brings us to the last element: the commitment to the common whole, which consists of the awareness that the transnational orders form a bigger, closely intertwined and therefore mutually dependent picture. Again, the presence of this element appears to be growing with the maturity of the legal orders involved. EU law and *lex sportiva* act in mutual awareness that the success of the fight against doping, as a shared objective, necessarily depends on the contribution of both. In that way, the two legal orders travel in the same boat, even if sometimes they do not partake of exactly the same means or understanding of the means for achieving a shared objective. In the relationship between EU law and *lex informatica*, this awareness is also present, out of the pure fact that the Internet spans the globe and perforce affects everyone. Nevertheless, because in regulatory terms this vast Internet space remains legally uncharted territory to an important extent, the EU has tried to leave an important regulatory mark on it, perhaps even to establish itself as a leading regulator.[120]

In short, the relationship between EU law and the transnational law of sport fits the normative requirements of principled legal pluralism. This is less the case in the relationship between EU law and the transnational law of the Internet, whereby the latter's legal underdevelopment affords the EU with an opportunity to make regulatory inroads in a relatively self-centred and therefore monistic way. Nonetheless, even in this relationship it is possible to identify the important elements of self-reflexivity and of the commitment to the common whole, which could and will be strengthened as the relationship between EU law and *lex informatica* becomes more legally balanced. That this will undoubtedly occur stems from the fact that, while the EU legally and institutionally, and therefore also politically, has the upper hand, the Internet has a factual technological advantage over it, as it can be predicted that the EU's regulatory attempts will always trail behind the swift technological development of the Internet, which is growing, like a universe, without any limits and beyond borders.

For this reason, it is all the more important that the EU, as well as other national orders, develop a legally pluralist relationship with *lex informatica* and private transnational corporate actors. This might be the only possible way of optimising the disparate values and interests involved, as well as, and most importantly,

---

[119] The European Commission has similarly targeted other companies whose activities are, at least indirectly, related to the global internet governance, most notably Apple. See European Commission, 'State Aid: Ireland Gave Illegal Tax Benefits to Apple Worth up to €13 Billion', europa.eu/rapid/press-release_IP-16-2923_en.htm.

[120] The *Schrems* case ((n 79) para 73) is again of relevance here as it marks the EU's ambition to ensure that third countries guarantee 'the protection of fundamental rights and freedoms, [in particular the right to privacy], that is essentially equivalent to that guaranteed within the European Union by virtue of Directive 95/46 read in the light of the Charter'.

of ensuring effective protection of the right to privacy. Even if the EU harbours hope that it alone can ensure this right to individuals all over the globe, this is simply technically unfeasible and per se requires a joint approach by the other national legal orders, *lex informatica* and the transnational corporate actors inside it. Simultaneously, this is not to say that due to the existence of a legally pluralist relationship between EU law and *lex sportiva* there is no room for improvement in the level of protection of the right to privacy in the anti-doping procedures. This need is certainly present, but the existence of the legally pluralist relationship between EU law and *lex sportiva* fills us with hope that it will emerge in a desirable dialogical, pluralist way.

7

Justice, the EU and Transnational Law

I. INTRODUCTION

IN THE PRECEDING chapters we have examined the effects of transnational law on the rule of law, democracy and human rights protection in the EU. This was done on the basis of relatively narrow case studies, which have also attempted to draw some more general conclusions, either embedded in or critically examined against the normative idea(l) of principled legal pluralism. Drawing on this debate, this chapter will address the implications of transnational law for justice in the EU. The question of justice is a perennial one. It has occupied humanity since time immemorial, receiving numerous conflicting theoretical responses and giving rise to real and also not infrequently bloody conflicts in practice. The history of questioning justice, the agreements and disagreements it has raised, discloses that justice is perhaps the most intuitive and therefore also the most emotive[1] social concept. It is an essential ingredient of every individual's relationship to the social world. And yet, even on the most abstract philosophical level, among the brightest minds, the conceptual question of the definition of justice has not received unequivocal answers, nor has it been furnished with answers that would, even in the eyes of their authors, let alone their critics, be coherent and persuasive all the way down.[2] If the very concept of justice thus remains undefined, it is all the more difficult to answer the question of what justice actually requires in practice in particular contexts and across them.

If anything, this demonstrates that the concept of justice is an extremely difficult one.[3] It therefore requires modesty on behalf of the academic observer.[4]

---

[1] S Douglas-Scott, *Law after Modernity* (Oxford, Hart Publishing, 2013) 175.

[2] See, for example, J Rawls, *A Theory of Justice* (Cambridge, MA, Harvard University Press, 2000); A Sen, *The Idea of Justice* (London, Penguin Books, 2009); A Ryan (ed), *Justice* (Oxford, Clarendon Press, 1993); D Miller, *Principles of Social Justice* (Cambridge, MA, Harvard University Press, 1999); J Gray, *Two Faces of Liberalism* (New York, New Press, 2002); KJ Arrow, *Social Choice and Justice: Collected Papers of Kenneth J. Arrow*, vol 1 (Cambridge, MA, Harvard University Press, 1983); GA Cohen, *Rescuing Justice and Equality* (Cambridge, MA, Harvard University Press, 2008); JE Roemer, *Theories of Distributive Justice* (Cambridge, MA, Harvard University Press, 1996); TW Pogge, *Realizing Rawls* (Ithaca, Cornell University Press, 1989).

[3] It has even been described as a philosophical failure; see Douglas-Scott (n 1) 395.

[4] The same is, of course, not necessarily true of those who pursue their own visions and conceptions of justice, and who fight for a more just world.

This does not suggest that justice should be shied away from. It cannot, because it is—simply staying faithful to Giddens' double hermeneutic[5]—a quintessential social question that social actors have been posing again and again. However, addressing justice from a theoretical perspective requires circumspection about the claims made as well as about the capacity to produce a compelling theoretical justification for those claims. Hubris has to be avoided by all means possible.

It is against this backdrop that this chapter proceeds to answer the question of transnational law's effects on justice in the EU. This question is raised rarely, if at all. In fact, as a recent monograph has persuasively shown, the very question of justice in and of the EU has hardly been raised at all.[6] While Europe has, for example, been busy addressing its democratic deficit, it has remained largely silent on its recently discovered justice deficit. The reasons for the absence of justice from EU academic and political speak might be numerous. Justice could have been perceived as an issue reserved exclusively for the (Member) States, which the EU as a *sui generis* entity is not.[7] This political stance would not be surprising because it still enjoys support from many eminent philosophers of justice[8] and because it might, especially at the integration's early stage, correspond well to the actual situation on the ground. Related to this latter sociological point, the question of justice might not be raised due to the overall increase in prosperity that the EU integration has long been marked by. In good times, that is, in the relative absence of injustice, the question of justice is simply not raised. This confirms, on the other hand, why in times of economic crisis, which in some Member States has bordered on economic cataclysm, the question of justice has emerged so vigorously.[9] Moreover, the question of justice might have always been present, but it has been blended with more profane, more politically accessible notions of legitimacy and democracy. Again, the very philosophical difficulty in drawing a watertight conceptual distinction between the concepts of justice, democracy and legitimacy might attest to this point.[10]

Be that as it may, the question of justice is now undoubtedly posed. It has been so in two different ways: in relation to justice in the EU and of the EU. Thus, the inside question and the inside-out question have been asked.[11] Neither of them will be of direct interest to us here. We are instead going to focus on the outside-in

---

[5] A Giddens, *New Rules of Sociological Method: A Positive Critique of Interpretative Sociologies* (Stanford, Stanford University Press, 1993) 9.

[6] D Kochenov, G de Búrca and A Williams, *Europe's Justice Deficit?* (Oxford, Hart Publishing, 2015).

[7] For a strong critique of this view, see D Kochenov, 'The Ought of Justice' in ibid.

[8] Who have therefore found justice beyond the state, or even global justice more or less inconceivable; see, for example, T Nagel, 'The Problem of Global Justice' (2005) 33 *Philosophy and Public Affairs* 113. See also early Rawls, who has subsequently at least partly amended his views: J Rawls, *Political Liberalism* (New York, Columbia University Press, 2005).

[9] See, for example, a vibrant discussion on *Verfassungsblog*: http://verfassungsblog.de/category/debates/europes-justice-deficit.

[10] This dilemma is especially visible in the context of the EU; see N Walker, 'Justice in and of the European Union' in Kochenov, de Búrca and Williams (n 6).

[11] ibid.

question: examining what transnational law does to justice in the EU. In answering this question, we will be guided by the required modesty. Rather than pursuing ideal justice in the EU, as has traditionally been part and parcel of the so-called transcendental institutional approach to justice,[12] we will be interested in a much narrower question. Have transnational law and its actors improved or worsened the conditions of justice in the EU? And to the extent that the latter has occurred, can our theory of principled legal pluralism contribute in any way to reducing injustice in the EU?

Facing an equation entailing justice, transnational law and the EU, we are standing in front of a demanding task, which has by virtue of the discussion in the preceding chapters nevertheless been made slightly easier. At least we are no longer dealing exclusively with mere variables. On the contrary, the case has been made for a pluralist conception of the EU as a union and the map of transnational law has been drawn too. The two main elements of our equation are therefore specified relatively well or certainly sufficiently enough to study their interaction also with regard to justice. The latter's definition, for the reasons spelled out above, will not be attempted. Instead, we are only going to focus on the specific circumstances of justice in the EU in an attempt to sketch out possible solutions for limiting injustice potentially created or exacerbated by transnational law and its actors. In so doing, we will limit ourselves again to three particular examples of injustice in which transnational law has been directly and/or indirectly implicated. They will be presented under the tags of: justification, economic justice and human dignity.

II. SPECIFICITIES OF JUSTICE IN THE EU

Justice has traditionally been thought of and argued about in the context of a state. The latter has stood for a fully fledged polity in which legal and political authority has been exercised over a well-defined community, ideally in its name and for its benefit. The concept of justice too has thus emerged as a statist concept. Moreover, and as a result, the concept of justice has been inextricably tied to the idea (and practice) of a self-contained political entity.[13] To a certain extent, it has been developed as a monist and particularistic concept. Justice has traditionally stopped at the well-defined boundaries of a sovereign state.[14] In a less conservative

---

[12] Sen (n 2). For a similar departure from ideal theories of justice, see Douglas-Scott (n 1) 388.

[13] See, for example, Nagel (n 8) 121: 'Justice is something we owe through our shared institutions only to those with whom we stand in a strong political relation. It is, in the standard terminology, an associative obligation.'

[14] This is certainly true for the most prominent theory of justice of the twentieth century defended by Rawls (n 2), as well as for the Dworkin's legal philosophy; R Dworkin, *Sovereign Virtue* (Cambridge, MA, Harvard University Press, 2002). However, both of these authors in their later work endorse a more cosmopolitan or universalist approach to justice; see J Rawls, *The Law of the Peoples* (Cambridge, MA, Harvard University Press, 2001); and R Dworkin, 'A New Philosophy for International Law' (2013) 41 *Philosophy and Public Affairs* 1.

sense, it has been portrayed as a concept contingent on proximity,[15] according to which justice is always more pertinent, more binding and fuller among us than in the relationship with the others. The EU challenges most of that. It is certainly not a state, which makes its polity status dubious too. We have suggested that it should be conceived of as a union. What does that entail in terms of justice?

To recall, the EU is a pluralist constitutional form of a three-level entity: national, supranational and the common whole, which consists of 29 legal orders and of an equal number of polities. The EU as a common whole is thus not a singular polity, but a composition of a plurality of polities (both national and supranational) which do not stand in mutual isolation, but constitute a common whole that itself does not have the status of a polity.[16] The polity status of Member States is fairly uncontested, even though by virtue of being a *Member State*,[17] the nature of the EU state polity certainly cannot be likened to a self-contained state, whose boundaries are impermeable and whose considerations of justice are sealed off from external influences. The same is, of course, true of the supranational level, whose polity status, since it is not a state, can be more easily questioned. Nevertheless, I have argued before that a supranational level is a polity too. It exercises real political authority over the EU community consisting of EU citizens, who were initially only legally constructed, but have over time also appropriated this construction in sociological terms of the necessary community 'we feeling'.[18]

The EU as a plurality of polities features a plurality of political communities and therefore also a plurality of schemes of justice. To paraphrase Rawls, a scheme of justice draws together the polity's political and social institutions as one system of cooperation, which is publicly known to rely on principles of justice that all polity members consider just and therefore generally comply with.[19] The scheme of justice is a central choice about the fundamental values in a polity that the latter arrives at autonomously.[20] Elsewhere, I have also described it as a public order of a

---

[15] J Waldron, 'Who is My Neighbour? Proximity and Humanity' (2003) 83 *The Monist* 333.

[16] Certainly not in the conventional sense. As Walker observed, when faced with pluri-political common whole, we outrun the conventional conceptual limits of a polity idea and the latter consequently turns out a 'little hard-edged for what we are trying to get at in understanding pluralistic constellations'. In other words, the EU as a common whole does not require the existence of a third-level 'common whole political authority' and a corresponding 'common whole community'. The common pluralist political whole—a kind of pluri-polity, as it were, like and parallel to the common pluralist legal whole—is at the same time not merely presupposed as a theoretical metaphor of some sort. It in fact exists as a set of practiced sociopolitical relationships, described in Chapter 3 above.

[17] See CJ Bickerton, *European Integration from Nation-States to Member States* (Oxford, Oxford University Press, 2012), who argues that the EU is a state-driven and a state-based process in which the state has been fundamentally transformed. It has become a Member State.

[18] KW Deutsch, *Political Community and the North Atlantic Area* (Princeton, Princeton University Press, 1957) 36.

[19] Rawls (n 8) 35.

[20] This corresponds to what Weiler has labelled as a fundamental boundary. See JHH Weiler, 'Fundamental Rights and Fundamental Boundaries: On Standards and Values in the Protection of Human Rights' in N Neuwahl and A Rosas (eds), *The European Union and Human Rights* (Leiden, Martinus Nijhoff Publishers, 1995) 52: 'Fundamental boundaries are about the autonomy and self-determination of the communities.'

polity, which stands for a balance or equilibrium of fundamental values of a polity. It encompasses a comprehensive set of values in a given polity and orders them in terms of their importance for that polity.[21]

When talking about justice or its absence in the EU, it is therefore necessary to query whose justice.[22] There is not a single scheme of justice in the EU, but at least 29 of them and they should ideally make up an appropriate pluralist balance of the common whole. Furthermore, these different schemes of justice, contrary to what the idea of a single scheme of justice might suggest, are not necessarily internally completely unified and without any contradiction.[23] If anything, they are certainly not in perfect harmony between themselves, across the polity boundaries of the Member States. What might be perceived as just in one polity need not be so in another. When assessing the impact of transnational law on justice in the EU, we must remain mindful of both the EU's many justices as well as of the many diverse positive and negative impacts of transnational law on them. As the complexity of the question on the abstract level is thus more than apparent, let us move on to some more concrete examples to illustrate the previous points.

III. THREE EXAMPLES OF INJUSTICE UNDER TRANSNATIONAL LAW

We shall focus on three examples of injustice in the EU that could have been attributed to transnational law. These examples, as we shall see, proceed from different conceptions of justice and concern disparate segments of transnational law. The first example is injustice as a lack of justification, which results, as will be argued below, directly from transnational law as a whole. The second example is economic injustice caused indirectly by sector-specific economic transnational law. And, finally, the last example is injustice as an affront to human dignity also stemming, albeit even more indirectly, from specific segments of mostly private transnational law. We shall look at all of them in turn.

A. Injustice of Transnational Law as a Lack of Justification

To understand the type of injustice allegedly caused by transnational law under this title, it is first necessary to elucidate the conception of justice on which these allegations are built. The conception of justice relied upon here is essentially tied to the right and duty of justification. The conception appears to come in two

---

[21] M Avbelj, 'Security and the Transformation of the EU Public Order' (2013) 14 *German Law Journal* 2057.

[22] For a similar point, see AJ Menendez, 'Whose Justice? Which Europe' in Kochenov, de Búrca and Williams (n 6).

[23] For a critique of Rawls on this point, demonstrating that the consensus on the principles of justice even in an ideal original situation behind the veil is simply not plausible, see Sen (n 2) 58.

versions: thicker and thinner. The former's intellectual father is Rainer Forst. He has argued in favour of a political conception of justice rather than some 'otherworderly abstract idea',[24] according to which social relations and institutions are just if they are free of domination, understood as a form of arbitrary, unjustifiable rule.[25] In this conception, justice is closely connected to democracy (and vice versa). 'Democracy is the basic practice of justice'.[26] Accordingly, the rule-making authorities must be constituted by those subject to its norms. As subjects, they must be considered free and equal, and act not only as recipients but also as agents of justification in a fair procedure.[27] They must be enabled to discursively produce, contest, reject and construct justification with others.[28] In short, 'those subjected to norms can be the authors of these norms'.[29]

On the other hand, pursuant to a thin conception defended by Jurgen Neyer, justice is 'the outcome of a justificatory process in a justified structure of political decision-making'.[30] On this basis alone, it is impossible to distinguish it from a thicker conception. This can, however, be done once we add a thin conception's insistence on divorcing justice from democracy. This renders it—at least in the eyes of its critics—much less demanding (and therefore much less persuasive).[31] It can apparently do without a constituent power.[32] It satisfies itself with the conception of a subject of a norm mainly as a recipient rather than as an agent of justification.[33] In other words, while a thick conception primarily emphasises the point of input, where norms are being made in a justifiable way,[34] the thin conception privileges the receiving end, eg, how the outcome of norms is justified to their addressees.[35]

Naturally, measuring the impact of transnational law on justice in the EU against the criteria of the two conceptions of justice as a justification cannot lead to an identical outcome. From the perspective of a thick conception, transnational law as a whole in the EU creates considerable injustice. As we saw in Chapter 1,

---

[24] R Forst, 'Transnational Justice and Democracy' (2011) 4 *Normative Orders Working Paper* 1, 2.

[25] R Forst, 'Justice, Democracy and the Right to Justification: Reflections on Jürgen Neyer's Normative Theory of the European Union' in Kochenov, de Búrca and Williams (n 6) 229. For a more in-depth discussion, see also R Forst, *The Right to Justification: Elements of a Constructivist Theory of Justice* (New York, Columbia University Press, 2012).

[26] R Forst, 'Justice, Democracy and the Right to Justification: Reflections on Jürgen Neyer's Normative Theory of the European Union' in Kochenov, de Búrca and Williams (n 6) 229.

[27] ibid.

[28] ibid.

[29] ibid 232.

[30] J Neyer, *The Justification of Europe: A Political Theory of Supranational Integration* (Oxford, Oxford University Press, 2012).

[31] Forst (n 26) 230 has thus observed that 'Neyer argues for a watered-down conception of justice'.

[32] Neyer (n 30), especially ch 3.

[33] Forst (n 26) 229.

[34] ibid 232.

[35] J Neyer, 'Justice and the Right to Justification: Conceptual Reflections' in Kochenov, de Búrca and Williams (n 6) 213.

transnational law, especially its administrative and private examples, does not come into being in a democratic way. It is a product of special, specialised and narrow functional communities that are mostly concerned with maximising the efficiency and utility of their functional domains. However, in so doing, they are creating norms that by no means affect only the subjects of the said functional communities, but cause a plethora of direct and indirect externalities for other communities that have no say in the production of transnational norms. The thick conception's requirement that 'those subjected to norms can be the authors of these norms' is therefore clearly violated.

This already becomes visible at the level of the supranational law of the EU, which is an example of public transnational law. While the norms of public international law can still be considered just because they mostly cannot be adopted in the absence of the consensus of the participating states, which ensures their justice through an admittedly distant and long chain of national democratic justification, the laws of the EU can already be adopted against the wishes of several Member States and hence their democratic constituencies and can—indeed, shall—be enforced against them due to the principle of primacy and direct effect. Yet the supranational law of the EU has tried to compensate for this emerging injustice by setting up its own justificatory (eg, democratic) framework. But, as we saw in Chapter 5, the results have been mixed. However, moving beyond the EU, to administrative and private transnational law, the problem of justice and the degree of injustice, at least in the eyes of a thick conception, is only getting worse.

For example, private administrative transnational law is created by standard-setting and certifying bodies in which states or other public entities, such as the EU, are involved only indirectly or not at all. Their rules bind or regulate the collective practices of numerous entities in designated functional sectors, sometimes without the prior assent of the addressees, but even more often without any input of the users of those rules. We could refer here to the International Accounting Standards Board (IASB), the International Organization for Standardization (IOS) and the Internet Corporation for Assigned Names and Numbers (ICANN) as perhaps the best-known examples of such non-governmental autonomous, transnational standard-setting bodies. The rules of private administrative transnational law therefore do not comply with a justificatory framework required by a thick conception. Most clearly, the constituencies of these rule-making authorities do not overlap with all those that are affected by them. The same, perhaps even a reinforced, conclusion applies to the new *lex mercatoria* in the EU as well as to the private transnational law of global corporations.

The most obvious private transnational actors, whose actions directly affect the lives of millions of people throughout the EU without any involvement by them in the norms produced, are credit rating agencies (CRAs). In Chapter 5, we discussed their negative effects on EU democracy and hence—by virtue of the thick conception—inevitably also on justice in the EU. From the perspective of the thick conception, the actions of CRAs are unjust and most likely beyond repair, since it is difficult to envisage how all the affected subjects—Member States, the

EU and their citizens—could be turned into a constituency of the CRAs without transforming their character completely. If the CRAs were to be changed into a just actor following the requirements of the thick conception, they would need to be altered beyond recognition. In fact, this conclusion applies across the board of transnational law to all the existing and still-emerging private transnational regulators, which of course cannot remain private if they are to be constituted by all the subjects of their norms. The crux, novelty and difficulty of transnational law lies precisely in the fact that it affects the lives and behaviour of many more subjects than they have in any way contributed to its development.

Having said that, the thick conception of justice—even when reduced to a more limited, context-sensitive, 'practice-dependent' approach to justice,[36] which somehow detracts from its own democracy requirements—appears to be too demanding for transnational law. The latter's effects in the EU will therefore always be, by and large, assessed as unjust. This is not necessarily true of the thin conception. The latter requires that the adopted norms must be justified to their addressees. They must be given good reasons to comply with them, but they do not need to be themselves involved in the production of these norms. As a thin conception of justice is divorced from democracy, it does not insist on the ideal of self-legislation; rather, it satisfies itself with reason giving for the norms adopted and the actions they require. In this way, the requirements stemming from the thin conception of justice as justification come very close to the normative prescription of principled legal pluralism. The overlap is most notable in the pluralist element of a dialectic open-self entailing a reflexive attitude in and among the entities forming a plurality.

It was thus argued in Chapter 2 that principled legal pluralism requires interacting or conflicting legal regimes to justify their ultimate positions by taking the interests and claims of the opposing legal order into account. This should be done, to paraphrase Welsch, transversally through reciprocal interpretation.[37] A legal order should reconstruct a claim of another legal order within its own framework to discover the inevitable situatedness and framework dependedness of each claim. On this basis, it would gain a detached view from its own position, opening itself up to the consideration of alternatives and (perhaps) identifying flaws or lacunae in one's own argument. It would reach a final but always situational and temporally specific decision after having 'frankly and extensively considered all potential objections to one's own description of the situation and determination of the position'.[38]

The foregoing is the thin conception of justice translated into the language of principled legal pluralism. It was, for example, adopted in Chapter 5 in the case

---

[36] Forst (n 24) 12.

[37] Drawing on W Welsch, 'Reason and Transition: On the Concept of Transversal Reason', https://ecommons.cornell.edu/bitstream/handle/1813/54/Welsch_Reason_and_Transition.htm?sequence=1&isAllowed=y, 6.

[38] ibid 15.

of CRAs, where we insisted that they need to be aware of and mitigate the consequences of their ratings beyond the immediate economic ones. In so doing, they have to develop a reflexive self-openness, which requires a reform of the key elements of the rating process along the lines of the rule of law and greater accountability. This, however, cannot remain exclusively on the level of aspiration or normative orientation, but should gradually adopt a more concrete institutional form of a direct justificatory engagement with the EU. To conclude this section, if the relationship between transnational law and the EU is conducted pursuant to the requirements of principled legal pluralism, this will prevent new instances of injustice emerging in the EU and might even strengthen justice inside it. However, this conclusion can only be drawn from the vantage point of the thin conception of justice as justification. The thick conception imposes excessive, most notably democratic demands, on transnational law, whose effects in the EU will therefore always be, more or less, perceived as unjust.

B. The Economic Injustice of Transnational Law

The second example of injustice in the EU is associated with the economic crisis. Its roots date back to 2009 after the collapse of Lehman Brothers, which provoked an investment scare on the global markets. The revelation of the enormous Greek public deficit further ignited the crisis. This soon led to a domino effect of sovereign debt in the peripheral Member States, resulting in unsustainably high yields on sovereign bonds. The euro thus came under huge pressure from the global markets, its survival being threatened directly. As we know, and as was described in Chapter 5, the EU reacted by building a monetary firewall around the single currency and by implementing political and legal mechanisms to ensure that the conditions on which the euro is built are indeed complied with by all members of the eurozone. In so doing, the EU wanted to achieve two things: to prevent the same events happening again and to endow its currency with the credibility needed to win back the trust of the global markets and investors. For those Member States falling short of the European Stability Pact criteria, this meant that spending had to be rolled back, sometimes significantly. This set of requirements has come to be known as the programme of austerity.

Austerity, especially in Greece, which is the Member State that has fared worst in the crisis, has been subject to potent critiques. Its critics have argued not only that it does not work economically and politically,[39] but they have also insisted that it breeds huge social injustice.[40] Living standards in Greece have fallen dramatically

---

[39] See, for example, P Krugman, 'Ending Greece's Bleeding' *New York Times* (5 July 2015), www.nytimes.com/2015/07/06/opinion/paul-krugman-ending-greeces-bleeding.html.

[40] See, for example, D Schraad-Tischler and C Kroll, *Social Justice in the EU: A Cross-national Comparison* (Gütersloh, Bertelsmann Stiftung, 2014).

in both absolute and relative terms, whereby those who were already less well-off have been hit the hardest.[41] It is said that this has benefited the global markets, whose exclusive concern has been to have their credits repaid by any means necessary, as well as the richer EU Member States in the north. They are seen as doing their best to maintain the stability of their banks, which have also been major creditors in Greece. At the same time, the richer Member States, especially Germany, are said to have drawn numerous advantages from the currency union, not infrequently also at the expense of the southern Member States, in particular in terms of greater internal and external competitiveness. This has stifled economic development in the south, forcing the southern Member States to preserve their living standards on the basis of foreign loans. As a result, austerity should be abandoned and ought to be replaced with solidarity, taking the form of writing down the loans and by providing new ones. In short, the north should finance the economic recovery of the south. Naturally, the former is deeply opposed to this. It is not only that the Treaty of Lisbon with its no-bail-out clause does not permit any debt sharing, it is also, so the argument goes, that Greece alone is responsible for its own economic despair after years—indeed, decades—of economic and political mismanagement by the state.

What we are faced with here is a classical problem of distributive justice, distilled in the principle that all may get their due (*suum cuique*). Of course, unlike in the case of injustice as a lack of justification, this distributive problem has not been created directly by transnational law as a whole. The role of transnational law here is more indirect, mediated and sector-specific as it only involves private administrative transnational law and private transnational economic law. The seeds of the economic problems in Greece were sown by the Greek state and its citizens. The EU has contributed to this by its laws, their inconsistent implementation and by a half-built political house, locking into the mechanisms of a single currency a state that did not meet its criteria at the very beginning and which has, apparently, been falling short of them ever since.[42] If the responsibility for the crisis is thus both individual and shared by Greece and the EU, the solution to the crisis is not exclusively in their hands. To make the euro a trustworthy currency, which is a *conditio sine qua non* for the viability of the economy in the EU, it has to win the support of the global financial markets and their intermediaries: the CRAs. It is here that private transnational law and their actors distantly, indirectly, albeit decisively, enter the picture and inevitably impinge on the question of economic justice in the EU.

How precisely do they do that? Do they cause justice or injustice? If the latter, how could that be prevented? Who is to say this: the Greeks, the wealthier others of

---

[41] G Cavero, *The True Cost of Austerity and Inequality: Greece Case Study* (London, Oxfam, 2013).

[42] Greece apparently falsified data already prior to 2004 as well as in 2010; see C Wienberg, 'Greece "Cheated" to Join Euro' *Bloomberg* (26 May 2011), www.bloomberg.com/news/articles/2011-05-26/greece-cheated-to-join-euro-sanctions-since-were-too-soft-issing-says; see also A Willis, 'EU Report Slams Greece over False Statistics' *EU Observer* (13 January 2010) euobserver.com/economic/29258.

the eurozone or transnational actors, who all argue about and especially for their own due? Does principled legal pluralism come with any normative prescriptions for such a situation? These questions are not easy to answer, but are further complicated by the specificity of justice in the EU described above. We should recall that since in the EU there are 29 polities, there is also an equal number of different conceptions of justice. The questions asked and especially the answers given thus depend fundamentally on which of the 29 polities one is situated in. Greece thus believes that it has already given its due; Germany on the other hand wants its due back and so do the international and transnational creditors. Similarly, Greece asserts that austerity has already taken too high a social toll, it is causing too much human suffering and is therefore unjust, whereas the creditors insist that justice requires that *pacta sunt servanda* and the loans should be paid back. If they are not, this would mean that somebody else has to pay for the debts they have neither caused nor used for their own benefit. This would, again, be unjust. So who is right? What is a just solution in this case?

Drawing on the work of Sen and following his departure from the transcendental or ideal conception of justice, we are bound to conclude that there is no ideal, just solution in this case. There is a plurality of ideal answers, each of them polity- or entity-specific, which might mean, as Sen concludes, that 'there may not indeed exist any identifiable perfectly just social arrangement on which impartial agreement would emerge'.[43] However, this cannot be the end of the story. This would be the case if we were dealing with the problem inside a sealed-off, self-contained entity. Instead, we are addressing a union, consisting of a plurality of polities, in the context of transnational law where interactions between the two are numerous and boundaries are more than porous. In such a pluralist situation, our principled legal pluralism can be put to work again.

A plurality of just solutions, as perceived and maybe even practised by different polities and entities, can just be a point of departure rather than a final destination. This plurality must be respected: each of the entities involved must therefore award the other with the benefit of possibly getting its own justice answer right and question itself that possibly its answer is wrong. This is what a dialectical open self of pluralism requires and it has to be practised through an intense dialogue of claims and counterclaims, essentially through the process of justification. This process of justification must again be underlined by a commitment to the common whole: that we are all in the same boat. If so, while a perfectly just solution will remain beyond the reach of all the actors involved, they could, by following the described normative spirit of pluralism, agree on removing insular examples of injustice, even if only incrementally and on a case-by-case, practical basis. In this way, the problem of the economic injustice in the EU, stemming from the multitude of divergent epistemic, normative and practical aspects, involving a

---

[43] Sen (n 2) 15 and 105: 'A systematic theory of comparative justice does not need, nor does it necessarily yield, an answer to the question "what is a just society".'

plethora of independent as well as closely connected endogenous and exogenous factors, will not disappear. Yet, it will be under control and somehow tamed. We have a normative map provided by the principled legal pluralism, which helps us steer these conflicts away from searching and arguing about the ideally just solutions that will never be found to practical attempts at removing the most flagrant examples of injustice on a case-by-case basis.

C. Injustice as an Affront to Human Dignity

The last example of injustice to be discussed here is even more remotely, but nevertheless still importantly connected to transnational law. It concerns the human dignity of thousands of those who seek refuge in the EU, but either disappear in the rough waters of the Mediterranean Sea, are fended away by the recently erected walls on the EU's external borders or, if they manage to reach EU soil, become stuck in the limbo of one of the many provisional detention centres for immigrants in different, usually distant corners of the EU Member States.[44] The causes of migrations are, of course, numerous. While the traditional actors, the states fostering their regional and global interests, continue to bear the most important share of the responsibility for the present situation, the influence of transnational law and its less traditional actors cannot be neglected either. The recent biggest waves of refugees have been provoked by state failure in North Africa and the Middle East, where the power vacuum has enabled radical religious groups to connect transnationally and establish their rule over vast swaths of territory, which formally still belongs to 'sovereign states'. The most successful, powerful and violent among these groups has been the so-called Islamic State (IS), which, in its own words, is building a new caliphate.[45] However, other groups, some of them 'global', like Al-Qaida, and others more local, have joined them in a similar endeavour, characterised by terrorist assaults against any community which does not fit their conception of the world. To escape persecution or even massive killings or simply for want of a better life, local populations have been fleeing these territories in huge numbers.

Before looking at the question of which concerns for justice in the EU this development has brought about, let us dwell a little more on the precise character of these terrorist groups. They are non-statist, private actors. On the basis of their religious objectives, they could be qualified as transnational private NGOs. However, their terrorist methods and the physical power they wield over large geographical areas obviously argue against this classification. They are best seen as what they really are: transnational private terrorist networks, a conceptual

---

[44] For a good critical overview, see AJ Menendez, 'The Refugee Crisis: Between Human Tragedy and Symptom of the Structural Crisis of European Integration' (2016) 2 *European Law Journal* 388.

[45] J Sekulow, J Sekulow, RW Ash and D French, *Rise of ISIS: A Threat We Can't Ignore* (Brentwood, Howard Books, 2014).

and practical novelty made possible by the process of globalisation described in Chapter 1. As such, they are, of course, also producers of transnational law, which however has nothing to do with the rule of law, but it is still law: autonomous regulations that govern the horizontal power relations among the leaders of these networks as well as the vertical power relations against those subjugated to them in and across the states. It is this kind of private administrative transnational law that is driving refugees to the doorsteps of the EU.

Two questions of justice can be raised in this context. One is external and the other is internal. The external question asks what justice requires from the EU in relation to these terrorist groups in the places where they cause extreme suffering to the local population. The internal question, on the other hand, asks what justice demands from the EU once the refugees knock on its door because of the actions of the transnational terrorist groups that the EU might have originally inadequately addressed in situ. What kind of guidance, if any, does the principled legal pluralism provide for answering these questions?

In the case of private transnational terrorist groups, our principled legal pluralism runs out. Not in terms of normative proposals, but in terms of its capacity to connect to the plurality represented by the terrorist networks. No normative spirit of pluralism can be developed with regard to them. Their plurality is unworthy of recognition because it violates the exclusive foundation of pluralism: equal human dignity. There can thus be no commitment to IS, nor can it and the EU be seen as part of a common whole. After all, the normative objective of IS is precisely the opposite: to physically destroy and subjugate the world represented by the EU and its liberal, secular counterparts. However, our principled legal pluralism requires more from the EU than just not committing to IS. Even tolerance or a simply passive stance, a hands-off approach, is incompatible with principled legal pluralism. In this case, principled legal pluralism demands action because it is the human dignity of individuals that is at stake. If the EU is to allow the ongoing violation of human dignity by IS, even if of certain foreign individuals living in distant and highly remote places, it would be effectively betraying its exclusive substantive foundation. For one cannot, other than rhetorically and therefore disingenuously, claim to be founded on equal human dignity while staying passive when this very human dignity is being massively violated by another entity. Doing precisely this would run contrary to the spirit of principled legal pluralism, but it would simultaneously also be unjust.

This unjustness would manifest itself in the sense that the respect for equal human dignity is a minimum content of any conception of justice. No rule or action which fails to respect equal human dignity can be considered just. It cannot even be considered civilised because a violation of human dignity is an act of barbarism. Allowing acts of barbarism is illegal, immoral and ultimately unjust by way of doing it as well as in terms of its outcome. Preventing violations of human dignity is thus a legal obligation of the EU, underlined by the normative spirit of pluralism, moral duties and requirements of justice. This legal obligation grows, both in terms of its strength and scope, with proximity to those whose human dignity is violated. If the EU therefore cannot remain aloof from the actions of transnational terrorist networks where these take place, it can even less disregard the calamities their victims undergo on their risky road to a better life in Europe. The EU must act to stay faithful to the normative requirements of principled legal pluralism and in order not to cause even more injustice.

So far, the EU has performed this task poorly. Its inaction has caused injustice both for the refugees as well as the relationships inside the EU. The lives of thousands have been lost in the Mediterranean Sea, while thousands of others are kept in inhumane conditions in immigration centres. The brunt of the refugee burden has been borne by the southern Member States with external borders to the Schengen Area. Incidentally, these are the same Member States that also find themselves in the worst economic situations. On top of lacking resources for their own citizens, they must exclusively accommodate thousands of refugees, as the EU Dublin Regulation mandates that the refugees must stay in the Member State in which they first arrived.[46] The Member States are explicitly prohibited from allowing the refugees to continue their journey on to the Member States of their choice inside the Schengen Area. This situation again raises the question of distributive justice. However, in contrast with the case of economic injustice discussed above, the contest here is not just about the distribution of funds, but also of actual people.

The very thought of this creates an atmosphere of injustice. If all may get their due, the refugees are certainly not getting theirs when their human dignity is imperilled or even directly violated. Similarly, the financial, material and organisational solidarity of the internal Schengen Area Member States shown towards the external Member States has for years been clearly inadequate too. Only recently has this trend been reversed and financial solidarity increased with the establishment of several emergency funds.[47] Also, talks about the refugee quota, in which the Member States were bargaining about the numbers of refugees they would be willing to accept, were almost indecent. However, just talking the talk, but not walking the walk is even worse: it is not just indecent, it is creating and perpetuating injustice. Despite the fact that the Council adopted two decisions on relocating 160,000 refugees from Italy and Greece, the decisions have remained effectively unimplemented[48] and the Visegrad countries took their bitter opposition to the relocation plan to the CJEU.[49]

At this point, we can see how the inaction of the EU in its relationship with transnational terrorist networks leads to its internal refugee problem, where

---

[46] Council Regulation (EC) No 343/2003 of 18 February 2003 establishing the criteria and mechanisms for determining the Member State responsible for examining an asylum application lodged in one of the Member States by a third-country national [2003] OJ L50.

[47] For a more in-depth discussion, see S Carrera, S Blockmans, D Gros and E Guild, 'The EU's Response to the Refugee Crisis: Taking Stock and Setting Policy Priorities' (2015) 20 *CEPS Essay* 1.

[48] According to the Commission's report by January 2017, fewer than 12,000 people have been relocated to other Member States: ec.europa.eu/home-affairs/sites/homeaffairs/files/what-we-do/policies/european-agenda-migration/press-material/docs/state_of_play_-_relocation_en.pdf.

[49] See, for example, the pending Case 647/15 *Hungary v Council of the European Union*, lodged on 3 December 2015.

similar inaction essentially creates a double injustice, both external and internal. Had the EU followed the normative prescriptions of principled legal pluralism towards the transnational terrorist networks, the problems would be far less significant and the injustice thus created would also be less significant. Again, what we notice is an apparently positive correlation between legal pluralism and justice. It is to the analysis of this point that we turn in the conclusion.

IV. PRINCIPLED LEGAL PLURALISM AND JUSTICE

That legal pluralism as defended in this book has a positive correlation with justice should not be a surprise. This has been a deliberate and self-explanatory choice. After all, no theory with a bona fide motivation can be expected to do the opposite: to be in the service of injustice rather than justice. The theory of principled legal pluralism has been developed to achieve three objectives: to describe the social objects under examination more accurately; to explain the functioning of the social phenomena under review and the causal relations in and between them more persuasively. Finally, its purpose has also been explicitly normative: to put the relationship between EU law and transnational law in a better light and provide normative guidance for their normatively appealing development in the future. It is in this last explicitly normative part of our theory that another objective—that of furthering justice or at least preventing injustice—can also be found.

There are five main elements of our theory which gear it towards justice. The first is a normative choice for pluralism as opposed to monism. Pluralism is about the recognition of diversity, plurality, which is considered good and is to be preserved. Unlike monism, pluralism does not recognise any privileged normative sites or arguments. It hence disqualifies attempts at imposing 'justice' or privileging one specific form or source of it. All normative sites, polities, entities, legal orders and orderings have, in principle, equal weight as long as they derive from and respect equal human dignity.

This is the second element of our theory: a normative foundation which any conception of justice must take as its indispensable point of departure. There can be no conception of justice that would permit the violation of equal human dignity. The same is valid for pluralism, which means that our legal pluralism and every meaningful conception of justice share a minimal, thin normative core. By virtue of respect for equal human dignity, legal pluralism and justice are thus normatively united at their foundation.

The third element is the recognition of irreconcilability. This flows naturally from pluralism's requirement to respect plurality. Among the plurality of sites, which are always first epistemic and then imbued with a plethora of values and topped by layers of socially constructed particularistic identities, in the absence of any privileged Archimedean point, there are simply no socially accessible ideal solutions and, more importantly, there can be no one who could claim he or she has such access. As indicated above, this conclusion echoes the non-transcendental, non-ideal approach to justice advocated by Sen and Douglas-Scott, which is however not a mainstream approach. For those who seek an ideal solution to the justice conundrum in the relationship between EU law and transnational law, our theory of legal pluralism will thus ultimately come as a disappointment.

The fourth element complements the third element and concerns self-reflexivity. As there are no ideal solutions and privileged positions, what is required is a self-reflexive sincere dialogical approach among equals in which the arguments are made and challenged in pursuit of the best possible outcome. These outcomes should be arrived at, the fifth element insists, in a principled way rather through a pragmatic, ad hoc accommodation. This means that the outcomes ought to be justified with arguments, which are intended to genuinely persuade their audience, even if only provisionally and for that specific occasion, so that in all similar situations, everyone participating in them would be making and adhering to the same arguments. In short, in order to be principled, these arguments must be applied against oneself as well as others in all similar situations, consistently and with integrity. Since our theory is a theory of *legal* pluralism, this is a legal duty as well as a moral one in and among the communities of principle. It is also, doubtlessly, in consonance with the conception of justice built around the right to justification.

In conclusion, we can state that there are two main overlaps between our theory of principled legal pluralism and the idea of justice. They are both substantive and procedural. Substantively, legal pluralism and justice share the same normative foundation of equal human dignity. Procedurally, they are both built on the framework of justification, which requires the giving of reasons, self-reflexivity and a dialogical relationship between the participant, be it in conflicting or harmonious practices. It is because of these two overlaps that principled legal pluralism can contribute to justice. And this is also, as this book has tried to argue on an abstract level as well as in concrete case studies, why the admittedly dynamic and complex relationship between EU law and transnational law should be conducted pursuant to the normative guidance of principled legal pluralism.

8

Principled Legal Pluralism, EU Law and Transnational Law

I N THE PRECEDING four chapters we have studied the relationship between EU law and transnational law to establish to what an extent this relationship in descriptive and explanatory terms fits the proposed theory of principled legal pluralism. The contours of the relationship have been examined on the basis of four case studies in which we have focused on transnational law's impact on the rule of law, democracy, human rights protection and justice in the EU. Each of the foundational values of the EU has been researched in relation to different type of transnational law to establish whether the modalities of the relationship between EU law and transnational law also depend on the type of transnational law involved. The purpose of this chapter is to round off the discussion, on the one hand, by drawing some conclusions of the book, as well as, on the other hand, to look at the challenges ahead and to alternative scenarios to that defended in this treatise.

I. THE MAIN FINDINGS OF THIS BOOK

This book has set an ambitious objective: to conceptualise the relationship between EU law and transnational law. The pursuit of this objective, as we have seen, is burdened at least by two sets of problems. First, there is no established, widely shared conceptualisation of the EU and transnational law. Theoretical disagreements have reigned instead. Second, examining the nature of the relationship between EU law and transnational law amounts to solving an equation with two variables whose outcome is ultimately uncertain, while the outcome itself essentially determines the meaning of the variables. This book has decided to cut through this ultimate open-endedness of the research project by situating the equation into a normative theoretical premise of the theory of principled legal pluralism. The latter has been used to conceptualise transnational law *qua* law; to define the EU in pluralist terms as a union, as well as to expound, by way of four case studies, the relationship between the hence-defined transnational law and EU law in pluralist terms.

The theory of principled legal pluralism is the most important original contribution of this book to transnational legal studies. As explained in Chapter 2, this theory eschews the ambition of mechanically translating the old modernist, essentially statist, legal paradigm, whereby the normative scope for legal theory and praxis has been caught between two monist extremes of constitutionalism and international law, to the legal and political world beyond the state. Instead, on the basis of a constructive, collaborate and inclusive approach, our theory draws on the modernist legal paradigm, but upgrades it conceptually, descriptively, analytically and normatively to a new theory for the polycentric legal landscape of the twenty-first century. This theory takes its cues from other refined constitutional, pluralist constitutional and pluralist theoretical approaches to the legal phenomena beyond the state. While it shares many characteristics with them, it also importantly differs from all of them by being simultaneously legal, principled and normative.

Accordingly, the theory of principled legal pluralism has been defended as a general theory of law describing, explaining and normatively guiding the situation of plurality of legal orders. Its starting point is a recognition of legal plurality: the existence of multiple legal orders, which are recognised *qua* legal orders since they are intelligible to the other, foremost statist legal orders, as legal orders. Second, the principled legal pluralism requires the identified legal plurality to be connected into a common whole without exhausting the autonomous standing of its constitutive legal orders. To do so, it is necessary to develop a normative spirit of pluralism. This necessitates a double commitment: to the plurality and to the common whole, both at the same time. However, as this commitment is subject to the inherent epistemic differences of the legal orders involved, the potential conflicts over the divergent formal and substantive claims to authority cannot always be resolved, but their resolution must always be attempted in a principled legal manner in line with the substantive and formal transcontextual legal principles of human dignity and integrity.

This theory has informed our conceptualisation of transnational law, while the praxis of transnational law has, simultaneously, prompted the development of the theory. This is an example of a reflexive equilibrium between praxis and theory in action. Proceeding from the refined, pluralist concept of law, according to which not every normative order can be considered as a legal order, while simultaneously the state is not its only source either, we have conceived of transnational law as its own, autonomous and separate field of law. This is composed of three broader groups of transnational law: public, administrative and private transnational law, each of which contains a number of subtypes of transnational law, as explained in Chapter 1. Several types of transnational law have been then examined in their relationship with the EU for their impact on its selected four foundational values.

The influence of international law, which belongs to public transnational law, on the rule of law in the EU has been analysed first. We have established that the development of international law, which is now able to target the individuals directly, has not only affected human rights of concrete individuals, but has also undermined the rule of law in the EU. This has happened for two reasons. The first is related to international law and the second to the EU. Since public international law, with the UN at its apex, is undernourished in terms of the rule of law, the duty to comply with it has put the higher EU rule of law standards under pressure. As we have seen, the EU's reaction to this has not been fully in line with the normative expectations of principled legal pluralism and nor has it contributed to the protection of the rule of law.

The EU has recognised the international law's autonomous existence and has committed itself to its preservation, but it has failed to develop sufficient dialectical openness towards international law. Rather than engaging with the UN pluralistically, so as to eventually encourage the development of the rule of law in international law, the EU has instead acted in a self-referential way by strongly defending its own autonomy against international law. The outcome for the rule of law in the EU has been negative. The EU's protection of the rule of law was only rhetorical. Its sociological dimension has remained unimplemented, but other objectives, most notably the collective security, which the UN is there to ensure, have thereby been undermined too.

The monistic impulse of the EU judiciary, which is reflected in the overzealous defence of the EU's autonomy against international law, has been explained by the EU's internal structure as well as by the reasons related to international law. As is well known, the EU's autonomy has foremost resulted out of its judiciary's claim to a distinct legal order, separate from international law. The EU's legal autonomy in relation to the Member States thus essentially depends on the EU's capacity to remain different, eg, autonomous from international law. If the EU gives way to international law, especially in a situation where the latter fails to protect the rule of law, its autonomy is undermined not just against international law, but also against the Member States. In the absence of the EU's proper reaction, the Member States themselves would need to defend their established domestic rule-of-law standards against their lowering by EU law under transnational law, falling back on the *Solange I* scenario.

The internal need for the protection of the autonomy was thus high, but so was the external need. International law is an example of public transnational law. It is a legal system that is institutionalised to a relatively high degree. It is well-entrenched, robust and backed up by a considerable degree of public power. As such, when observed through a monist lens, it presents serious competition to the EU's own legal and political authority. Against a strong legal order, a strong protection of one's legal autonomy is necessary too. This is a monistic conclusion. A pluralist one is different. The more the legal orders involved are established and fully fledged, the greater the need for a more intense pluralist engagement between them. This is all the more important when the rule of law is at the heart of the interaction between legal orders.

With regard to the rule of law, Chapter 4 has thus also taught us that in a situation of transnational legal plurality, the rule of law cannot be ensured within the exclusive confines of a single legal order, eg, in a monistic manner. Even if the EU built an ideal rule-of-law system, which of course (still) is not the case, this would be under a constant pressure of the external rule-of-law undernourished legal orders with which the EU would formally or de facto need to co-operate for the achievement of joint objectives. Achieving the rule of law in one legal order, which is no longer self-contained, thus necessarily depends on the rule-of-law quality of other legal orders with which this legal order interacts.

A similar lesson has been learnt about democracy. Like in the case of the rule of law, this book has also opted for an integral conception of democracy, drawing together the collectivist, the procedural and the substantive elements of democracy. We have proceeded from the assumption that at the heart of democracy, there is an idea of self-determination, standing for the capacity of the members of a particular polity to decide together on the resolution of collective problems, issues and challenges autonomously in a procedurally predetermined way. This capacity is dependent on the political sovereignty and economic sovereignty of the state, which are closely related and in fact interdependent. Democracy existing in practice, a veritable democracy, requires that the polity retains meaningful political competences for self-regulation, which are backed up by sufficient economic resources permitting the exercise of the political powers in practice. If either or both elements of sovereignty are lacking, we speak, following Scharpf, of the pre-emption of democracy. This has gradually been taking place in the EU due to a specific interaction between the internal constitutional structure of the EU and the external influence by the actors of transnational law.

If Chapter 4 has focused on public transnational law, Chapter 5 has centred on private administrative law, concretely on the rules and practices created by the credit rating agencies (CRAs). These played a decisive role during the economic crisis, acting as a de facto, if not even a de jure, gatekeeper to the global financial markets on whose funds the EU and its Member States came to existentially rely in the absence of domestic resources. The CRAs estimated the Member States' credit capacity and issued a rating, on the basis of which the global lenders determined the interest rate to be paid on the loans requested by a Member State. A low rating means a high interest rate and expensive money for the borrowing Member State, which incrementally leads to its incapacity to raise any money under viable economic conditions, so that the state can eventually run out of funds. In such conditions of economic pre-emption, democracy is, of course, practically devoid of self-determination and becomes a mere empty shell.

The critical side of this development is that due to the EU's internal economically and politically half-built constitutional structure, the EU and its Member States under the impact of transnational law essentially lost control over their own democratic processes. For some time, the EU appeared to be literally helpless under the rating pressure of the CRAs in the hands of the volatile global financial markets. The CRAs' products caused the economic pre-emption of supranational democracy in the context of the pre-existing political and economic pre-emption of national democracies without the EU or the Member States having any say in the process of creation of the respective ratings. As explained in Chapter 5, the ratings are private administrative transnational norms adopted unilaterally by the CRAs. They bind through acceptance by the global financial markets the collective practices of states without their assent or even input to these rules, irrespective of the far-reaching public and private economic and political consequences that they cause.

The EU's reaction to this situation has been twofold: internal and external. Internally it has tried to perfect its economic structure by laying the grounds for a fiscal union and a banking union, and by establishing a permanent financial mechanism, a kind of monetary firewall, to limit the consequences of an eventual new economic crisis in any of its Member States. Part of the internal reshaping was also a rhetorical figure by the Governor of the European Central Bank (ECB), according to which the ECB will do whatever it takes to save the euro. This has, also under more favourable global economic conditions, helped to build trust and to quell the concerns of the global financial markets. Externally, the EU has fought back against the CRAs through a double strategy: first, by increasing control over them; and, second, by undermining their relevance through decreasing the regulatory reliance on the CRAs ratings inside the EU and by their pluralisation in the form of an attempted breaking-up of the monopoly of the big three.

The external strategies have been unsuccessful, since they have also been based on a monist approach. The CRAs have overgrown not just the national but also the supranational regulatory capacity. The EU's attempts to bring the CRAs back under its territorial regulatory regime have not succeeded as the CRAs' addressees, the global financial markets, keep following them, the EU's regulatory attempts notwithstanding. Chapter 5 has thus argued that the effects of the economic crisis on democracy in the EU would have been less grave had the relationship between the EU and CRAs been conducted more in line with the principled legal pluralism. The reasons why this was not the case ought to be sought both on the side of the CRAs and the EU. The CRAs obviously acted entirely self-referentially, paying little or indeed no heed to the (in)direct implications of their economic ratings on the entire plethora of social dimensions in the affected states, including democracy. It seems that these broader non-economic and public dimensions have been simply beyond the CRAs' epistemic self-conception. Chapter 5 has argued that this ought to be changed by increasing the transparency, accountability and rule-of-law commitments of the CRAs.

On the other hand, the monistic stance of the EU can be explained by the type of transnational law involved in this case. If the relative strength of public transnational law explains the EU's relentless defence of its autonomy against international law, it is the relative weakness of CRAs that explains the EU's aggressive stance towards them. The EU, as an autonomous, public supranational legal order, feels and acts in a superior way to CRAs as private transnational legal entities. The absence of pluralist elements, of the very readiness to recognise the CRAs autonomous legal status, can be also explained by the nature of interests or the objectives pursued by CRAs. These are predominantly economic and private in character, tailored to the needs of the global financial markets. This contrasts them, for example, with the UN objective of collective security, which is of a general, public interest and has hence enjoyed more, even if still insufficient, respect by the EU.

In the EU's relationship with transnational law, a pattern thus appears to be emerging. Accordingly, the pluralist elements of the relationship depend on the public/private character of transnational law and the type of interest a particular form of transnational law is devoted to. The relationship between EU law and public transnational law, which pursues more general, less specifically economic interests, tends to be better adapted to the normative requirements of principled legal pluralism. The opposite is true of the relationship between EU law and private transnational law with prevailing economic interests. Such a relationship is conducted in less pluralist terms. This pattern can also be identified in the case study of transnational law's impact on the right to privacy in Chapter 6.

Chapter 6 fittingly compared the EU's relationship with two types of transnational law: *lex sportiva* and *lex informatica*. *Lex sportiva* is an example of hybrid transnational law, in which both general and more particular economic interests overlap. Sport plays an important social function by fostering a sound, inclusive, healthy society and is an important economic activity too. On the other hand, *lex informatica*, as studied in Chapter 6, where the focus was on Google's accountability for respecting the right to privacy, has been used as an example of private corporate transnational law. It subjects are predominantly concerned with maximising the private economic interests. The difference between the more public and (also) general welfare-oriented *lex sportiva* and Google's predominantly private, profit-gaining *lex informatica* is reflected in the nature of their relationship with EU law. The EU's relationship with *lex sportiva* is much more pluralist in character than its relationship with *lex informatica* in the context of private corporate transnational law.

With regard to *lex sportiva*, the European Commission and the CJEU have demonstrated a considerable degree of self-restraint, paying heed to the relative autonomy of *lex sportiva*. The pluralist relationship, marked by the hands-off approach, has been at times so deferential to *lex sportiva* that the outcome has been unfavourable to the human right to privacy. Chapter 6 has explained this by the fact of greater maturity, density and indeed institutionalisation of the *lex sportiva* as a hybrid transnational legal order. On this basis, it has been argued that the maturity, the robustness of a legal order and its recognition in wider legal circles positively correlate with all four elements of principled legal pluralism. Conversely, *lex informatica* is still an example of transnational legal order in *statu nascendi*; less mature, less established and less entrenched. As a result, EU law again tries to play a pre-emptively superior and hence more monist role in relation to it. The fact that *lex informatica* in the context of private transnational corporate law pursues purely economic interests has led the EU judiciary to grant it less recognition and deference than to the sporting objectives of *lex sportiva*, which are directed at the general welfare and are simultaneously, in principle, shared by EU law. It was thus again the type of interests that a particular form of transnational law has pursued that has also determined the more or less pluralist/monist relationship with EU law.

Finally, Chapter 7 has turned to the question of transnational law's impact on justice in the EU. To avoid a grand philosophical discussion of the meaning of justice, the chapter has centred on its denial, eg, on injustice and the role of transnational law in relation to it. Three instances of injustice caused or deepened by transnational law were under review: injustice as a lack of justification; economic injustice; and injustice as an affront to human dignity. We have established that the contribution of transnational law to injustice as a lack of justification grows as we move from public transnational law to administrative and finally private transnational law. While few, if any, transnational law actors meet the criteria of thick justice, the normative expectations of thin justice, which overlap with those of principled legal pluralism, are better complied with by public rather than private transnational law actors. The latter thus still have a lot of room for improvement in light of our theory.

The challenge of economic injustice has turned out to be even more vexed. It poses a question of distributive justice among 29 different polities of the EU under the impact of global economic forces mediated by CRAs as private transnational law actors. Following Sen, we have acquiesced that such a complex question lends itself to no ideal answer and have suggested that the internal and the external actors having sway over the economic justice in the EU should act in accordance with principled legal pluralism and work at least on removing insular examples of economic injustice, even if only incrementally and on a case-by-case, practical basis.

Last but not least, the injustice as an affront to human dignity has been analysed through the perspective of the ongoing immigration crisis. This has been caused by several factors, including private non-statist, but state-emulating transnational terrorist groups, to which the EU has found no meaningful response. The external inaction and the internal shameful migrant quota disputes under the pressure of transnational terrorism has led to and deepened injustice as an affront to human dignity, both internally and externally. Here the theory of principled legal pluralism, of course, does not compel the EU 'to commit' to the terrorist groups, as transnational actors, but to fight them in order to stay faithful to the monistic foundation of principled legal pluralism: human dignity. Again the conclusion was a normative one: had the EU followed the normative prescriptions of principled legal pluralism towards transnational terrorist networks, the problems and the injustice thus created would be less significant. The theory of principled legal pluralism is therefore closely related to the pursuit of justice or at least to preventing further cases of injustice. In fact, this is at the heart of its normative agenda.

II. PLURALISM VERSUS THE OLD AND NEW MONISMS

It follows from the above that this book has tried to make several original contributions at the intersection of EU law and transnational legal studies. First, it has asked research questions that have either not been raised before or have not received satisfactory answers. Second, this has been used as a springboard for making three original conceptual contributions. The book has developed a new account of legal pluralism and has endorsed a pluralist concept of law. On this basis, it has proposed a more rigorous conception of transnational law, which has been missing in the otherwise growing transnational scholarship. Finally, it has advanced a unique pluralist conception of the EU as a union. Having rounded up the conceptual part, it has provided new theoretical instruments for a fresh take on questions that are of enormous theoretical and practical importance to the EU of today: the questions of rule of law, democracy, human rights protection and justice under the influence of transnational law.

While the literature on the rule of law and the democratic deficit in the EU has abounded, the external, transnational dimension, which further complicates the conditions for ensuring both values inside the EU, has been explored much less. The same conclusion can be arrived at with regard to human rights, where the mainstream concern has been how to ensure their protection against potential violations by the Member States or the EU, whereas the influence of transnational non-public actors has mostly been out of sight. The book has also tried to fill this lacuna. Finally, in addressing the question of justice in the relationship between EU law and transnational law, the book has had to tread an entirely new path. While the recently discovered justice deficit has been analysed with regard to the internal and external functioning of the EU, the consequences for justice in the EU deriving from transnational law and its actors have not been studied at all.

The book's normative decision in favour of the theory of principled legal pluralism eventually appears to be justified. Principled legal pluralism has been confirmed as a compelling theory of law in transnational environment. It provides a roadmap for adapting the conventional understanding of law to new forms of legal regulation beyond the state. Principled legal pluralism is not just a theory of adjudication, eg, on how judicial institutions should act when EU law and different forms of transnational law meet. On the contrary, principled legal pluralism is a general theory of law addressed to all power-wielding actors, public and private, political, administrative and hybrid. In this way, it offers itself as a compelling theoretical account for describing transnational law and EU law, as well as for explaining and normatively (re)shaping the relationship between the two.

This book has demonstrated that in many ways this relationship is already now structured and conducted in terms of principled legal pluralism. It has been shown that in practice, the actual pluralist character of this relationship largely depends on the maturity and robustness of a concrete transnational legal order as well as on its primary purpose (private economic or other). More mature and established transnational bodies of law, whose purpose is not exclusively economic, are given greater recognition by EU law and better comply with the normative expectations of principled legal pluralism.

On a lower level of abstraction, in terms of practical findings, this book has clearly shown that the relationship between the EU and most, if not all, types of transnational law exhibits a tendency of dejudicialisation (but not delegalisation)—in other words, of avoiding direct legal conflicts and their judicial resolution, and pushing the frictions into the domain of experts whereby, following the prescriptions of principled legal pluralism, these are resolved through a self-reflexive dialogue, underlined by the principle of proportionality. The latter has been established as the structural legal principle, which mediates the relationship between EU law and transnational legal regimes to ensure, for example, an appropriate standard of human rights protection as these legal orders overlap and intersect.

On the other hand and simultaneously, this book has shown that the relationship between EU law and transnational law in important parts still falls short of the pluralist requirements. This has resulted in many negative consequences for foundational values of the EU. The book has offered several normative prescriptions for the improvement of this state of affairs. It has been central to this writing project not to be satisfied exclusively with conceptualisations, descriptions and analytic treatment of the many challenges transnational law poses to the EU. This is why this book has attempted to provide clear and compelling normative guidance as to how the relationship between EU law and transnational law should be developed to foster the rule of law, democracy, human rights protection and justice inside this relationship.

Nevertheless, the argument of this book is not that principled legal pluralism is an exclusive, comprehensive and absolutely correct theory of a transnational legal regulation. On the contrary, our theoretical ambition has been guided by modesty and complementarity. We have only tried to make a persuasive descriptive, explanatory and normative case for the theory of principled legal pluralism on the example of EU law and transnational law without taking credit away from other competing theoretical approaches. Inevitably, each theory, more or less successfully and comprehensively, captures certain elements of the phenomena under investigation. Progress in science and praxis is ultimately achieved through the integration of different theories and their co-operation, as well as through the competition between them.

The question, of course, remains whether the advocated theory is viable, in the sense that in the future it will be influencing the actual praxis in the transnational realm to an even greater degree. The book has argued that this would come with notable positive consequences. However, only time will tell whether this will really happen. Recent developments point to the plausibility of an alternative scenario under which we shall be witnessing the reinforcement of the old or the emergence of new monisms. The re-invention or comeback of the nation state as the principal, aspiring to be the dominant, actor in transnational affairs is an example of the old monism. This aspiration is not limited, as has traditionally been the case, to the semi-autocracies on the brink of the Western world, but has found strong resonance right at the heart of the West. There is Donald Trump's America First and Theresa May's Global Britain, which both smack more of outlived imperial times than they are approximating any pluralist ideals in a globalised transnational world of the twenty-first century.

As a reaction to the new trend of old monisms, we could, not entirely para-doxically, see the emergence of the new monism too. This could take place with regard to the EU that could, under the pressure of many crises, both internal and external, try to respond to them with the process of etatisation. In order to escape the alternative scenario of reverting to the position of former Member States, the EU would rather opt for a fast-forward option of becoming a (federal) state itself. In this way, the pluralist character inside the EU would be lost, which would naturally reduce (or even eliminate) the chances for the prevalence of principled legal pluralism outside it in relation to other legal entities in the transnational realm.

I am convinced that the prevalence of old and new monisms over pluralism would not have favourable consequences either for the particular entities, legal orders and polities in transnational law or for the global order and stability as a whole. We should therefore be hopeful for the success of a pluralist scenario. The writing of this book has been inspired by a desire of contributing, even if no more than just a little, towards that goal.

Bibliography

Abdelal, R, *Capital Rules: The Construction of Global Finance* (Cambridge, MA, Harvard University Press, 2007).

Ahmed, M, Waters, R and Robinson, D, 'Google Risks Legal Action over "Right to Be Forgotten" Report' *Financial Times* (5 February 2017).

Almeida, H, Cunha, I, Ferreira, MA and Restrepo, F, 'The Real Effects of Sovereign Ratings: The Sovereign Ceiling Channel' (2014) 72(1) *Journal of Finance*.

Alter, K, *Establishing the Supremacy of European Law: the Making of an International Rule of Law in Europe* (Oxford, Oxford University Press, 2001).

Amar, AR, 'Of Sovereignty and Federalism' (1987) 96 *Yale Law Journal*.

Arrow, KJ, *Social Choice and Justice: Collected Papers of Kenneth J. Arrow, vol 1* (Cambridge, MA, Harvard University Press, 1983).

Avbelj, M, 'The EU and the Many Faces of Legal Pluralism' (2006) 2 *Croatian Yearbook of European Law and Policy*.

——. 'Questioning EU Constitutionalisms' (2008) 9 *German Law Journal*.

——. 'Theory of European Union' (2011) 36 *European Law Review*.

——. 'Can European Integration Be Constitutional and Pluralist—Both at the Same Time?' in M Avbelj and J Komarek (eds), *Constitutional Pluralism in the European Union and Beyond* (Oxford, Hart Publishing, 2012).

——. 'Supremacy or Primacy of EU Law—(Why) Does it Matter?' (2012) 6 *European Law Journal*.

——. 'Differentiated Integration: Farewell to the EU-27' (2013) 14 *German Law Journal*.

——. 'Security and the Transformation of the EU Public Order' (2013) 14 *German Law Journal*.

——. 'Crises and Perspectives of Building a European Nation: The Case of Slovenia' in P Jambrek (ed), *Nation's Transitions: Social and Legal Issues of Slovenia's Transitions: 1945–2015* (Brdo, Graduate School of Government and European Studies, European Faculty of Law, 2014).

——. 'Theorizing Sovereignty and European Integration' (2014) 27 *Ratio Juris*.

——. 'Central Europe as a Legal Phenomenon' (2015) 7 *European Perspectives*.

——. 'Integral Pre-emption of EU Democracy in Economic Crisis under Transnational Law' (2015) 4 *Cambridge Journal of International and Comparative Law*.

——. 'Global Constitutionalism as a Grammar of Global Law?' (2016) 3 *Critical Quarterly for Legislation and Law*.

——. 'Transnational Law between Modernity and Postmodernity' (2016) 7 *Transnational Legal Theory*.

Avbelj, M, Fontanelli, F and Martinico, G (eds), *Kadi on Trial: A Multifaceted Analysis of the Kadi Trial* (London, Routledge 2014).

Avbelj, M and Komarek, J (eds), *Constitutional Pluralism in the European Union and beyond* (Oxford, Hart Publishing, 2012).

——. (eds), Four Visions of Constitutional Pluralism (2008) 2 *European Journal of Legal Studies*.

Avbelj, M and Roth-Isigkeit, D, 'The UN, the EU, and the *Kadi* Case: A New Appeal for Genuine Institutional Cooperation' (2016) 17 *German Law Journal.*

Backer, LC, 'The Extra-national State: American Confederate Federalism and the European Union' (2001) 7 *Columbia Journal of European Law.*

——. 'Principles of Transnational Law: The Foundations of an Emerging Field' *LC Backer Blog* (9 March 2007).

——. 'Private Actors and Public Governance beyond the State: The Multinational Corporation, the Financial Stability Board and the Global Governance Order' (2011) 18 *Indiana Journal of Global Legal Studies.*

Balassa, B, *The Theory of Economic Integration* (Sydney, Allen & Unwin, 1961).

Banks, K, 'Trade, Labor and International Governance' (2011) 32 *Berkeley Journal of Employment and Labor Law.*

Baquero Cruz, J, 'The Legacy of Maastricht-Urteil and the Pluralist Movement' (2008) 14 *European Law Journal.*

Bartelson, J, *A Genealogy of Sovereignty* (Cambridge, Cambridge University Press, 1995).

Beal, JC and Restall, G, *Logical Pluralism* (Oxford, Oxford University Press, 2006).

Beaud, O, 'Fédéralisme et souveraineté, Notes pour une théorie constitutionnelle de la Fédération' (1998) 114 *RDP.*

Bellamy, R and Steiger, U (eds), *The Eurozone Crisis and the Democratic Deficit* (Florence, European University Institute, 2013).

Berman, PS, *Global Legal Pluralism* (Cambridge, Cambridge University Press, 2012).

——. 'Global Legal Pluralism' (2007) 80 *Southern Californian Law Review.*

Berger, KP, *The Creeping Codification of the New Lex Mercatoria* (The Hague, Kluwer Law International, 2010).

Berger, PL and Luckmann, T, *The Social Construction of Reality: A Treatise in the Sociology of Knowledge* (London, Penguin Books, 1971).

Bickel, A, *The Least Dangerous Branch* (Indianapolis, Bobbs-Merrill, 1962).

Bickerton, C, *European Integration: From Nation-States to Member States* (Oxford, Oxford University Press, 2012).

Blockmans S, Carrera S, Gros D and Guild E, 'The EU's Response to the Refugee Crisis Taking Stock and Setting Policy Priorities' (2015) 20 *CEPS Essay.*

Bodin, J, *Six livres de la Republique* (1576).

Brandsma, GJ, *Controlling Comitology* (Basingstoke, Palgrave Macmillan, 2013).

Brest, P et al, *Process of Constitutional Decisionmaking* (Alphen aan den Rijn, Aspen Law & Business, 2000).

Bugarič, B, 'Protecting Democracy and the Rule of Law in the European Union: The Hungarian Challenge' (2014) 79 *LSE 'Europe in Question' Discussion Paper Series.*

Burgess, M, *Federalism and European Union: The Building of Europe* (London, Routledge, 2000).

Burley, AM, 'The Alien Tort Statute and the Judiciary Act of 1789: A Badge of Honor' (1989) 83 *American Journal of International Law.*

Burrell, SA, Deutsch, KW, Kann, R and Lee, M, Jr, *Political Community and the North Atlantic Area* (Princeton, Princeton University Press, 1957).

Calliess, PG, 'Reflexive Transnational Law: The Privatisation of Civil Law and Civilisation of the Private Law' (2002) 23 *Zeitschrift fur Rechtssoziologie.*

Casini, L, 'The Making of *Lex Sportiva* by the Court of Arbitration for Sport' (2010) 12 *German Law Journal.*

Cassese, S (ed), *Research Handbook on Global Administrative Law* (Cheltenham, Edward Elgar, 2016).

Chalmers, D, 'The European Redistributive State and a European Law of Struggle' (2012) 18 *European Law Journal*.

Charnovitz, S, 'Non-governmental Organizations and International Law' (2006) 100 *American Journal of International Law*.

Claes, M, 'Constitutionalizing Europe at its Source: The "European Clauses" in the National Constitutions: Evolution and Typology' (2005) 24 *Yearbook of European Law*.

Claeys G, Leandro, A and Mandra, A, 'European Central Bank Quantitative Easing: The Detailed Manual' (2015) *Bruegel Policy Contribution*.

Closa, C and Kochenov, D (eds), *Reinforcing Rule of Law Oversight in the European Union* (Cambridge, Cambridge University Press, 2016).

Cohen, GA, *Rescuing Justice and Equality* (Cambridge, MA, Harvard University Press, 2008).

Cohen, JL, *Globalization and Sovereignty: Rethinking Legality, Legitimacy and Constitutionalism* (Cambridge, Cambridge University Press, 2012).

Congleton RD, 'America's (Neglected) Debt to the Dutch: An Institutional Perspective' (2008) 19 *Constitutional Political Economy*.

Cotterrell, R, 'Transnational Communities and the Concept of Law' (2008) 21 *Ratio Juris*.

Cozzillio, MJ, Dimino, MR, Feldman, GA and Levinstein, MS, *Sports Law: Cases and Materials* (Durham, NC, Carolina Academic Press, 1997).

Craig, P, 'Formal and Substantive Conceptions of the Rule of Law: An Analytical Framework' (1997) 16 *Public Law*.

Cramme, O, 'The EU's War against Credit Rating Agencies is Symptomatic of a New Struggle between Politics and the Market, But it Also Lays Bare Growing Tensions in the European Project and Globalisation as a Whole' *LSE Blogs* (19 July 2011).

Cruz, JB, 'The Legacy of the Maastricht-Urteil and the Pluralist Movement' (2008) 14 *European Law Journal*.

Curtin, D, 'Challenging Executive Dominance in European Democracy' in C Joerges and C Glinski (eds), *The European Crisis and the Transformation of Transnational Governance* (Oxford, Hart Publishing, 2014).

Dalacoura, K, *Islamist Terrorism and Democracy in the Middle East* (Cambridge, Cambridge University Press, 2011).

Darbellay, A, *Regulating Credit Rating Agencies* (Cheltenham, Edward Elgar, 2013).

Davies, B, *Resisting the ECJ: Germany's Confrontation with European Law, 1949–1979* (Cambridge, Cambridge University Press, 2012).

Davis, SR, *The Federal Principle: A Journey through Time in Quest of a Meaning* (Berkeley, University of California Press 1978).

Dawson, M and Muir, E, 'Hungary and the Indirect Protection of EU Fundamental Rights and the Rule of Law' (2013) 14 *German Law Journal*.

Dawson, M and de Witte, F, 'Constitutional Balance in the EU after the Euro-Crisis' (2013) 76 *Modern Law Review*.

De Búrca, G, 'The European Court of Justice and the International Legal Order after *Kadi*' (2010) 51 *Harvard International Law Journal*.

——. 'The Road Not Taken: The European Union as a Global Human Rights Actor' (2011) 105 *American Journal of International Law*.

——. 'After the EU Charter of Fundamental Rights: The Court of Justice as a Human Rights Adjudicator' (2013) 20 *Maastricht Journal*.

De Búrca and Craig, P, *The Evolution of the EU Law* (Oxford, Oxford University Press, 1999).

De Búrca, Kochenov, D and Williams, A, *Europe's Justice Deficit?* (Oxford, Hart Publishing, 2015).

De Búrca and Weiler J (eds), *The Worlds of European Constitutionalism* (Cambridge, Cambridge University Press, 2012).

De Haan, J and Amtenbrik, F, 'Credit Rating Agencies' (2011) 278 *DNB Working Paper*.

De Sousa Santos, B, *Toward a New Common Sense: Law, Science and Politics in the Paradigmatic Transition* (London, Routledge, 1995).

De Tocqueville, A, *Democracy in America* (East Orange, NJ, Clark, 2003).

De Wet, E, 'From Kadi to Nada: Judicial Techniques Favouring Human Rights over United Nations Security Council Sanctions' (2013) 12 *Chinese Journal of International Law*.

De Witte, B, 'Direct Effect, Supremacy, and the Nature of the Legal Order' in P and G de Búrca (eds), *The Evolution of the EU Law* (Oxford, Oxford University Press, 1999).

Delmas-Marty, M, *Le Pluralisme Ordonné* (Paris, Seuil, 2005).

Dibadj, R, 'Panglossian Transnationalism' (2008) 44 *Stanford Journal of International Law*.

Diamond, M, 'The Federalist on Federalism: "Neither a National nor a Federal Constitution, But a Composition of Both"' (1977) 6 *Yale Law Journal*.

Domingo, R, *The New Global Law* (Cambridge, Cambridge University Press, 2010).

Douglas-Scott, S, *Law after Modernity* (Oxford, Hart Publishing, 2013).

Dworkin, R, *Law's Empire* (Cambridge, MA, Harvard University Press, 1986).

——. *Sovereign Virtue* (Cambridge, MA, Harvard University Press, 2002).

——. 'Hart's Postscript and the Character of Political Philosophy' (2004) 24 *Oxford Journal of Legal Studies*.

——. 'A New Philosophy for International Law' (2013) 41 *Philosophy and Public Affairs*.

Eberlein, B and Kerwer, D, 'New Governance in the European Union: A Theoretical Perspective' (2004) *Journal of Common Market Studies*.

Eckes, C, 'International Law as Law of the EU: The Role of the Court of Justice' (2010) 6 *CLEER Working Papers*.

Ehrlich, E, *Grundlegung der Soziologie des Rechts* (Munich, Duncker & Humblot, 1989).

Elazar, DJ (ed), *Federalism and Political Integration* (Ramat Gan, Turtledove Publishing, 1979).

Eleftheriadis, P, 'Pluralism and Integrity' (2010) 23 *Ratio Juris*.

Fabbrini, S (ed), *Democracy and Federalism in the European Union and the United States* (London, Routledge, 2005).

Fassbender, B and Peters, A (eds), *The Oxford Handbook of the History of International Law* (Oxford, Oxford University Press, 2012).

——. 'Triepel in Luxemburg—Die dualistische Sicht des Verhältnisses zwischen Europa- und Völkerrecht in der Kadi-Rechtsprechung des EuGH als Problem des Selbstverständnisses der Europäischen Union' (2010) 63 *DÖV*.

Fischer-Lascano, A and Teubner, G, 'Regime-Collisions: The Vain Search for Legal Unity in the Fragmentation of Global Law' (2004) 25 *Michigan Journal of International Law*.

Fontanelli, F, 'Kadieu: Connecting the Dots—from Resolution 1267 to Judgment C-584/10 P' in M Avbelj, F Fontanelli and G Martinico, (eds), *Kadi on Trial: A Multifaceted Analysis of the Kadi Trial* (London, Routledge, 2014).

Forst, R, 'Transnational Justice and Democracy' (2011) 4 *Normative Orders Working Paper*.

——. *The Right to Justification: Elements of a Constructivist Theory of Justice* (New York, Columbia University Press, 2012).

——. 'Justice, Democracy and the Right to Justification: Reflections on Jürgen Neyer's Normative Theory of the European Union' in D Kochenov, Ge de Búrca and A Williams (eds), *Europe's Justice Deficit?* (Oxford, Hart Publishing, 2015).

Foster, K, '*Lex Sportiva* and *Lex Ludica*: The Court of Arbitration for Sport's Jurisprudence' in R Siekmann and J Soek (eds), *Lex Sportiva: What is Sports Law?* (The Hague, Asser Institute, 2012).

Fuller, L, *The Morality of Law* (New Haven, Yale University Press, 1964).

Follesdal, A and Hix, S, 'Why There is a Democratic Deficit in the EU: A Response to Majone and Moravcsik' (2006) 44 *Journal of Common Market Studies*.

Forsyth, M, *Unions of States: The Theory and Practice of Confederation* (Leicester, Leicester University Press, 1981).

Friedmann-Goldstein, N, *Constituting Federal Sovereignty: The European Union in Comparative Perspective* (Baltimore, Johns Hopkins University Press, 2001).

Galanter, M, 'Justice in Many Rooms: Courts, Private Ordering, and Indigenous Law' (1981) 19 *Journal of Legal Pluralism*.

Galston, AG, 'Pluralist Constitutionalism' (2011) *Social Philosophy and Policy*.

Ginsborg, L and Scheinin, M, 'You Can't Always Get What You Want: The *Kadi II* Conundrum and the Security Council 1267 Terrorist Sanctions Regime' (2011) *Essex Humam Rights Review*.

Giddens, A, *New Rules of Sociological Method: A Positive Critique of Interpretative Sociologies* (Stanford, Stanford University Press, 1993).

Glenn, HP, *The Cosmopolitan State* (Oxford, Oxford University Press, 2013).

——. 'Transnational Legal Thought: Plato, Europea and Beyond' in M Maduro, K Tuori and S Sankari (eds), *Transnational Law: Rethinking European Law and Legal Thinking* (Cambridge, Cambridge University Press, 2014).

Gray, J, 'Pluralism and Toleration in Contemporary Political Philosophy' (2000) 48 *Political Studies*.

——. *Two Faces of Liberalism* (New York, New Press, 2002).

Griffiths, J, 'What is Legal Pluralism?' (1986) 24 *Journal of Legal Pluralism and Unofficial Law*.

Habbel, M, Kotz, HH, Mußhoff, J, Rall, W, Mattern, F and Windhagen, E, *The Future of the Euro: An Economic Perspective on the Eurozone Crisis* (Berlin, McKinsey Germany, 2012).

Habermas, J, *Between Facts and Norms* (Cambridge, MA, MIT Press, 1996).

——. 'Why Europe Needs a Constitution' (2000) 11 *New Left Review*.

——. 'Constitutional Democracy: A Paradoxical Union of Contradictory Principles?' (2001) 29 *Political Theory*.

——. *The Divided West* (Cambridge, Polity Press, 2006).

——. *The Crisis of the European Union* (Cambridge, Polity Press, 2012).

——. 'Democracy, Solidarity and the European Crisis' (lecture delivered at KU Leuven, 26 April 2013).

——. *Im Sog der Technokratie* (Berlin, Suhrkamp Verlag, 2013).

Habermas, J and Halberstam, D, 'Local, Global and Plural Constitutionalism: Europe Meets the World' in G de Búrca and JHH Weiler (eds), *The Worlds of European Constitutionalism* (Cambridge, Cambridge University Press, 2012).

Habermas, J and Stein, E, 'Constitutional Heterarchy: The Centrality of Conflict in the European Union and the United States' in JL Dunoff and JP Trachtman (eds), *Ruling the World* (Cambridge, Cambridge University Press, 2009).

——. 'The United Nations, the European Union and the King of Sweden' (2009) 46 *Common Market Law Review*.

Halliday, TC and Shaffer, G (eds), *Transnational Legal Orders* (Cambridge, Cambridge University Press, 2015).

Hallstein, W, *Der Unvollendete Bundesstaat* (Düsseldorf, Econ Verlag, 1969).

Halt, J, 'Where is the Privacy in WADA's "Whereabouts Rule"?' (2009) 20 *Marquette Sports Law Review.*

Hart, HLA, *The Concept of Law* (Oxford, Clarendon Press, 1994).

Hartley, TC, 'The Constitutional Foundations of the European Union' (2011) 117 *Law Quarterly Review.*

Haynes, J, 'Transnational Religious Actors and International Order' (2009) 17 *Perspectives.*

Hirvonen, A, 'Reinventing European Democracy: Democratization and the Existential Crisis of the EU' in M Fichera, S Hänninen and K Tuori (eds), *Polity and Crisis* (Farnham, Ashgate, 2014).

Holovaty, S, 'Rule of Law in Action' in Venice Commission, The Rule of Law as a Practical Concept—Reports (Venice, 2012).

Hongju Koh, H, 'Why Transnational Law Matters' (2005–06) 24 *Penn State International Law Review.*

Ip, EC, 'Globalization and the Future of the Law of the Sovereign State' (2010) 8(3) *International Journal of Constitutional Law.*

Ipsen, H P, 'Europaische Verfassung—Nationale Verfassung' (1987) 195 *Europarecht.*

Isiksel, T, 'Global Legal Pluralism as Fact and Norm' (2013) 2(2) *Global Constitutionalism.*

Jakab, A and Kochenov, D, *The Enforcement of EU Law and Values: Ensuring Member States' Compliance* (Oxford, Oxford University Press, 2017).

Jančič, D, 'Representative Democracy across Levels: National Parliaments and EU Constitutionalism' (2012) 8 *Croatian Yearbook of European Law and Policy.*

——. 'Countering the Debt Crisis: National Parliaments and EU Economic Governance' (2014) 1 *LSE Law: Policy Briefing Papers.*

Jessup, C, *Transnational Law* (New Haven, Yale University Press, 1956).

Joerges, C, 'European Economic Law, the Nation-State and the Maastricht Treaty' in R Dehousse (ed), *Europe after Maastricht: An Even Closer Union?* (Munich, Beck, 1994).

——. '"Economic Order"—"Technical Realization"—"The Hour of the Executive": Some Legal Historical Observations on the Commission White Paper on European Governance' (2001) 6 *Jean Monnet Working Paper*, Symposium: Mountain or Molehill? A Critical Appraisal of the Commission White Paper on Governance.

Jurcys, P, Kjaer, PF and Yatsunami, R (eds), *Regulatory Hybridization in the Transnational Sphere* (Leiden, Brill, 2013).

Karmis, D and Norman, W (eds), *Theories of Federalism* (New York, Palgrave Macmillan, 2005).

Kant, I, *Perpetual Peace* (London, George Allen & Unwin, 1917).

Kedzior, M, 'Effects of the EU Anti-doping Laws and Politics for the International and Domestic Sports Law in Member States' (2007) 1–2 *International Sports Law Journal.*

Kerwer, D, 'Holding Global Regulators Accountable, The Case of Credit Rating Agencies' (2004) 11 *School of Public Policy Working Paper Series.*

Kidd, C, *Union and Unionism: Political Thought in Scotland* (Cambridge, Cambridge University Press, 2008).

King, P, *Federalism and Federation* (London, Croom Helm, 1982).

Kingsbury, B, 'The Concept of "Law" in Global Administrative Law' (2009) 20 *European Journal of International Law.*

Kingsbury, B, Krisch, N and Stewart, RB, 'The Emergence of Global Administrative Law' (2005) 68 *Law and Contemporary Problems.*

Kochenov, D, 'The Ought of Justice' in D Kochenov, G de Búrca and A Williams, *Europe's Justice Deficit?* (Oxford, Hart Publishing, 2015).

Kokott, J and Sobotta, C, 'The *Kadi* Case: Constitutional Core Values and International Law—Finding the Balance' (2012) 23 *European Journal of International Law*.

Kolev, B, '*Lex Sportiva* and *Lex Mercatoria*' in R Siekmann and J Soek (eds), *Lex Sportiva: What is Sports Law?* (The Hague, Asser Institute, 2012).

Koncewicz, TT, 'Of Institutions, Democracy, Constitutional Self-Defence and the Rule of Law: The Judgments of the Polish Constitutional Tribunal in Cases K 34/15, K 35/15 and beyond' (2016) 53 *Common Market Law Review*.

Koskenniemi, M, 'The Fate of Public International Law: Between Technique and Politics' (2007) *Modern Law Review*.

Krisch, N, 'Europe's Constitutional Monstrosity' (2005) 25 *Oxford Journal of Legal Studies*.

——. *Beyond Constitutionalism* (Oxford, Oxford University Press, 2010).

——. 'Global Administrative Law and the Constitutional Ambition' in M Loughlin and P Dobner (eds), *The Twilight of Constitutionalism* (Oxford, Oxford University Press, 2010).

——. 'The Case for Pluralism in Postnational Law' in G de Búrca and JHH Weiler (eds), *The Worlds of European Constitutionalism* (Cambridge, Cambridge University Press, 2012).

Krygier, M, 'The Rule of Law: Legality, Teleology, Sociology' (2007) 65 *University of New South Wales Faculty of Law Research Series*.

——. 'Four Puzzles about the Rule of Law: Why, What, Where? And Who Cares?' (2010) 22 *University of New South Wales Faculty of Law Research Series*.

Krugman, P, 'Ending Greece's Bleeding' *New York Times* (5 July 2015).

Kumm, M, 'The Jurisprudence of Constitutional Conflict: Constitutional Supremacy in Europe before and after the Constitutional Treaty' (2005) 11 *European Law Journal*.

——. 'The Cosmopolitan Turn in Constitutionalism: On the Relationship between Constitutionalism in and beyond the State' in JL Dunoff and JP Trachtman (eds), *Ruling the World* (Cambridge, Cambridge University Press, 2009).

——. 'Rethinking Constitutional Authority: On the Structure and Limits of Constitutional Pluralism' in M Avbelj and J Komarek (eds), *Constitutional Pluralism in the European Union and beyond* (Oxford, Hart Publishing, 2012).

——. 'What Kind of a Constitutional Crisis is Europe in and What Should Be Done about it?' (2013) WZB 801 Discussion Paper.

Kuner, C, 'The Court of Justice of the EU Judgment on the Data Protection and Internet Search Engines' (2015) 3 *LSE Law, Society and Economy Working Papers*.

Ladauer, KH (ed), *Public Governance in the Age of Globalization* (Aldershot, Ashgate, 2004).

Latty, F, *La lex sportiva: Recherche sur le droit transnational* (Leiden, Martinus Nijhoff Publishers, 2007).

Lavranos, N and Vatsov, M, 'Protecting European Law from International Law' (2010) 15 *European Foreign Affairs Review*.

——. 'Kadi II: Backtracking from *Kadi I*' in M Avbelj, F Fontanelli and G Martinico (eds), *Kadi on Trial: A Multifaceted Analysis of the Kadi Trial* (London, Routledge, 2014).

Leben, C, 'A propos de la nature juridique des Communautés Européennes' (1991) 14 *Droits*.

Leibfried, S and van Elderen, K, '"And They Shall Beat Their Swords into Plowshares"—The Dutch Genesis of a European Icon and the German Fate of the Treaty of Lisbon' (2012) 10 *German Law Journal*.

Lenaerts K, 'Constitutionalism and the Many Faces of Federalism' (1990) 38 *American Journal of Comparative Law.*

Lejour, A, Linders, GJ, Möhlman, J and Straathof, B, 'The Internal Market and the Dutch Economy' (2008) 168 *CPB Netherlands Bureau for Economic Policy Analysis.*

Lipschutz, RD, 'Reconstructing World Politics: The Emergence of Global Civil Society' (1992) 21 *Millennium, Journal of International Studies.*

Loughlin, M, 'Ten Tenets of Sovereignty' in N Walker (ed), *Sovereignty in Transition* (Oxford, Hart Publishing, 2003).

Mac Amhlaigh, C, Michelon, C and Walker, N (eds), *After Public Law* (Oxford, Oxford University Press, 2013).

MacCormick, N, 'The Maastricht-Urteil: Sovereignty Now' (1995) 1 *European Law Journal.*

——. *Questioning Sovereignty: Law, State and Nation in the European Commonwealth* (Oxford, Oxford University Press, 1999).

MacMahon, AW (ed), *Federalism: Mature and Emergent* (New York, Doubleday, 1955).

Maduro, M, 'Contrapunctual Law: Europe's Constitutional Pluralism in Action' in N Walker (ed), *Sovereignty in Transition* (Oxford, Hart Publishing, 2003).

Maduro, M, Tuori, K and Sankari, S (eds), *Transnational Law: Rethinking European Law and Legal Thinking* (Cambridge, Cambridge University Press, 2014).

Mair, P, *Ruling the Void: The Hollowing of Western Democracy* (London, Verso, 2013).

Majone, G (ed), *Regulating Europe* (London, Routledge, 1996).

Mannheim, K, *Ideology and Utopia: An Introduction to the Sociology of Knowledge* (Eastford, Martino Fine Book, 2015).

Margulies, P, 'Aftermath of an Unwise Decision: The UN Terrorist Sanctions Regime after *Kadi II*' (2014) 6 *Amsterdam Law Forum.*

Martinico, G, 'The Autonomy of EU Law' in M Avbelj, F Fontanelli and G Martinico (eds), *Kadi on Trial: A Multifaceted Analysis of the Kadi Trial* (London, Routledge, 2014).

——. 'Constitutionalism, Resistance, and Openness: Comparative Law Reflections on Constitutionalism in Postnational Governance' (2016) 35 *Yearbook of European Law.*

Mason, L, 'The Intractably Unknowable Nature of Law: *Kadi*, Kafka, and the Law's Competing Claims to Authority' in M Avbelj, F Fontanelli and G Martinico (eds), *Kadi on Trial: A Multifaceted Analysis of the Kadi Trial* (London, Routledge, 2014).

Mattarocci, G, *The Independence of Credit Rating Agencies* (Amsterdam, Elsevier, 2014).

McCrudden, C, *Understanding Human Dignity* (Oxford, Oxford University Press, 2014).

McFall, L, 'Integrity' (1987) 1 *Ethics.*

Melissaris, E, *Ubiquitous Law: Legal Theory and the Space for Legal Pluralism* (London, Routledge, 2009).

Menendez, AJ, 'Whose Justice? Which Europe?' in D Kochenov, G de Búrca and A Williams (eds) *Europe's Justice Deficit?* (Oxford, Hart Publishing, 2015).

——. 'The Refugee Crisis: Between Human Tragedy and Symptom of the Structural Crisis of European Integration' (2016) 2 *European Law Journal.*

Merry, SE, 'Legal Pluralism' (1998) 22 *Law and Society Review.*

Michelman, F, *Brennan and Democracy* (Princeton, Princeton University Press, 1999).

Michaels, R, 'Global Legal Pluralism' (2009) 5 *Annual Review of Law and Science.*

Micklitz, H-W, 'Rethinking the Public/Private Divide', in M Maduro, K Tuori and S Sankari (eds), *Transnational Law* (Cambridge, Cambridge University Press, 2014).

Miller, D, *Principles of Social Justice* (Cambridge, Cambridge University Press, 1999).

Milward, AS, *The European Rescue of the Nation State* (London, Routledge, 2000).

Mitten, MJ and Opie, H, '"Sports Law": Implications for the International, Comparative and National Law and Global Dispute Resolution' in R Siekmann and J Soek (eds), *Lex Sportiva: What is Sports Law?* (The Hague, Asser Institute, 2012).

Monnet, J, *Memoires* (New York, Doubleday & Company, 1978).

Morgan, G, *The Idea of European Superstate* (Princeton, Princeton University Press, 2005.

Müller, JW, 'The Hungarian Tragedy' (2011) *Dissent Magazine.*

——. *What is Populism?* (Philadelphia, University of Pennsylvania Press, 2016).

Muller, T, 'Customary Transnational Law: Attacking the Last Resort of State Sovereignty' (2008) 15 *Indiana Journal of Global Legal Studies.*

Muller-Mall, S, *Legal Spaces: Towards a Topological Thinking of Law* (Berlin, Springer, 2013).

Muniz-Fraticelli, M, *The Structure of Pluralism: On the Authority of Associations* (Oxford, Oxford University Press, 2014).

Neuwahl, N and Rosas, A, *The European Union and Human Rights* (Leiden, Martinus Nijhoff Publishers, 1995).

Neyer, J, *The Justification of Europe: A Political Theory of Supranational Integration* (Oxford, Oxford University Press, 2012).

——. 'Justice and the Right to Justification: Conceptual Reflections' in D Kochenov, G de Búrca and A Williams (eds), *Europe's Justice Deficit?* (Oxford, Hart Publishing, 2015).

Nicolson, A, *A Sketch of the German Constitution and the Events in Germany from 1815 to 1871* (Longmans, Green & Co, 1875).

Nourse, V and Shaffer, G, 'Varieties of New Legal Realism: Can a New World Order Prompt a New Legal Theory?' (2009) 95 *Cornell Law Review.*

Oklopčić, Z, 'Provincializing Constitutional Pluralism' (2014) 5 *Transnational Legal Theory.*

Paradiso, M, 'Google and the Internet: A Mega-project Nesting within Another Mega-project' in DS Brunn (ed), *Engineering Earth* (Berlin, Springer 2011).

Partnoy, F, 'The Siskel and Ebert of Financial Markets?: Two Thumbs Down for the Credit Rating Agencies' (1999) 77 *Washington University Law Quarterly.*

Payandeh, M, 'Rechtskontrolle des UN- Sicherheitsrats durch staatliche und überstaatliche Gerichte' (2006) 66 *ZaöRV.*

Patrikios, A, 'Resolution of Cross-border E-Business Disputes on the Basis of Transnational Substantive Rules of Law and E-Business Usages: The Emergence of the Lex Informatica' (21st Bileta Conference, Malta, 2016).

Pearson, G, 'Sporting Justifications under EU Free Movement and Competition Law: The Case of the Football "Transfer System"' (2015) 21 *European Law Journal.*

Pellet, A, 'Les fondement juridique internationaux du droit communautaire' in Academy of European Law Staff (ed), *Collected Courses of the Academy of European Law* (Vol V, Book 2, The Hague, Kluwer Law International 1997).

Perez, F, *Political Communication in Europe: The Cultural and Structural Limits of the European Public Sphere* (Basingstoke, Palgrave Macmillan, 2013).

Pernice, I, 'Multilevel Constitutionalism in the European Union' (2002) 27 *European Law Review.*

Pescatore, P, 'Aspects judiciaires de l' "acquis" communautaire' (1981) 17 *Revue trimestrielle de droit europeen.*

Peters, A, *Beyond Human Rights: The Legal Status of the Individual in International Law* (Cambridge, Cambridge University Press, 2016).

Pospisil, L, *Anthropology of Law: A Comparative Theory* (New Haven, HRAF Press, 1971).

Pogge, TW, *Realizing Rawls* (Ithaca, Cornell University Press, 1989).

Rasmussen, M, 'Revolutionizing European Law: A History of the *Van Gend en Loos* Judgment' (2014) 12 *International Journal of Constitutional Law*.

Rawls, J, *Political Liberalism* (Cambridge, Cambridge University Press, 1993).

——. *A Theory of Justice* (Cambridge, MA, Harvard University Press, 2000).

——. *The Law of the Peoples* (Cambridge, MA, Harvard University Press, 2001).

——. *Political Liberalism* (New York, Columbia University Press, 2005).

Raz, J, *The Authority of Law: Essays on Law and Morality* (Oxford, Clarendon Press, 1979).

Reidenberg, JR, '*Lex Informatica*: The Formulation of Information Policy Rules through Technology' (1998) 76 *Texas Law Review*.

Riker, WH, 'Dutch and American Federalism' (1957) 18 *Journal of the History of Ideas*.

Roemer, JE, *Theories of Distributive Justice* (Cambridge, MA, Harvard University Press, 1996).

Roughan, N, *Authorities: Conflicts, Co-operation and Transnational Legal Theory* (Oxford, Oxford University Press, 2013).

Rosenfeld, M, 'Habermas' Call for Cosmopolitan Constitutional Patriotism in an Age of Global Terror: A Pluralist Appraisal' (2007) 14 *Constellations*.

Ryan, A (ed), *Justice* (Oxford, Clarendon Press, 1993).

Sabel, CF and Zeitlin, J, 'Experimentalism in the EU: Common Ground and Persistent Difference' (2012) 6 *Regulation and Governance*.

Salinas de Frias, AM, Samuel, K and White, N (eds) *Counter-terrorism: International Law and Practice* (Oxford, Oxford University Press, 2012).

Sand, I-J, 'Globalization and the Transcendence of the Public/Private Divide: What is Public Law under Conditions of Globalization?' in C-M Amhlaigh, C Michelon and N Walker (eds), *After Public Law* (Oxford, Oxford University Press, 2013).

Sartori, G, 'Understanding Pluralism' (1997) 8 *Journal of Democracy*.

Sassen, S, 'Neither Global nor National: Novel Assemblages of Territory, Authority and Rights' (2008) 1 *Ethics & Global Politics*.

Scharpf, F, 'The Joint-Decision Trap: Lessons from German Federalism and European Integration' (1988) 66 *Public Administration*.

——. 'Monetary Union, Fiscal Crisis and the Preemption of Democracy' (2011) *MPIfG Discussion Paper*.

Schilling, T, 'Who in the Law is the Ultimate Umpire of European Community Law?' (1996) *Jean Monnet Working Paper*.

Schmitt, C, *Verfassungslehre* (Berlin, Duncker & Humblot, 1993).

Schraad-Tischler, D and Kroll, C, *Social Justice in the EU: A Cross-national Comparison* (Gütersloh, Bertelsmann Stiftung, 2014).

Schönberger, C, 'Die Europäische Union als Bund, Zugleich ein Beitrag zur Verabschiedung des Staatenbund-Bundesstaat-Schema' (2005) 129 *Archiv des öffentlichen Rechts*.

Schütze, R, 'Supremacy without Pre-emption? The Very Slowly Emergent Doctrine of Community Preemption' (2006) 43 *Common Market Law Review*.

——. *From Dual to Cooperative Federalism* (Oxford, Oxford University Press, 2009).

Schwartz, PM and Solove, DJ, 'The PII Problem: Privacy and a New Concept of Personally Identifiable Information' (2011) 86 *NYU Law Review*.

Scott, C, 'Transnational Law as Proto-Concept: Three Conceptions' (2009) 10 *German Law Journal*.

Sekulow, J, Sekulow, J, Ash, RW and French, D, *Rise of ISIS: A Threat We Can't Ignore* (Brentwood, Howard Books, 2014).

Sen, A, *The Idea of Justice* (London, Penguin Books, 2009).

Searle, JR, *The Construction of Social Reality* (New York, Simon & Schuster, 1995).

Shaffer, G, 'A Transnational Take on Krisch's Pluralist Postnational Law' (2012) 23 *European Journal of International Law*.

——. 'Transnational Legal Process and State Change (2012) 37(2) *Law and Social Inquiry*.

——. (ed), *Transnational Legal Ordering and State Change* (Cambridge, Cambridge University Press, 2013).

Siekmann, R and Soek, J (eds), *Lex Sportiva: What is Sports Law?* (The Hague, Asser Institute, 2012).

Somek, A, 'The Concept of "Law" in Global Administrative Law: A Reply to Benedict Kingsbury' (2009) 20 *European Journal of International Law*.

Stein, E, 'Toward Supremacy of Treaty Constitution by Judicial Fiat: On the Margin of the Costa Case' (1964) 63 *Michigan Law Review*.

——. 'Lawyers, Judges and the Making of Transnational Constitution' (1981) 75 *American Journal of International Law*.

Stone Sweet, A, *The Judicial Construction of Europe* (Oxford, Oxford University Press, 2004).

——. 'The New *Lex Mercatoria* and Transnational Governance' (2006) 13 *Journal of European Public Policy*.

Tamanaha, BZ, 'A Non-essentialist Version of Legal Pluralism' (2000) 27 *Journal of Law and Society*.

Tetley, W, 'The General Maritime Law: The *Lex Maritima*' (1994) 20 *Syracuse Journal of International Law and Commerce*.

Teubner, G, 'Autopoiesis in Law and Society: A Rejoinder to Blankenburg' (1984) 2 *Law and Society Review*.

——. (ed), *Global Law Without a State* (Dartmouth, Ashgate, 1997).

——. 'The King's Many Bodies: The Self-Deconstruction of Law's Hierarchy' (1997) 31 *Law & Society Review*.

——. *Constitutional Fragments: Societal Constitutionalism and Globalization* (Oxford, Oxford University Press, 2012).

Tietje, C and Nowrot, K, 'Laying Conceptual Ghosts of the Past to Rest: The Rise of Philip C. Jessup's Transnational Law' in C Tietje, A Brouder and K Nowrot (eds), *The Regulatory Governance of the International Economic System* (2006) 50 *Halle-Wittenberg: Beitrage zum Transnationalen Wirtschaftsrecht*.

Trebilcock, MJ and Daniels, RJ, *Rule of Law Reform and Development: Charting the Fragile Path of Progress* (Cheltenham, Edward Elgar, 2008).

Tully, J, *Strange Multiplicity: Constitutionalism in an Age of Diversity* (Cambridge, Cambridge University Press, 1995).

Tuori, K, 'Transnational Law: On Legal Hybrids and Perspectivism' in M Maduro, K Tuori and S Sankari (eds), *Transnational Law: Rethinking European Law and Legal Thinking* (Cambridge, Cambridge University Press, 2014).

Twinning, W, *Globalization and Legal Theory* (Cambridge, Cambridge University Press, 2000).

Unger, RM, *Free Trade Reimagined: The World Division of Labor and Method of Economics* (Princeton, Princeton University Press, 2007).

Vanderlinden, J, 'Return to Legal Pluralism: Twenty Years Later' (1989) 28 *Journal of Legal Pluralism*.

Vauchez, A and de Witte, B (eds), *Lawyering Europe: European Law as a Transnational Social Field* (Oxford, Hart Publishing, 2013).

Von Bogdandy, A and Sonnevend, P (eds), *Constitutional Crisis in the European Constitutional Area* (Oxford, Hart Publishing, 2015).

Von Danwitz, T, 'The Rule of Law in the Recent Jurisprudence of the ECJ' (2014) 35 *Fordham International Law Journal.*

Waldron J, 'Is the Rule of Law an Essentially Contested Concept (in Florida?)' (2002) 21 *Law and Philosophy.*

——. 'Who is My Neighbour—Proximity and Humanity' (2003) 83 *The Monist.*

Walker, N, 'The Idea of Constitutional Pluralism' (2002) 65 *Modern Law Review.*

——. 'Late Sovereignty in the European Union' in N Walker (ed), *Sovereignty in Transition* (Oxford, Hart Publishing, 2003).

——. 'EU Constitutionalism in the State Constitutional Tradition' (2006) 21 *EUI Working Papers—Law Department.*

——. 'Beyond Boundary Disputes and Basic Grids: Mapping the Global Disorder of Normative Orders' (2008) 6 *International Journal of Constitutional Law.*

——. 'Flexibility within a Meta-constitutional Frame: Reflections on the Future of Legal Authority in Europe' (2009) 12 *Jean Monnet Working Paper.*

——. *Final Appellate Jurisdiction in the Scottish Legal System* (Edinburgh, 2010).

——. 'Reconciling MacCormick, Constitutional Pluralism and the Unity of Practical Reason' (2011) 3 *Ratio Juris.*

——. 'Constitutionalism and Pluralism in Global Context' in M Avbelj and J Komarek (eds), *Constitutional Pluralism in the European Union and Beyond* (Oxford, Hart Publishing, 2012).

——. 'The Post-national Horizon of Constitutionalism and Public Law: Paradigm Extension or Paradigm Exhaustion', in C Mac Amhlaigh, C Michelon and N Walker (eds), *After Public Law* (Oxford, Oxford University Press, 2012).

——. *Intimations of Global Law* (Cambridge, Cambridge University Press, 2014).

——. 'Justice in and of the European Union' in D Kochenov, G de Búrca and A Williams (eds), *Europe's Justice Deficit?* (Oxford, Hart Publishing, 2015).

Watts, RL, 'Federalism, Federal Political Systems and Federation' (1998) 1 *Annual Review of Political Science.*

Weatherill, S, 'Competence Creep and Competence Control' (2004) 23 *Yearbook of European Law.*

——. 'Is There Such a Thing as EU Sports Law?' in R Siekmann and J Soek (eds), *Lex Sportiva: What is Sports Law?* (The Hague, Asser Institute, 2012).

——. *European Sports Law: Collected Papers* (Berlin, Springer, 2013).

Weiler, JHH, 'The Transformation of Europe' (1991) 100 *Yale Law Journal.*

——. 'Fundamental Rigths and Fundamental Boundaries: On Standards and Values in the Protection of Human Rights' in N Neuwahl and A Rosas (eds), *The European Union and Human Rights* (Leiden, Martinus Nijhoff Publishers, 1995).

——. 'European Neo-constitutionalism: in Search of Foundations for the European Constitutional Order' (1996) XLIV *Political Studies.*

——. 'In Defence of the Status Quo: Europe's Constitutional Sonderweg' in JHH Weiler and M Wind (eds), *European Constitutionalism beyond the State* (Cambridge, Cambridge University Press, 2003).

——. 'Prologue: Global and Pluralist Constitutionalism—Some Doubts' in G de Búrca and JHH Weiler (eds), *The Worlds of European Constitutionalism* (Cambridge, Cambridge University Press, 2012).

Weiler, PC, *Sports and the Law* (Rochester, NY, American Case Book Series, 2010).

Welsch, W, 'Rationality and Reason Today' in DR Gordon and J Niznik (eds), *Criticism and Defense of Rationality in Contemporary Philosophy* (Amsterdam, GA: Rodopi, 1998).

Wessel, RA, 'Reconsidering the Relationship between International and EU Law: Towards a Content-Based Approach' in E Cannizzaro, P Palchetti and RA Wessel (eds), *International Law as Law of the European Union* (Leiden, Martinus Nijhoff Publishers, 2011).

Yang, N, 'Constitutional Dimension of Administrative Co-operation: Potentials for Reorientation in *Kadi II*' in M Avbelj, F Fontanelli and G Martinico (eds) *Kadi on Trial: A Multifaceted Analysis of the Kadi Trial* (London, Routledge, 2014).

Ziegler, K, 'Strengthening the Rule of Law, But Fragmenting International Law: The *Kadi* Decision of the ECJ from the Perspective of Human Rights' (2009) 9 *Human Rights Law Review*.

——. 'The Relationship between EU Law and International Law' (2015) 4 *University of Leicester School of Law Research Paper*.

Zumbansen, P, 'Transnational Law' (2008) 9 *CLPE Research Paper*.

——. 'Transnational Legal Pluralism' (2010) 1 *Transnational Legal Theory*.

——. 'Neither "Public" nor "Private", "National" nor "International": Transnational Corporate Governance from a Legal Pluralist Perspective' (2011) 38 *Journal of Law and Society*.

——. 'Defining the Space of Transnational Law: Legal Theory, Global Governance, and Legal Pluralism' (2012) 21 *Transnational Law & Contemporary Problems*.

Index